THE HORSEMEN

The Horsemen

COMMISSIONER

C. W. HARVISON (RTD.)

Royal Canadian Mounted Police

MCCLELLAND AND STEWART

LIMITED

TORONTO/MONTREAL

CONTENTS

➛➛➛➛➛➛➛➛➛➛

CONTENTS

-»»-»»-»»-»»«-«««-«««-«««-«««

TO DORIS

Foreword

When I retired as Commissioner of the Royal Canadian
Mounted Police in October of 1963, friends – among them some members of the Press Gallery and publishers – suggested that I should try my
hand at writing. But I was determined that I would not give in to a
temptation that faces most retired persons who have lead reasonably active
lives. It seemed doubtful that my experience could provide material of
sufficient interest to justify another book about the Force. Furthermore,
during my years of service, I had looked forward to the time when I would
be able to concentrate on the enjoyment of long-neglected hobbies. My
determination began to waver after several months of retirement, when
I found that photography, painting, fishing, and gardening were not
enough to hold my interest or to keep me happily occupied.

At about this time I came across a series of articles that had appeared
in a popular magazine in one of the Scandinavian countries. The writer
– whose photographs showed her to be an extremely attractive young
woman – told a harrowing tale of her experiences in coming to Canada,
joining the Royal Canadian Mounted Police, earning promotion to the
rank of Sergeant, and eventually securing an appointment as riding master
at the Force school in Fort William. According to her story, this curvace-
ous little blonde had had some difficulty in exerting authority over the
towering recruits under her command. The yarn contained a great deal
of seemingly authentic detail – particularly her problems holding the
eager young recruits at bay. Undoubtedly her readers were convinced that
the writer was a very resourceful and determined young woman. Certainly
she deserved full marks for resourcefulness. She had sold the editors a

ix

series of articles that did not contain one word of truth. Not only does the Force not recruit women into its uniformed ranks, it does not have a riding school at Fort William!

These articles of fiction, which were presented as actual fact, started me thumbing through many of the books that have been published on the Royal Canadian Mounted Police and its forbears, the North West Mounted Police and the Royal North West Mounted Police. I found that they fell into two main categories: official, authoritative works (such as those of Turner, Fetherstonhaugh, and Kemp); and those of the fictitious, "they-always-get-their-man" variety. A little research disclosed the fact that the latter category had most influenced the public image of the Force. Fiction has outweighed fact and created an image of the RCMP officer that is closer to the Hollywood-style, Rose Marie kind of Mountie than the real thing.

The tremendous tasks performed by the three hundred original members and their close successors in bringing law and order to the "vast lone land" of the West and North brought the Force well-deserved recognition. In turn, this gave rise to many tales of adventure, romance, and derring-do. Fact and fiction combined to create a distinctive Canadian legend – one that is popular around the world. But the Force cannot rest and has not rested on the laurels of legend. It has moved with the times to meet new challenges. Its motto, which appears on its official crest, is *Maintiens le Droit* – "Maintaining the Right."

The horses and scant equipment of the early days have been replaced by cars and planes and launches. Laboratories, computers, wire-photo apparatuses, and other law-enforcement aids are now necessary in the fight against the more complicated and changing patterns of crime. The original strength of three hundred has now grown to almost ten thousand. The annual budget has increased from a few thousand to more than a hundred million dollars. The whole structure of the Force has changed.

The Horsemen is an attempt to show some of these changes taking place. At the same time I have tried to show that in another sense there has been no change at all through the years. I believe that the strong *esprit de corps* and legendary devotion to duty that the Force has enjoyed from the beginning are with us today.

->>>->>>->>>->>><<<-<<<-<<<

Preface

The Royal Canadian Mounted Police is now ninety-three years old. The author's experiences with "The Force," as it is always referred to by its members, began in 1919 – almost at the half-way point.

Those years saw a tremendous growth and development in the Force; they saw increased duties, extended jurisdiction; they saw what had been a frontier police force change into a modern, highly skilled, efficient law-enforcement body – a Force which in the opinion of many experienced critics has had few equals and no superiors. Certainly no other police force is called on to perform the wide variety of duties that make up the work of the Force today.

In announcing my retirement as Commissioner, Prime Minister Pearson said (in Hansard, October 21, 1963):

> *Mr. Speaker, I should like to announce that the Government has with regret accepted the resignation of Commissioner C. W. Harvison of the Royal Canadian Mounted Police to take effect on October 31, 1963. Commissioner Harvison first submitted his resignation in April of this year at the termination of thirty-five years of service. At the request of the Government, he agreed to retain his post as Commissioner for a further period but has now requested to be allowed to retire as of the end of October.*
>
> *Commissioner Harvison joined the Royal North West Mounted Police in 1919 and is the last serving officer who began his service in the force when it bore that historic name.*

> *Both in the ranks and as a commissioned officer he has not only participated in but has made a distinguished contribution to the development of the RCMP from a frontier police force into one of the finest modern law-enforcement agencies of any country in the world.*
>
> *On behalf of all members of the house and of the people of Canada, may I express our sincere appreciation of Commissioner Harvison's long years of outstanding service to the country and to the Royal Canadian Mounted Police. He has good reason to be proud of his record, just as we can all take pride in the force he has served.*

Throughout this book I will tell of many of the changes that have taken place in narcotics, espionage, security, organized crime, and in the development of the Force. But these new duties could not have been successfully undertaken, the growth and development could not have taken place, had it not been for the foundation, the tradition, laid down by the men who served in the original force before 1919. To understand this, one must look back to the beginning, to the North West Mounted Police and the part they played in the pages of Canadian history.

In 1868, a year after the Confederation of the eastern provinces had brought the Dominion of Canada into being, Canada acquired the Northwest Territories as a result of an act passed by the Imperial Government. The Territories comprised "Rupert's Land and the areas beyond," a vast region of 2,300,000 square miles, reaching from the boundary of Ontario westward to the Rockies, and from the United States border northward across the prairies, on through the forests and into the wastes of the Arctic. Three years later, British Columbia entered Confederation.

East and west were separated by almost a thousand miles of unmapped country which was known only to the Indians and a handful of traders and trappers. The Indians consisted of the Crees, Blackfeet, Sarcees, Peigans, and Assiniboine – about thirty thousand of whom were said to inhabit the Territories, most of whom were believed hostile. There were further serious problems and complications. An uprising by the *métis* or half-breeds at Fort Garry (now Winnipeg) had been settled, but the peace was an uneasy one. Louis Riel, the *métis* leader, had enjoyed the active support of Americans, some of whom belonged to the anti-British and anti-Canadian group known as the Fenians. There were wide-spread rumours of a movement in the United States to annex the Territories. These stories were kept alive by unscrupulous traders from south of the border, and by United States Army deserters and veterans of the Civil War. There were stories, too, of massacres of Indians by whites and whites by Indians, and of the debauchment by outlaw whisky-traders of entire Indian tribes. In order to secure accurate information regarding conditions in the Territories, the Government of Canada, located in Ottawa, five hundred miles from the eastern edge of the Territory, invited Lieutenant W. F. Butler (later Lieutenant-General Sir William Butler), an Imperial Army officer, to make a survey. Butler accepted, and after a trying and hazardous journey of nearly three thousand miles, submitted a very detailed and informative report.

Butler dwelt at some length on the pressing need for law and order in the Territory and pointed out that "robbery and murder for years have gone unpunished. Indian massacres are unchecked." The report went on, "The wrong-doer does not appear to violate any law because there is no law to violate." Of the fighting ability of the prairie Indians, he said that warfare was considered a normal and desirable way of life. He warned, "Accustomed to regard murder as honourable and war, robbery, and pillage as the traits most ennobling to mankind – free from all restraint – these warring tribes of Crees, Assiniboine, and Blackfeet form some of the most savage among even the wild races of western America."

After Butler covered in great detail the difficulties and hazards of trying to settle the Territory, and emphasized the paramount importance of establishing the rule of impartial law and justice, he recommended the organization of a mobile, mounted police force of from one hundred to one hundred and fifty men. His report must rank as one of the foremost documents on the history of Western Canada. It should also rank, surely, as an extreme example of economy in police planning. The maximum strength recommended by Butler allowed one policeman for each 155,000 square miles of hostile territory.

In the United States, the opening of the western regions had started some years earlier, but American developments offered little comfort or encouragement to the Canadian Government. United States Congressional Records show that between 1862 and 1868 no less than eight hundred settlers were murdered in the Southwest. During the first week of the big Sioux War which began in 1868, seven hundred whites perished throughout the Northwestern frontier, and two hundred were taken prisoner. Only incomplete records exist as to the number of Indians killed during that period. The opening of the West was costing the Government of the United States $20,000,000 a year, an amount equal to the total revenue of the Canadian Government.

Certainly the opening and settling of the West posed problems of awesome but magnificent proportions to the newly formed Government of Canada. Decisions and actions could not be long delayed. Threats of annexation from the United States of all or part of the Territory seemed very real. Delay would serve only to increase that threat. Further, British Columbia had entered Confederation on the understanding that a transcontinental railway would be built without delay. Canadian legislators were fortunate, for they had learned from the experience of the United

States that to encourage settlers into a new region before the establishment of the rule of impartial law was to invite lawlessness. That lesson led to a decision to recruit, equip, and train a mobile, mounted police force that would move onto the plains ahead of the settlers.

During the preparation of the necessary legislation, it was decided that a suitable name for the proposed police force would be the "North West Mounted Rifles." News of this appeared in the press. In the tense atmosphere of the 1870's, the news caused concern in Washington. Critics and alarmists held that Canada was organizing an armed military body to patrol the border. The view was taken by some that this was a war-like action, and this is somewhat remarkable in that the United States Armed Forces had been active south of the border for several years. Common sense and cool heads prevailed, however, and eventually Ottawa received an apology from Washington. Probably the Force should be grateful to the Washington critics. The furore had not been lost on the Prime Minister, Sir John A. Macdonald, who drew his pen through the words "Mounted Rifles," which appeared in the official draft, and replaced them with "Mounted Police." That seemingly small change may have profoundly affected the nature and spirit of the Force and its acceptance by settlers and Indians. A force of "Mounted Rifles" might not have survived beyond the frontier days.

The North West Mounted Police Act was given Royal Assent on May 23, 1873. Recruiting started a few months later and resulted in one hundred and fifty men being sent over the Dawson route to Fort Garry for winter training. In the spring of 1874, another group of about the same number of men was recruited and sent through the United States, with the authority of the United States Government, to Fargo, North Dakota. The two groups joined forces at Fort Dufferin, just north of the international border. On July 8, 1874, this small group started the long march west to the Rockies and into the history of Canada. The Government of Canada had gambled heavily on the ability of a handful of men to carry law and order into the prairies. The spirit of those men made the gamble pay off. When the settlers came in their thousands, they found peaceful communities in which the rule of law prevailed, even in the most remote settlements. The prairies grew and developed without lynch law, massacres, or "the rule of the six gun." The present Force could not have asked for a stronger or richer heritage.

THE HORSEMEN

I

-»>-»>-»>-»>«<-«<-«<-«<

The Early Years

The barrack buildings, mess halls, offices, stables and side-walks had been scrubbed and cleaned and polished. Windows shone. Fences and stone markers glistened white. Even the old artillery pieces at the base of the flagstaff had been burnished until they gleamed in the sunlight. On the barrack square – formed by the officers' quarters, the barracks, and the administration building – a squadron of mounted men, smart in their historic red coats, was drawn up for inspection. The magnificent, carefully groomed horses, made restive by the waiting, shifted and tossed their heads against the gentle restraint of their riders.

Behind the mounted men, a dismounted squadron stood stiffly at ease. On the lawn in front of their mess, a small group of officers lead by Commissioner A. Bowen Perry chatted while awaiting the arrival of an important visitor. Everything – or almost everything – fitted into the picture of a proud, well-trained, well-disciplined corp, fully prepared for a special event. Clearly something important was in the making at the Regina Headquarters of the Royal North West Mounted Police on that October day in 1919.

There was one incongruous flaw in the picture. A single rank of about thirty men lined the curb in front of the barrack buildings. Dressed in nondescript clothes, part stable uniform, part civvies – most of them distinctly unmilitary in their bearing – these were clearly the raw recruits, the awkward squad. Only at the last minute had the Commissioner, probably with some misgivings, countermanded an order that would have banished them from sight – or, in the words of the Sergeant Major, "kept them from mucking up the landscape."

1

Some of these men were veterans of World War I that had just ended. Long experience had innured them to the thrill of inspection, or it had at least trained them not to allow their excitement to show. But many of us in the awkward squad that day were young, too young to have served in the War. I was not yet eighteen, and only my height of six feet had enabled me to convince the recruiting sergeant that I had passed that minimum age requirement. Most of us had been in the Force only a few days. It was thrilling, even as a member of the awkward squad, to be on the drill square of a Force that had played a large part in the settlement and building of Western Canada. It was thrilling to recall the events and engagements to which men had gone from these very barracks. It was thrilling, too, to think that someday, if we made the grade, we might take our places as trained men and be considered worthy of wearing the "Red Serge."

Suddenly, sharp words of command brought the squadrons to ramrod-straight attention, then to the "Present Arms." Several cars entered the barracks area and drove slowly around the parade ground to the officers' mess. Dignitaries and aides alighted and were followed by a slight, boyish figure in military uniform. The Prince of Wales, later King Edward VIII, had arrived to inspect the old headquarters on the banks of Pile of Bones Creek.

After welcoming the Prince, who was then at the height of his popularity and an almost-idolized figure in Canada, Commissioner Perry presented his officers. Then, accompanied by several aides and officers, the Prince and the Commissioner moved to the parade ground for the inspection of the assembled troops. The inspection went smoothly. The Prince, an old hand at spotting medals, stopped frequently to chat with men who had served overseas with the squadrons sent from the Force to France or Siberia, or with veterans who had served with other units. There were many medals on parade that day.

Having completed his inspection of the smartly turned-out troops, the Prince hesitated for a moment while he glanced across the square at the odd assortment of men lining a bit of the curb. We must have looked strangely out of place, strange enough to arouse his curiosity, for he came across the square to get a closer look at us. His Royal Highness walked slowly along our line. There was no stopping to speak to any of us, but it did seem that he was studying each face carefully, and that his scrutiny was much more detailed than had been the case with the properly uniformed squadrons. Probably some of us thought that we were making an impression on the Prince, which indeed we were. At the end of our line he turned to study us collectively for a while, before saying to the Commissioner in a loud, clear voice, "These, I take it, are the prisoners."

As they moved off in the direction of the stables, the Commissioner said something to the Prince. I never will know whether or not he admitted that this odd-looking group actually belonged to the Force.

A year earlier, I had been attending a technical school in Hamilton, Ontario, where my parents lived. The hope had been that I would be able to complete the course there and go on to university, but family fortune – or rather lack of it – made that hope somewhat dim.

The War ended in November of 1918. Victory celebrations were scarcely over before the signs of hard times to come began to appear. It was only a few months and the family budget could no longer support me and pay for my schooling. The only decision possible was that I leave school to help bolster the income. Further education would have to be acquired by way of night school and correspondence courses.

The decision was a hard and disappointing one for my parents, who had cherished great plans for their two sons. My brother William, three years my senior, was still in the army overseas. He had set the precedent I was to follow later, by using his height to mislead a recruiting sergeant regarding his age. Recruiting sergeants did not pay too much attention to birth certificates during World War I.

My parents knew nothing of his enlistment until he had been accepted. They could have stopped him then, but in the spirit of those days, thousands of youngsters were stretching their ages to join the Colours. Kipling was still regarded as an authority on Empire and Glory. King, Flag, and Country were next only to God, and beyond question God was on the side of the Allies. Most parents felt bound by loyalty and duty to let their youngsters join up and serve. However, great pride in his service did not offset my parents' concern over my brother's education and future. Now hard times brought them worry about my future.

Although I liked school and had been doing quite well in my studies, the decision that I must leave was not as disappointing to me as it was to my parents. During the War years, I shared with all my friends an eager anticipation of the day we would be able to join one of the services. Our planning for the future never went much beyond the hope of getting overseas, and of glamorous homecomings as conquering heroes. But even during the War years, I had a second ambition. Vaguely formed at first, this gradually became part of my overall plan for the future.

From my reading and from tales told by visitors to our home, I had learned something of the West, the prairies, the Indians, the settlers, the putting through of the railways, and of the Royal North West Mounted Police. It seemed that whenever tales were told of the West, a mounted policeman was in the picture. What better plan could a young man have than of joining one of the services and going overseas – to return covered with medals and glory – to enjoy for a time a hero's welcome before applying to the Royal North West Mounted Police! The War record would assure acceptance by the Force.

My youthful dreams ended with the War, and I was forced to adjust to the likelihood of a less exciting career. That settled, there seemed to be more point in schooling and studies. I had begun to tackle these with increased interest when the Depression dictated that I leave school. I was not yet seventeen, and disappointment and doubt about the future ought not to ride very heavily at that age. Apart from youth, I still had one dream to take the keen edge from my disappointment. Someday I might be able to go West to join the Force. My parents encouraged me in this hope, probably more from a desire to keep my interests high than from any expectation that the hope might be realized.

My father, the youngest of a large family, was born in a little Lincolnshire village with the improbable name of Chapel-in-Mumby. When he was four, the family came to Canada, where they settled near Hawksbury, Ontario, a centre of the lumbering industry then thriving in the Ottawa Valley. For awhile the family prospered. Grandfather, a veterinarian, ranged far and wide among the lumber camps, and fees were plentiful. Prosperity ended tragically when grandfather suffered severe and crippling injuries in a logging accident. He lingered on for a year or two but was no longer the breadwinner.

The entire burden of raising the large family fell to my grandmother. As a boy, I heard from my father and my visiting aunts and uncles many stories of how they grew up on the farms on which they lived: stories of hardships met and overcome, of chores assigned to each, of efforts to get work done for themselves and for neighbours, all in time to allow for schooling. Into these tales there were always woven threads of love and affection for the mother who, while imposing hard work and discipline on her children, applied an even harder code to herself. Many times during those troubled years she had brought the family through on little more than courage and hope.

I met my grandmother only once when she visited us in Hamilton. I was very young, but one of the clearest of my memories is of a tall, erect, elderly lady who looked severe and strict, yet she was always on hand to smooth over my troubles. She was always on hand at bedtimes, too, to read a few verses from the Bible.

There was no estate when she passed on. Her children were already possessed of those touchstones that had guided her: a strong, unshakeable belief in the Bible, in hard work, in being under obligation to no one. Her children were also imbued with a belief that my Father had adopted regarding the beneficial effects of discipline, especially when applied to growing boys in the place and manner most suited to the occasion.

Having left England at the age of four, my father's memories of the Old Country were vague. Nevertheless, he retained a deep-rooted loyalty to England, the Crown, and the Flag. Even today, at eighty-eight, he will do ready battle with anyone who implies the slightest criticism of that triumvirate. Although radio and television now bring many such critics into his home, he refuses to be swayed or moved from his old anchors to windward. In some ways, I am thankful for the critics and detractors; they provide Dad with the interest and joy of furious battle.

My Mother was born Elizabeth Butler in Ogdensburg, New York. Her family moved to Cornwall, Ontario, some years later, and then to Montreal, where she met and married my father. A devout and practising Methodist, her interests were her husband, her sons, her home, and her Church. She, too, was a firm believer in the values of hard work and discipline, rules by which she lived and which she applied with firmness well mixed with humour and love.

Mother had a gift of understanding and sympathizing with the difficulties of others. She had another quality that impressed me deeply and which I have recalled many times. Almost automatically, she cut through the complications and side-issues of problems or troubles in order to arrive at the nub. Thus isolated, the problem or trouble usually lost dimension. Mother would then proceed methodically to examine alternative courses of action. Having decided on the course most likely to prove successful, she refused to be moved by doubt or to be worried by misgivings.

Church, Sunday school, Junior Epworth League meetings, prayers, work assignments, and chores were a regular part of our lives. A first offence against the rules laid down for the behaviour of brother Bill or myself would bring a stern warning of punishment for future offenses, a warning that was always fulfilled if we had the temerity to repeat the misbehaviour. Trips to the woodshed, where the old-fashioned strap hung in readiness, were not infrequent. Years later, I discovered that these conducted trips should have caused feelings of repression, of resentment and rebellion. My brother and I, according to some modern theories, should have been twisted and torn by inhibitions whacked into us by that strap. Fortunately for us, we were not aware of these theories and took the trips to the woodshed as a part of the process of growing up. Even now when I think back, I am without resentment. Every forced meeting I had with the strap was richly deserved.

Sundays were days of rather mixed blessings. On the one hand, I could not regard Sunday clothes, Church, Sunday school, the rule that games must not be played, and the fact that the gramophone must remain silent, with any great joy or enthusiasm. On the other hand, there was usually "company" for Sunday night dinner, and this brought a touch of excitement and change and, sometimes, wonderful stories.

Tom McKay, our next-door neighbour and a close friend of my Father, was a frequent visitor. He told marvellous tales of his boyhood in Scotland and of the old wars of the clans and of battles fought and victories won by kilted regiments. Somehow, while speaking to the adults, his stories seemed to be aimed at the children. At such times, I regretted that I had not been born a Scot.

Then there was my wandering uncle. His occasional visits were looked forward to with eager anticipation. He was a marvellous story-teller and had visited in many parts of Canada. He seemed always on his way from a job in one part of the country to make a million dollars somewhere else. The million, or even a very small part of it, never materialized, but he had a lot of fun in the pursuit. Our parents were always rather guarded in talking about this wanderer, but my brother and I picked up enough to know that he was a "drinking man" with a knack for finding trouble and getting into the middle of whatever fracas happened to be taking place. My uncle did not hold with the rule that children should not be heard and, in fact, insisted on addressing himself to us and seeking our views. This flattering approach, his ability as a story-teller, his travels, plus the guarded comments regarding his drinking and fighting abilities, made him a prime favourite.

It was from my wandering uncle that I first heard about the Royal North West Mounted Police. He avoided going into details about how he had acquired his very considerable knowledge of the day-to-day work of the Force, but he did know a great deal about their ability to bring a quick end to over-exuberant disturbances, about their impartiality in maintaining law and order in the rapidly developing prairie country, and even about the insides of their buildings and jails. Whichever way he had gained this knowledge, his experiences had left him with a high regard for the Force and a fund of tales about their prowess. The kilted clansmen of Tom McKay had to make way in my mind for the "red-coated riders of the West."

Another frequent guest at Sunday dinner was the pastor of our Church, the Reverend Todd, always referred to by his senior parishioners as the "Young Preacher" with emphasis on the "Young." Calvary Methodist was a small Church in one of the less well-to-do sections of Hamilton. I suspect that only a young bachelor could have existed on whatever salary was paid, and then only with the bounty of meals taken with members of the congregation. The young preacher was thoroughly dedicated to his work and to the well-being of his flock, but he was also a hungry young man. Mother was an outstanding cook, and it was my great good fortune that the attractions of her table brought the Reverend Todd to our home often, Sundays and week days.

His elders did not always see eye-to-eye with the young preacher. For one thing, he did not put the usual and expected emphasis on hellfire and brimstone. His sermons leaned more to the need for understanding and forgiveness than to punishment. At times his sermons were filled with humour, and in some way many of the older parishioners regarded this as not quite proper or in keeping with the spirit of a religious service.

He managed to overcome the resistance, and under his guidance Sunday school sessions and meetings of the youth groups became enjoyable rather than simply the carrying out of a duty. While some parents found fault with his theory that the solemnity of church gatherings could and should be tempered by a little fun and happiness, the children loved him. I became such an admirer that for a time, under his urging, aided and abetted by Mother, kilts and red-coats seemed less attractive than a clerical collar.

The Reverend Todd talked to youngsters at their own level, and it was easy to sense that this was not a sham or an act like those put on by many adults. He was really interested, and he understood the wants, the dreams, and the reasons for many questions. His understanding brought a return flow of confidence in him and in his views.

It was a surprise to me to learn that he too had been addicted to the *Boy's Own Annual* and Horatio Alger, and even to the occasional "Dime Novel," the paperbacks of the time. We talked about some of these yarns, and gradually a practice developed of discussing my current reading during each of his visits. He always seemed curious about my views and wanted my reasons for thinking a story good or bad. These discussions increased my interest in books. I learned to read with more care and concentration in order that I might be prepared for the next session.

After a time he began to bring me books from his own library and from the public library. I opened the first of these books with some misgiving. Despite his grounding in the *Boy's Own Annual* and despite our discussions, I still clung to the vague notion that clergymen were limited in their reading to the Bible, Sunday school tracts, and *Pilgrim's Progress*. But the book was *Treasure Island*. I wish I could again experience the excitement and pleasure of that first reading, and of the session that followed, during which every twist of the story was studied and every character analyzed. We went through many books that way.

After a few years, Calvary Methodist Church moved into a grand new building. The eastern part of the city of Hamilton was developing rapidly, and the congregation had outgrown the old frame house of worship. The new prosperity touched the pastor. He was provided with quarters that were sumptuous by comparison with the broading-house room in which he had lived. His salary was brought into line with the brand-new Church. But the Reverend Todd was not much interested in prosperity. Shortly after the opening of the new building, he accepted a call to a tiny church in a small remote town in Northern Ontario. I never saw him again. I am forever indebted to him for his friendship, for having shown me the meaning of dedication, and for his gift of the enjoyment of reading.

A very rare and welcome visitor was my uncle Jack, my Father's eldest brother. As a young man, he was one of the first homesteaders in the Big Quill Lake area of Saskatchewan. He had watched the lonesome land fill with settlers from the east and from foreign lands. Growth was slow at first, until the building of a railway through the area brought a rush of settlers and a fair measure of prosperity. And many times during the development of the new country, he had given shelter to Mounted Policemen when they stopped by on their long patrols, patrols that meant a visit to every homestead, just to make sure that all was well. Listening to Uncle Jack reminisce about the early days and of the pleasure of seeing a lone red-coat coming across the prairie to visit with him, and realizing the regard in which these men were held by the settlers for their help in time of trouble, was powerful stuff indeed for a youngster. It took very little imagination to put oneself in the rider's place and to fight through heat and blizzard and sandstorm and rows of villains in order to bring help and peace and order to the homesteaders.

After leaving school early in 1919, I managed to secure several part-time jobs. Some of these were very interesting, such as running an overhead crane, operating an engine lathe, or assembling gramophones, but none was steady. That was before unions had gained enough power to correct working conditions, so the hours were long and the pay small. In the late spring of 1919, the newspapers carried a story about the RNWMP. It told of the squadrons sent from the Force to France and Siberia, and of the hundreds of men who had purchased their discharge in order to enlist for overseas service. The Force would not compete with the armed services for recruits. During the War years, the strength had dropped from nine hundred to three hundred, just about its strength when the Force marched West in 1874.

The article went on to say that the Government had authorized the Commissioner of the Force to carry out a recruiting campaign to engage about one thousand men, and that part of the recruiting would be done in Eastern Canada. A few days later, the local papers carried an advertisement saying that a recruiting sergeant would visit Hamilton for several days during the coming week. Recruits were required to be of sound health, of a minimum height of five-feet-eight inches, a maximum weight of one hundred and seventy-five pounds, and not less than eighteen years of age. They would be required to sign engagement papers for a period of not less than three years. Pay would be at the rate of two dollars *per diem*. It did not take a great deal of coaxing to get my parents' consent to apply. The stickler was the age limit. I had just passed my seventeenth birthday.

I believe I was the first applicant to appear before the recruiting sergeant, an imposing figure in his Red Serge, blue breeches, riding boots, and spurs. His Stetson hat, riding crop, and gauntlets were on the desk beside him. He was kindly and understanding, but he was also firm. No birth certificate, no engagement. This was my hometown. My parents were here; it should be a simple matter to produce a birth certificate. He was a good judge of age, for he suggested that I wait about a year and then try again. It was a very dejected boy who made way for the next applicant.

High hopes do not die easily. On the street car on the way home, I kept reviewing the conversation with the Sergeant. It soon became apparent that my weakness had stemmed from the fact that this was my hometown. Had I applied a thousand miles away, I might have given some plausible reason for not having a birth certificate. But travelling to far-away places costs money and, besides, I was sure that my parents would never agree to my going anywhere without money, friends, or a job. Then I recalled the harvest trains. By the time I arrived home, I had a new plan to place before my parents.

In those days, the railways ran special trains every August to carry workers from Eastern Canada to help harvest the crops on the prairies. The fare was twelve dollars to the dispersal point at Winnipeg. From Winnipeg, the workers were given very low rates to the places where they were to be employed. A certificate allowed the purchase of low-fare tickets to return to Eastern Canada when the crops were in. Uncle Jack was still living on his farm in Saskatchewan. Why couldn't I wait until August and then take advantage of the low-rate harvest trains to visit Uncle Jack? While there, I could earn some money harvesting and then go down to Regina to apply again to the Force.

My parents did not share my enthusiasm. The trip would be long and hard in so-called "immigrant" coaches of the special train. Further, the harvesters had a reputation for toughness and were not fit travelling companions for a seventeen-year-old boy. Why, just last year the papers had told of fighting and rioting by the harvesters in some of the towns where the trains had stopped. Besides, Uncle Jack might not want me to visit him just at harvest time.

It took several days and much persuasion before it was agreed that it would do no harm to write to Uncle Jack. There were days of anxious waiting for his reply, but when it came, his letter was everything I could have asked for. He would be delighted to have me and could keep me busy during harvest. After the crops were in, I could go down to Regina to try for the Force. If that didn't work out, I could go back to stay with him during the winter, until I had passed my eighteenth birthday in March, or I could stay on with him. He was a bachelor and getting on in years. He planned to return to the east before too long, and probably I would like to take over the farm when he had had enough. That settled the matter. The trip was on.

By the time August rolled around – and it was very slow rolling – I had saved enough for my fare and for the purchase of food on the way. Mother and Dad added what they could to my funds, and I was ready for the big day. The good-byes for this first trip away from home were not easy. I was grateful that the station was crowded and busy so that any show of emotion could be held off until the last minute. Then the "allaboard" sounded, there were hurried embraces, and I mounted the train with great expectations, enough money to see me through, and a large hamper of my mother's cooking.

I have made the trip across Canada many times since with good and sometimes luxurious accommodation, but never again did I experience the excitement and sense of adventure of that first journey. True, the slats of the "immigrant" coaches had not been designed for comfort. True, too, the train seemed to spend most of the time on sidings waiting for the regular trains to go through. Meals were a little sketchy in that any cooking required had to be done on a small coal stove in a tiny compartment at one end of the coach – but what did it matter? I was on my way to the prairies.

My companions were not toughs. They were good men trying to earn money during bad times, and they were willing to work hard and long to get it. Many were labourers who had made the trip before. Some were men who were out of regular employment because of the Depression – craftsmen, skilled workers, white-collar men, all bent on making a stake against what promised to be a rough winter. And there were some lads around my own age trying to find something to do, somewhere to start.

I wondered how the reputation for fighting and rioting by the harvesters had started and grown. A partial answer was provided at a few of the towns where the train stopped to allow passengers to purchase food. In most of the towns, the merchants charged prices a little higher than normal, but not outrageously so. In a few towns, however, the prices asked were little short of robbery: one dollar for a loaf of bread, or a bottle of milk, or a pound of tomatoes. Double prices for tobacco and cigarettes. Most of the harvesters were short of funds. Small wonder that there were fights and near riots. A few years later, I was to have the satisfaction of playing a small part toward correcting these conditions.

We arrived in Winnipeg on the morning of the fifth day of the trip. The station was filled with noisy bustle and activity as the seven hundred passengers from our train surged into the already crowded waiting room. Desks had been set up around the waiting room for the use of employment agents representing the various regions of the prairies. Many of the harvesters had not decided on a destination, and these moved from desk to desk seeking information regarding conditions and rates of pay being offered in the different areas. Having reached a decision, they registered for work and received a slip which permitted them to purchase cheap transportation to the desired point.

I had no problem as to destination. Kandahar, Saskatchewan, was the station closest to my uncle's farm. I registered for work there and lined up at the wicket to purchase my special-rate ticket. While waiting, I noticed several men making their way down the line of harvesters ahead of me. After a time, one of these chaps approached me with an offer of ten dollars for the ticket stub that allowed for the purchase of a low-rate return ticket to Eastern Canada after harvesting was over. I hesitated for a few moments. That return stub would get me back home if things went wrong. But optimism regarding the future, plus ten dollars, won out. I sold my return stub.

My Uncle Jack was waiting for me on the station platform at Kandahar and gave me a warm welcome. It was a little disappointing to find that he had a car. I had imagined a long drive in a wagon or, at least, in a buckboard. During the ride to the farm, I answered a barrage of questions regarding the health and welfare of Mother and Dad and of all the aunts and uncles and nephews and nieces back east. Uncle Jack, no great hand at writing, was eager for news of the family.

The farm house provided another surprise. This was not the sod shack that he had described during some of his visits but a new, comfortable, well-furnished home. The old sod-roofed cabin was still standing, although the general appearance of the farm would have been improved by its removal. Later, in discussing the early days with Uncle Jack, it became apparent that he had a great fondness for the old building that had sheltered him through many tough seasons in the early days. Eye-sore or not, it would stand as long as he was around.

Harvesting started a few days after my arrival. From the time the grain ripened until it was cut, stooked, dried, threshed, and stored, it was a hard steady race against the frost. Work was from dawn to dusk. My uncle owned the neighbourhood threshing machine. When threshing started, all the neighbours pitched in with a will in order to get the machine to their own farms as soon as possible. The women pitched in too, to provide tables groaning with good food.

Uncle Jack gave me an easy task. Most of the water in the area contained too much alkali for use in the steam engine that ran the threshing mill. I am not sure of the effect of the alkali water on a steam engine, but I did learn from somewhat painful experience that it packs much too much power for consumption by a greenhorn. Good water had to be hauled several miles. I was assigned a team, ancient in deference to my inexperience, and a stone-boat on which two barrels were mounted. My chore was to keep the engine serviced with good water. The ancient horses had lost their mettle and required some urging to break into a trot, but the job of driving them across the rolling prairie and occasionally flushing prairie chickens or sighting a coyote held a great deal of attraction for a city-bred boy.

I enjoyed every minute of my stay with Uncle Jack and left his place with some reluctance on the first day of October. He drove me to the station and made me promise that I would come straight back if the Force did not accept me. There had been no talk of pay for my work, but as I was boarding the train he thrust some bills into my hand and said, "Here's what you earned." When I counted it later, I found that he had paid me the top rate for experienced teamsters. I arrived in Regina with more money in my pocket than I had ever before possessed.

In Regina, I bought a new shirt and tie, got a haircut, and had my suit pressed. The following morning, after my first night in an hotel, I splurged and took a taxi to the headquarters of the Royal North West Mounted Police on the outskirts of the city.

I was directed to the administration building where, after a brief interview and an examination of my letters of reference, a corporal handed me an application form. Opposite the question "Date of Birth," I wrote, "March 26, 1901," instead of "1902." There was no request for a birth certificate, but this falsehood was to cause me some considerable difficulty in later years. Following completion of the application form, I was given several written tests. These were followed by a rather lengthy interview with an officer. I didn't know it at the time but the officer was Inspector Denny Lanauze, an almost-legendary figure in the Force because of his exploits in the far North. He must have been satisfied that I might have the makings of a policeman, for having warned me that if engaged I would be required to sign on for three years of service, but that I could be discharged as unsuitable at any moment, he instructed me to report to the hospital for a medical examination. By noon, and after much thumping and pounding by the doctor, I had passed the physical tests.

Following lunch, which I was permitted to have in the mess, I was required to write an essay on Canada. The product must have proven satisfactory, for I was then taken before an officer to be sworn in. He was in no hurry about the process. For almost half an hour he spoke to me of the history of the Force, of how it had played a full part in the settling and development of the West, and of the traditions that had been built up by many men since 1873. He spoke, too, of the low pay, the long hours, and the hardships to be expected in the service. He emphasized the need for strict discipline and that such discipline would be applied at all times, and he repeated the warning that, if found unsuitable, I would be dismissed forthwith. Certainly his talk would have achieved its main purpose, which was to discourage applicants who were not firm in their desire to serve the Force and live up to its requirements.

The swearing-in ceremony was carried out with all due solemnity. In the presence of several non-commissioned officers called in for the occasion, I took the Oath of Allegiance and the Oath of Office. The latter ends with words that have become well-known and which form an excellent guide for any law-enforcement officer: "I will well and truly obey and perform all lawful orders and instructions which I shall receive as such without fear, favour, or affection of, or toward, any person. So help me God."

The Force is now almost a hundred years old. My experience started at almost the half-way mark. Looking back, it is easy to see that I was privileged to join at a time when a new chapter was opening, a chapter that would see wide expansion of jurisdiction, many added duties and responsibilities, and great increases in manpower and resources. It is of these developments that I wish to write. But the growth and expansion would not have been possible, the new responsibilities could not have been undertaken and fulfilled without the loyalties, without the spirit and the tradition that were made a part of the fabric of the Force by the men who served between 1873 and 1919.

2

-»»-»»-»»-»»«-«-«-«-«-

Success —
On a Trial Basis

Immediately after the swearing-in ceremony, I was required to report back to the Corporal from whom I had received the application form that morning. During this second interview, it was very clear that my status had undergone a considerable change during the last few hours. His voice and attitude were no longer those of a public official supplying information to a civilian. There was no invitation to sit down. He was now a Corporal giving instructions to the lowest of the low, the most recently joined recruit. There could be no delay in the start of training. Using a chart, he described the badges of rank by which I could recognize officers and NCO's, and the forms of address to be used in replying to them. The "replying" was very clear. Recruits remained silent unless spoken to. On general deportment, the instructions were brief and to the point. "From the moment you leave this office, you will do everything at the double – and that means on the run."

He then handed me a slip of paper which assigned me to Three Troop of the junior squadron and to Tent 22. A second piece of paper instructed the quartermaster to issue to "Regimental Number 8758," a long list of articles of uniform, clothing, and kit. I was instructed to go to the supply stores on my way to the tent, and I was reminded that this was to be done "on the double." The Corporal ended the interview, somewhat disturbingly, with a curt, "Good luck – I think you'll need it."

In the supply stores, a blanket was spread on the floor, and into this the quartermaster and his assistant tossed a somewhat bewildering array of articles. Spare blankets, underwear, socks, a hoof pick, bandolier, Sam Browne belt, grooming kit, button stick, cleaning brushes, tooth

14

brush, hair brush, lanyard, gauntlets, spurs, moccasins, long woollen stockings, knitted toque, woollen and leather mitts, kid gloves, dunnage bag, kit bag, a Lee-Enfield Rifle, and a Colt .45 revolver.

Items of actual uniform were in short supply. The small mountain of kit that had accumulated on the blanket included one pair of canvas stable trousers and a pair of stable boots. So as far as dress was concerned, I remained a civilian from the waist up for some weeks.

Having assembled a fairly staggering load of equipment, the quartermaster sergeant advised me that further articles of uniform would be issued as received in stores, except for the Scarlet Serge. "You'll have to earn that," he said. Ammunition for the rifle and revolver would be issued at the appropriate time after I had received instructions in the handling of firearms. The issue of saddlery would wait until the start of riding instructions or, as it is always referred to in the Force, equitation.

After signing numerous receipts, there remained the task of transporting my new possessions. The blanket would not encompass the pile, so I draped the bandolier and Sam Browne belt around my neck, placed the revolver in the holster, tied the four corners of the blanket, and heaved the bundle to my shoulders. Grasping the Lee-Enfield rifle with my free hand, I started slowly for the door. An explosive "on the *double*" from the sergeant reminded me that from here on in there was to be no dawdling. I must have looked like a refugee from some rebel army as I trotted toward the tent lines.

It was the hour of the afternoon stable parade. The tent lines were deserted. After a time, I located and entered Number 22. The tents were of the "Bell" type, wherein one sleeps with his feet toward the centre pole. There were no floor boards or cots. From the arrangements of blankets on the ground, it was apparent that I would have four companions. I unloaded my belongings onto the remaining clear space and sat down on the bundle to review the events of the last few hours. This was not quite the picture I had had of joining the Force. Reality had displaced glamour, but the reality was still good. I had a small heap of kit to prove that I had been accepted, even though the acceptance had been somewhat tentative.

There was a great rush and bustle and noise in the tent lines as the recruits, just dismissed from stable parade raced to throw grooming kits into their tents and then raced to the long, cold-water troughs for a quick wash before lining up at the mess hall. My four tent-mates arrived on the run, hesitated for quick introductions, and invited me to join them in the hurry for dinner.

Our squadron ate in a building that had been erected as a temporary mess, pending the completion of new barracks. Only about a third of the squadron could be seated at one time. That, and ravenous appetites, explained the great rush. The mess door opened precisely fifteen minutes after the dismissal of the stable parade. The fortunate one-third at the head of the line got in quickly. The tardy waited in line to be admitted as vacancies occurred.

The brief delay caused by my presence placed us well back in line. Waiting gave us an opportunity to become better acquainted. Bill Flemming, a tall, solemn-looking man, several years older than the average recruit, was the obvious leader of our tent group. He had served in the army overseas and was, therefore, no stranger to recruit-training camps. I learned later that he had the good soldier's highly developed instinct for being in the right place at the right time, and far, far away when extra duties or some unpleasantness was in the air. He had acquired vast knowledge regarding the ways of officers and NCO's and the manner in which those ways could, at times, be turned to advantage. Parades, uniforms, firearms – all were old stuff to him and, more important, he was very willing to impart his knowledge to his young tent-mates. I was fortunate, indeed, to have landed in Tent 22.

The others were young men not yet turned twenty. Steve, tall, slim, blond, was from Vancouver. He had spent a short time at university before his love of the outdoors and riding lead him to join the Force. His knowledge of riding was most helpful to the rest of us when we reached that stage of our training. The third man, another Bill, was a quiet, cheerful, heavy-set lad from the maritimes. He was tremendously powerful and had been conditioned by work in lumber camps. His great strength was to prove a little embarrassing to our ju-jitsu and wrestling instructors. Bill completed three years of service and then left the Force to become a clergyman. I don't remember much about the fourth man, except that he seemed vastly unhappy in his new surroundings and talked only about his home. He lasted about a month. Shortly after we started learning to ride, he was let out as "unsuitable." The riding school is, in the well-worn words of the instructors, a good place in which to "sort the men from the boys."

The mess, in both appearance and food, was a far cry from the comfortable, spotless, and good dining-rooms that have been developed since. The temporary building was sheathed in quarter-inch lumber. Several months of prairie rain and heat had warped the thin lumber until it was no longer necessary to use the windows to see outside. The "air conditioning" was so advanced that when the snow and really cold weather came a few weeks later, the first comers into the seats near the wall had to brush small drifts of snow from the tables. By that time, we had been issued with our fur coats and hats and were permitted to wear them while eating. The furnishings were simple – wooden tables and benches, without curtains, tablecloths, pictures, or paint to mar the simplicity of the decor.

I don't know the source from which the cooks had been recruited, but it is certain that they had not been drawn from restaurants that had offered a variety of dishes. In fact, there is some room for doubt that they had ever seen the insides of a kitchen before being employed by the Force as civilian cooks. It took just two days to sample their entire range. Breakfasts never varied; scrambled eggs, cooked in huge pans, came out somewhat rubbery but were nevertheless fairly good. It would be an error to say that the cooks knew how to prepare two dishes for lunches and dinner, but they did turn out efforts at macaroni and cheese and a Mulligan stew. These preparations alternated with dreary monotony during the several months that this batch of cooks held sway in the kitchens. Their reign came to a sudden and fitting end when, during one noon-day inspection, the orderly officer dug a ladle deep into the stew pot. When withdrawn, it held a very large and straggley dishcloth. A crew of Chinese cooks appeared in the kitchen the next day. From there on we enjoyed excellent meals.

After dinner that first day, we proceeded – policemen never just go, they always proceed – to the notice board to look over the orders for the next day. Under Three Troop, I found evidence that the clerks worked with speedy efficiency. Constable C. W. Harvison was already shown as a member and mentioned for special duties. My first day in the Force would be spent on kitchen fatigue.

Back in the tent, my companions showed me how to make down my bed, which consisted of a mattress-cover filled with straw, and how equipment must be stored or arranged in order to comply with the regulations. This was followed by a brief description of daily activities. From Bill Flemming came advice regarding the cleaning and care of firearms, which, as an old soldier, he regarded as the most important of all duties. By the time I had arranged or packed everything in its proper place, it was close to "lights out," which sounded at ten-thirty, after a roll call in each tent. It was well to be in bed before the lantern had to be put out.

At five-thirty the following morning, the piercing notes of reveille were accompanied by loud whacks on the taut sides of the tents, as the night guards did their part toward stirring the camp into action. In just twenty-five minutes, everyone had to be on parade or at the post to which he had been detailed for the day. Beds had to be made, kit and equipment properly placed, and the tent prepared for morning inspection before the occupants could leave. Again there was no time for dawdling. There were just seconds to spare when I rushed into the kitchen to start a very full day of mopping, dishwashing, and potato-peeling. I was starting low on the ladder. There was nowhere to go but up.

The days that followed were busy and filled with interest. The newest recruits to the squadron went through the usual, awkward-squad days before being allowed to parade with their troops. Drill, and later riding parades, were interspersed with lectures and firearm-training and, of course, the extra duties; kitchen, stable guard, and general fatigues. It soon became obvious that our squadron was being readied to meet that part of the Government directive that called for the Force to be prepared to "assist the Civil Powers in the preservation of law and order." As our training advanced, it became increasingly concerned with subjects related to the controlling of riots and unlawful assemblies.

There were a few lectures on the Criminal Code, powers of a peace officer, and rules of evidence, but during the training in Regina, these were rather elementary. Then as now, however, great emphasis was placed on imbuing the recruits with the history and tradition of the Force. For the most part, talks on these subjects were given by members of the training staff, but occasionally retired members were brought in to tell us of very early days on the prairies or of the opening of the Northland. All of the lecturers were men of long experience in police work, but very few were trained as skilled speakers. Years of writing brief, curt, factual police reports had developed a uniformity in their style of recounting events. Most of them tended toward understatement. Dealing with feats of tremendous courage or endurance or both in such a way was, in fact, much more effective and lasting than any attempt at embellishment or exaggeration could have been. Thus courage and the willingness to undergo hardship in order to do a necessary job were shown to the recruits as being the normal and expected attributes of men, and not as characteristics to be regarded as rare or as fit subjects for boasting.

From these speakers, and especially from the retired men, we learned too that it had not been all work and hardship. There had been time out occasionally for a spot of fun. In relating adventures in this field, there was less inclination toward understatement. We gathered that those regulations which tended to rule out some of the more important forms of fun, celebration, and pleasure had suffered many fractures. The view seemed to be that, as regards those particular regulations, the offense was in being caught.

After a little more than a month of dismounted training, riding was added to our curriculum. This addition brought several changes in the daily routine. We were relieved of many of the fatigue duties which were taken over by newer recruits. In place of these chores, our squadron was now required to attend three one-hour stable parades daily, during which we cleaned the stables and fed and groomed the horses. Most of the horses were recent purchases of prairie stock: unbroken, unclipped, and unshod. These shaggy-looking animals were less than enthusiastic about recruits in general, particularly those recruits who attempted to apply curry comb and brush or tried to comb out matted manes and tails. Grooming them was not a dull, quiet operation.

Several corrals had been built between the stables. In these the "breaking staff" rode the new horses two or three times. In theory, this tamed the horses and prepared them for use by the recruits. The horses, however, were not disposed to be co-operative in this plan. The so-called breaking seemed to serve only to annoy them and to bring out hitherto unused streaks of meanness. Subsequent trips to the smithy, where their legs were tethered to stout posts, while they were being clipped, singed, and shod, did nothing to improve their tempers. As a result, the first few days in the riding school were a bit chaotic. We would have had a difficult enough task staying aboard trained horses, but the untamed broncos added immeasurably to the woes of the would-be riders. Here were opportunities galore to avenge themselves for the indignities suffered in the breaking corrals and in the smithy, and the horses took full advantage of the opportunities. The uneasy riders made many forced landings, the hazards of which were increased by flying hooves, as the late mounts attempted to get a few kicks at their tormentors. Eventually, and after many bumps and bruises, the time came when most of the riders could remain on horses most of the time. There followed hours and hours of riding at the trot without stirrups, or riding bareback. This was calculated to improve balance and harden the seats of the riders, but the latter purpose was not achieved without many applications of pipe-clay to the raw seats that were in the process of hardening. Just when we had reached the stage where we could ride a horse with some measure of confidence, another refinement was added.

We started our "riot" training, and chaos again visited the riding school. Riot training is designed to accustom the horses to noise, shots, quickly moving figures, and obstacles on the ground. It achieves this purpose but only after several sessions of lessening bedlam. Dummies with bells attached were suspended from the ceiling of the riding school so that they hung just above ground level. Logs and strips of white cloth were placed at various angles on the tanbark. A squad of men, carrying shotguns, tin pans, drums, and umbrellas, took up position in the centre of the menage. When a mounted troop entered the riding school, the doors were firmly closed, and the troop in single file was given the order to trot around the school.

At this point, minor difficulties arose as the horses shied away from the hanging dummies and the strips of white cloth. Then, just as the troop was getting into some semblance of order, the dummies started swinging, shotguns blasted off, tin cans clanged, and men rushed toward the horses raising and lowering umbrellas and waving white cloths. All hell broke loose as horses, with or without their riders, galloped madly about in a desperate effort to break clear of the uproar, and as thrown riders tried to avoid being run down. Surprisingly, the horses became accustomed to the clatter and moving objects after a few sessions. A few more sessions and they could be brought to "passage" against the dummies or to nuzzle men carrying shotguns and umbrellas. From that point on, noise-makers and shotguns were brought into the school periodically but caused little disruption to our mounted drill.

The old riding-school system was, in my view, unnecessarily and unwisely rough on horses and men. There were many accidents and injuries, a number of them serious. These methods did turn out good riders, but so do the better-planned, more humane methods of today.

Toward the end of November, rumours of impending changes in the Force started to circulate. It was said that the name was to be changed, that the jurisdiction was to be extended, that our squadron was to be transferred east, that the headquarters would be transferred to Ottawa. The rumours enlivened barrack-room conversation and led to an aroused interest in signs and portents. The stories gained strength, but we were left guessing for some time. The November weather had turned bitterly cold, and a great deal of snow had fallen. Tenting on the old camp grounds and eating in the weather-worn, temporary, wind-swept mess was hardly in keeping with the "food, lodging, and other accommodation" mentioned in recruiting circulars. We remained in the tents until December 20, when at long last the new C Block was completed. The new building, with its comfortable although crowded barrack rooms, warm, clean mess, library, and recreation room, was sheer luxury after the weeks of tent living.

Christmas Day was a memorable occasion. All members undergoing training or stationed in the Regina area were crowded into the mess hall in the new building gayly decorated for the occasion. Commissioner Perry and his officers had dinner with the other ranks. After dinner, the Commissioner rose to give the traditional "State of the Force" talk, a practice usually followed by a talk from the senior officer in each area. The content of the Commissioner's Christmas talk in 1919 was not unexpected. Most of the rumours that had been circulating were confirmed. He told us that, during the early part of 1920, the jurisdiction of the Force would be extended to cover all of Canada, and that this extension would entail the absorption of the Dominion Police, a federal agency that for years had carried out some federal duties, particularly in Eastern Canada. The name of the Force would be changed from Royal North West Mounted Police to Royal Canadian Mounted Police with its headquarters transferred to Ottawa. And our squadron would be the first group posted to Eastern Canada.

The Commissioner did not seem to share the excitement and enthusiasm of his audience as he told us of the changes to come. His service went back to 1882, almost to the beginning of the Force. Histories and the official reports make frequent mention of outstanding work performed by Inspector and later Superintendent A. Bowen Perry, not only in the field but in thoughtful, detailed study of the shifting problems as the prairies and Force developed. His services during the Northwest Rebellion of 1885 brought high commendation. In 1900, he was appointed Commissioner, and for nineteen years he had administered the Force with a firmness and determination that allowed for no deviation from the discipline, tradition, and principles within the service, nor for undue or improper interference from outside. He had brought the Force through many troublesome times, including the recent threat of disbandment.

A tall, greying man of commanding and dignified appearance, Perry was little given to displaying his feelings, but he seemed sad and disturbed when he spoke to us that day. At several points, he became quite emotional, as he dwelt on the changes to come. We were at a loss to understand his attitude toward expansion which, to us, seemed all to the good. Many years later, I learned that he thought in these changes he saw the beginning of the end. He had grave forebodings about the ability of the Force to maintain that impartiality in the carrying out of its duties that had been its keystone throughout the years. While the headquarters remained in Regina, he had been able to stay aloof from and clear of undue interference in the operation of the Service, particularly in the carrying out of actual law-enforcement work. His experience told him that the task would be much more difficult when the headquarters was within hailing distance of the seat of Government. He saw, too, increasing problems in maintaining the closely knit, almost family-like ties within the Force. In this he showed some lack of appreciation and confidence in the strong *esprit de corps* which he had helped inspire and build into the Service.

The confirmation of impending changes had one immediate effect on our squadron. What had been a stiff training program was tightened to a point that left no time for leisure. It became clear that everyone connected with our training was determined that the first representatives of the Force posted to Eastern Canada would leave Regina as thoroughly trained and disciplined as the officers and NCO's could make them. Drill and riding periods were increased. The schedules were extended into the evening so that lectures could be given. Inspections, scheduled and surprise, became more frequent and more searching. Time left clear of the parade ground, riding school, or lecture hall was fully taken up with cleaning kit and saddlery. Any indication that an individual could not keep up with the intensified training program was usually followed by his transfer out of the squadron to one of the new awkward squads or occasionally by his dismissal.

Early in the new year, we had an inspection by the Commissioner which, except in the case of a few unfortunates, led to the issue of Red Serges. By March, we were a well-trained, well-disciplined unit, but our training had been more that of a squadron of the cavalry than of police officers. The Government remained acutely concerned with the threat of disturbances and riots. Our role was still that of reserves to be used if a situation developed in which those normally responsible could not keep the peace and maintain good order.

New collar, shoulder, and cap badges bearing the new title of the Royal Canadian Mounted Police were issued a few days before our final inspection. We were instructed that they were to replace the old badges forthwith. We "old-timers" of a few month's service resented and resisted this change, and despite instructions turned out for several parades still wearing the RNWMP insignia. It was only after a number of us had been charged and severly reprimanded that all the old badges came down. Our instructors and lecturers had done a thorough job of indoctrination in a few months. The officer who heard the charges and administered the reprimand must have understood and to some extent shared our attitude. The charges were never entered in our service file.

The final inspection of men, horses, and equipment was completed by March 12. On that day we loaded the horses into box cars, and they started for the East under the care of twenty men detailed for that duty. That evening, the squadron boarded a special train and departed for Ottawa. We arrived in that city on March 17, 1920.

3

-»»-»»-»»-»»-«««-«««-«««-«««

With the RCMP
in
Ottawa

The trip East was an enjoyable break from the routine of training. We travelled in comfortable Pullman cars, a new experience for many of us. It was also a new experience to have a porter make up our berths. The special train made many stops to clear the way for regular rail traffic, but we had no thought of complaining. Why wish an end to this luxury, and to the wonderful meals that were provided in the diner, free of dish-washing or other fatigues?

Our porter was a huge, happy man who seemed to enjoy his somewhat exuberant passengers. Once he was out of the car when, at the usual time according to instructions, we prepared to turn in for the night. As a result of a small conspiracy, we placed our footwear in the aisle as though for cleaning. It was a startled and somewhat shaken porter who returned to the car and glanced down the aisle. Indeed, the sight of two long rows of high riding boots was enough to unnerve the most energetic porter. There was a great deal of head-shaking and muttering until he learned that we had been having a bit of fun with him. The high gloss on the riding boots can be achieved only after many hours of patient scrubbing, staining, boning, and polishing. Once achieved, the job of maintaining the mirror-like surface is a matter of personal pride and satisfaction.

Apart from surprise inspection parades, held at several of the stopping places along the way, discipline was relaxed during the trip, even to the point where we could risk playing poker and blackjack without taking the usual barrack-room precaution of posting a lookout. Regulations frowned on gambling but, nevertheless, extra-curricular

23

studies of the arts of poker and blackjack commenced in the very early recruit days. Able and experienced instructors were not lacking among the older men, with the result that most of us developed a reasonable degree of proficiency in these subjects by the time we had learned to drill and ride. This unauthorized and irregular part of training was to prove extremely useful a few years later when I was doing some under-cover work.

Money was in very short supply on the trip East, so most of the playing was for cigarettes. It was during that journey that I drew the only royal flush I have ever held in a game of stud poker. Under other circum-stances, the hand might have brought rich financial rewards. My royal flush netted me twenty-four cigarettes.

We arrived in Ottawa, and the wheels of the train had scarcely stopped turning when a trumpet sounding "fall in" reminded us that the holiday from discipline had ended. Buses were waiting to carry us to Landsdowne Park, where we were told one of the exhibition buildings had been prepared as our new barracks. We looked forward with hopeful anticipation to viewing our new living quarters. Strict economy in the spending of public funds had always been a matter of pride in the old Force. Such preparations as had been made for the squadron showed clearly that despite other changes the practice of economy, sometimes carried to the point of niggardliness, had not altered. The four troops of thirty-two men each that comprised the squadron were quartered in a huge room on the ground floor of a barn-like building which, if my memory is right, was then known as Howick Hall.

The troop areas were divided by lines of uprights that supported one row of shelving at the six-foot level. The shelving was necessary in order to comply with regulations that dictated that articles of uniform not in use were to be displayed in meticulously detailed order on a shelf over the head of each bed. The unpainted, trellis-like partitions contributed nothing toward privacy or quietude. A long table, plentifully supplied with taps and tin wash basins, ran along one wall. Another wall was lined with open showers. But again, economy had prevailed. Only cold-water plumbing had been installed. Off to one side of the room, a boxing ring stood as the sole gesture toward recreational facilities. Certainly the arrangements were compact. One room provided living, sleeping, work-ing, bathing, and boxing facilities for an entire squadron. Togetherness can be overdone.

While we were still contemplating the somewhat limited attractions of our new surroundings, trucks started to arrive with beds, mattresses, and our dunnage and kit bags from the train. The rest of the first day was taken up getting settled into the new quarters. By evening we were fairly well installed and prepared to resume the regular training schedule. The train carrying our horses, saddlery, jumping fences, lances, and other equipment arrived the following day. In the meantime, another special train had arrived carrying the staff, records, and equipment of headquarters.

Hollywood and fiction writers would colour and dramatize this event by showing the new national headquarters of the Force being set up in a spanking new police building, with flags fluttering, massed bands playing, and prominent citizens giving speeches to mark the historic occasion. Nothing could be further from the fact. Without fanfare, almost ashamedly, headquarters was crowded into limited office space over a ladies' dress shop in a somewhat dilapidated building. Some of the furniture and equipment had seen service during the Northwest Rebellion. Those of us who formed fatigue parties to assist in the setting up of the new national headquarters of the Force could see little cause for pride in the establishment. Economy and the continuation of a policy of parsimony on the part of a succession of Governments in dealing with the Force reduced the transfer of headquarters to something less than an auspicious occasion.

As might have been expected, the poor arrangements made for the location of our headquarters and for our squadron – or, as it was now known, as N Division – had an adverse effect on morale. The feeling of temporariness brought about by the makeshift character of the quarters dampened the hopes that had been raised by the extension of jurisdiction and brought back memories of the discussions in the House of Commons regarding disbandment. The future of the Force became a frequent subject of conversation in barracks, with many holding the view that, as soon as improving economic conditions brought an end to the threats of riots and unlawful assemblies, the Government's interest in maintaining the Force would end. We were not sufficiently well-informed to know that this barrack-room scuttlebut was, in fact, a fair summary of the situation. A year or two later, when employment conditions had returned to normal, the future of the Force was to hang in the balance for several months.

The drop in morale had an inevitable consequence. A number of men dropped out of the Service, either by purchasing discharge or by deliberately contriving discharge as unsuitable. Looking back, one is forced to question the wisdom of economy that brought about dissatisfaction and the loss of men whose training had cost a fair sum. But at that time, the Government or the Force – or for that matter other forces in Canada and the United States – did not and probably could not appreciate the effect and impact that social changes would have in the field of law enforcement. It would be several years before worsening conditions forced on Governments and police administrations the realization that the old methods of underpaid, under-staffed, poorly housed, and poorly equipped police would no longer serve the interests of the community.

While there were grounds for dissatisfaction following our arrival in Ottawa, there were bright spots. The citizens were friendly and sociable. Before long, most of us had developed interests outside the barracks that made life more pleasant and agreeable. The armed services welcomed us to their messes and recreational facilities, and this brought about much good companionship. Then, too, our crew of Chinese cooks, which had accompanied us, worked magic with the ration allotments and provided truly excellent meals.

Our training routine remained that of a squadron of cavalry, but there were some changes. Possibly as a gesture toward public relations, or probably in the hope of impressing members of Parliament, we rode in "full review order" through the city and passed the Parliament Buildings every Wednesday morning. The good people of Ottawa appeared to enjoy these parades, but if they had any effect on the parliamentarians, it was not visible.

Training was started for a musical ride, an old institution that had been neglected for some years. Another welcome change in the training schedule was the addition of mounted sports and trick riding. We were given an increased number of lectures on police subjects, but the emphasis remained on the handling of riots and unlawful assemblies. Our lecturers were men who had been through several riots, including the Winnipeg General Strike in which there had been bloodshed and fatalities among the strikers and police.

Over and over again they stressed the need for strict obedience to orders during times of stress. They pointed out that premature action on the part of any member of the police, even in the face of abuse or injury, might well aggravate a situation and bring an end to any hope of settling the disturbance before extreme violence occurred. They were frank, too, in expressing their opinion that riot duty was among the most difficult and distasteful jobs that the police can be called on to perform. They pointed out, and rightly so, that no matter how well or humanely their part had been carried out, and no matter who had been responsible for the violence, the police always ended up, in the view of many, as the brutal villains of the piece. Certainly our lecturers on this subject made no effort to glamourize riot duty or to minimize the difficulties that face the police in their efforts to carry out the essential maintenance of peace and good order in the face of mob violence.

4

➤➤-➤➤-➤➤-➤➤-❰❰-❰❰-❰❰-❰❰-❰❰

First Brushes
with Crime

While our days were active and crowded with the routine of training, it became increasingly apparent that the situation lacked permanence – not only for N Division but for the organization as a whole. A few new duties had been assigned to the Force, but the bulk of the members were stationed in divisions, such as ours, that had been set up across Canada as reserves of strength to be used by the Government to control such civil disturbances as might occur. From friends in other divisions, we knew that they too were living under temporary conditions and being trained almost entirely as riot squads.

In setting up this system of pools of riot police, the Government had acted expediently in the face of actual threatened violence, but the device had been adopted as a matter of dire necessity rather than of willing choice. So long as violence threatened, there was little criticism, since most critics find hindsight safer than attempting to forecast events. As economic conditions improved, and the country returned to normal, voices were raised in Parliament by both Government and Opposition parties, and by critics outside Parliament, against the maintenance of police for the sole purpose of quelling civil disturbances. The maintenance of such reserves of police power was found repugnant and contrary to Canadian ideals.

So far as the members of the Force assigned to this duty were concerned, there was fairly general agreement with the critics. But the agreement was tempered by the realization that, should violence erupt again anywhere in Canada, the wrath of the critics would be turned against the Force. Nevertheless, the thought of being continued in this

27

type of duty was distasteful to many of us. This was not the sort of career in police work we had in mind when we had joined the Force. All of this had a disturbing effect on morale, and men continued to leave the Force at a rate much higher than normal. Those of us who remained drew some perverse hope that things would change for the better from the very fact that the situation was so obviously makeshift.

While wavering somewhat in the face of criticism, the Government still insisted that every effort should be made to keep the Force up to authorized strength. This raised a serious problem. The inadequate rates of pay and poor living conditions, especially when coupled with extremely tight discipline and stringent regulations against marriage until the completion of seven years of service, did not present a very attractive employment opportunity. Suitable recruits could not be found in sufficient numbers in Canada. Eventually it was necessary to send a recruiting team to England, where two hundred and fifty men were found.

On the arrival of this contingent in Quebec, thirty-five men with prior riding, military, or police training were selected for posting to our division. The others went on to Regina. Some of these men remained with the Service for many years. Several achieved senior rank and contributed greatly in the development of the Force. I have in mind such men as George Curleigh, who retired in 1959 with the rank of Assistant Commissioner after an outstanding career, and Jim Churchman, who reached the rank of Superintendent and was to play a leading part in the development of scientific laboratories when, at long last, the Government decided on the role of the Force and steps were started toward modernization.

On the arrival of the thirty-five men from the English group, it happened that our division was on "stand-to" orders because of the threat of some disturbance in the Ottawa area. We were confined to barracks and, having nothing better to do, decided to give the new recruits a somewhat novel reception. Many of us had some article of cowboy trapping – chaps, polka-dot or embroidered shirts, Mexican spurs, ten-gallon hats, fancy gun-belts. Those not possessing the proper regalia could achieve reasonable imitation by altering the creases in the crown of the regulation Stetsons and by swinging the belt from the Sam Browne equipment low on the hips and tying the holster to the leg. With the consent of the sergeant-major and troop NCO's, saddles, bridles, blankets, and feed-bags were carted from the stables and thrown in great disorder on or under the beds. The meticulously arranged uniforms were removed from the shelves and replaced with an untidy assortment of whisky bottles, grooming kits, and bits of harnesses. A part of the washing table was set with rows of bottles and adorned with several girlie calendars. Lest our visitors think us inhospitable in not offering them the comforts of this bar, a sign was posted stating in large letters: "Bar closed from retreat until reveille." The transformation of the scrupulously clean and orderly barrack room, and of the normally neat and groomed inhabitants, was complete. Cowboys slouched about, with low-slung six-guns, or they sprawled on the beds, hat over eyes, in approved Western fashion, in many cases with whisky bottles within easy reach. Here and there a poker game was in progress.

The new arrivals from England had military backgrounds. Some of them had served in the Guards or other highly trained regiments, where tight discipline was almost a religion. Undoubtedly they had been told something of the reputation of our Force as a well-trained, well-disciplined body, and had drawn from their own experiences in imagining what to expect in their new Service. On arrival, the escorting sergeant held them near the entrance door until the entire group had entered. A number of us sauntered forward to form a semi-circle. The surprised, incredulous expressions as they looked us over, and as they glimpsed the unbelievable disorder and disarray in the room, showed plainly that they had not expected to be put down in a rendezvous of fugitives from the old Chisholm Trail.

The sergeant, who was in on our little plot, called the roll of the new group and assigned them to the various troops where beds had been set up for them. Having completed the task, the sergeant strolled quietly into the night, almost as though he had been on forbidden territory. Introductions followed, and the newcomers were escorted to their beds. The whole situation was so totally unexpected that they were in a state of shock that prevented them from suspecting that their legs were being pulled, and the farther they penetrated into the messy, untidy barrack room, the more shocked and incredulous they became.

Everyone was exceedingly friendly toward them, with a wide-open, uninhibited friendliness suited to our garb. Even the drunks, sprawled on some of the beds, came to long enough to wave a friendly bottle and mutter, "Hi, pa'dner!" At first, our new friends were almost speechless, but after a while wonder and curiosity led to cautious questions.

"Don't your officers and NCO's object to drinking and gambling?"

The answer to a question of that sort was easy: "Hell, we don't allow them in here."

"What about uniforms?"

Again, the answer fitted the surroundings: "Uniforms? We've got them stashed away somewhere, but we only wear them when the Commissioner comes around, and that's not very often."

In the centre of the room, a grim, high-stake poker game was being played. Gradually the newcomers were manoeuvred into position in that part of the room. Conversation died as the stakes grew higher and higher. Suddenly the quiet was broken as one of the players reached across to grab the wrist of another and shout, "You, bastard, you palmed an ace."

Stillness descended on the room, broken only by the rasp of chairs being pushed back from the table as accused and accuser rose to face one another, as other players scrambled out of the line of fire. Then, in a flash, revolvers were drawn. Shots rang out, and the man accused of cheating turned and grimacing in pain as he clutched at his heart, sank slowly to the floor. His accuser fell face down across a nearby bed. For a moment, there was complete stillness as the details registered.

But this was too much. Suddenly it dawned on the newcomers that the entire reception had been staged to mark their arrival. They were good sports and took our joke in the best of humour. Probably there was some relief at the discovery that they had not joined a wild west show. At any rate, they pitched in willingly to help us get everything back in order. Fun is fun, but our period of grace expired at lights out.

Those of us interested in boxing were fortunate in that several of the new arrivals were skilled in the sport. One had had some experience as a professional. Two or three had earned recognition in amateur ranks, both in and out of the armed services. Boxing became a favourite pastime. Tournaments were arranged, and the ring – off in one corner of our barrack room – was in use almost every evening. There was one strict rule regarding the ring. It was to be used for boxing, not fighting.

When a number of men live in close proximity day in and day out, it is to be expected that friction will develop and at times lead to fisticuffs. In Regina, it had been the practice to settle such matters behind the stables, with a few friends of the combatants present to guarantee fair play. Officers and NCO's kept out of sight on the principle that it was best to allow the antagonists to settle their differences. In N Division, a different rule was adopted, and woe betide the men who varied from that rule. Where frictions developed until in the opinion of the men involved it could only be settled by fighting it out, the quarrelling pair was required to report to their troop NCO who in turn reported to the Sergeant-Major. The Sergeant-Major fixed a time at which the fight would take place. But in the riding school, not in the boxing ring.

At these fights – and they were not infrequent – the Sergeant-Major acted as referee. Usually several officers and most of the personnel were in attendance. Since there was no ring, the combatants had the whole riding school in which to do battle, but there were handicaps. The tanbark on the floor of the school was ankle-deep; and this, plus the heavy boxing gloves that the men were required to wear, slowed the fighters down and tired them quickly. After four or five rounds in the heavy going of the tanbark, the men would be so utterly weary that they could scarcely lift their gloves. Most of these fights ended in a draw without too many bruises. It was an excellent method of allowing the men to settle their real or fancied grievances. In a surprising number of cases, the men involved became close friends.

In the late spring of 1920, I thought it time that I got back home for a visit with my parents, and to meet with my brother who had returned from overseas with an English bride. Accordingly, I applied for a week's leave to which, technically, I was entitled. The division was going through a period when an attempt was being made to improve sagging morale by the application of overly strict regulations and the curtailment of privileges: a not-to-well-considered policy. At any rate, my application was turned down. An attempt to secure a pass for an extended weekend – Thursday night until Monday morning – received similar treatment. Even an ordinary Saturday noon until Sunday night pass, which would have allowed only a few hours at home, was refused. I decided to go anyway.

It was a grand visit. My parents were well, as were my brother Bill and his wife. There was a great deal to talk about as we brought ourselves up-to-date on the news, experiences, and happenings within the family. There was also a great deal of visiting back and forth with old friends. Toward the end of the week, my brother, familiar with army ways, suggested that I should wire for an extension of leave. My parents thought this an excellent idea and applied pressure. There were a few embarrassing moments for me, while I thought of excuses to get around sending a wire asking for an extension of my non-existent leave.

I returned to N Division after an absence of six and a half days. To have delayed beyond seven days would, by regulation, have made me a deserter: a very serious offense. As expected, the night of my return was spent in a cell. The following morning, I was paraded before the Officer Commanding Superintendent R. L. Cadiz, with all the ceremony called for by regulations governing orderly room procedure. Superintendent Cadiz, resplendent in full uniform, with several rows of medals earned the hard way on the battle field, was a strict disciplinarian who brooked no deviation from the letter of the law. He disposed of my plea of guilty very quickly, and not too harshly, by imposing a fine of fourteen dollars, an amount equal to my pay during the period of absence, plus seven days confinement to barracks as a defaulter. The latter part of the sentence carried with it the penalty of arising for extra duties an hour before reveille each morning and of doing fatigue duties during the evenings until lights out.

I was detailed for raking and levelling the tanbark in the riding school each evening, a heavy and sweaty job when one man is required to cover the whole expanse. It was beyond imagining, as I raked the tanbark in atonement for my sins, that forty-three years hence I would take my last salute as Commissioner of the Force in this very riding school, or than an audience would see fit to give me the honour of a standing ovation.

During the early summer, it became necessary that the barracks be vacated in order that the building might serve its normal purpose during the summer and fall exhibitions and fairs. Accordingly, the old Bell tents were put to use again, and a camp was established in Sandy Hill near Hurdman's Bridge. The site, now an area of apartment buildings, was just across the river from the present headquarters of the Force.

In October, six of us were chosen for temporary duty in Quebec City. We were to remain there till winter closed the port, when we would go on to Halifax. The work was to assist the Department of Immigration. Trouble had been experienced in the handling of those immigrants who, on arrival, had been found undesirable and who were being held in confinement until arrangements could be made to return them to their homelands. We spent about two months in Quebec City and about five in Halifax. In both cities, fairly comfortable quarters were provided in the Immigration Building. The change from the routine of training was welcome, but the work was to some extent depressing.

Our duty was to act as guards in the area in which the so-called "undesirables" were confined. There had been fights, escapes, and near riots under guards provided by the Immigration Department, and it was our job to tighten the control. The immigrants were from all over Europe. We were told that in their haste to secure passengers, the shipping companies failed to pay proper attention to the regulations controlling immigration.

We were never entirely clear as to why the individuals being held had been ruled undesirable. Undoubtedly some rulings were on health grounds, but we were given to understand that for the most part these people could not be admitted because they lacked the required amount of money or because they lacked sponsors in Canada. Whatever the reason, an average of about one hundred undesirables were held in confinement for varying lengths of time, occasionally for several months. Most of them seemed to us to be good people who would have found a place in Canada. Certainly they were pathetically eager for the opportunity. Not much wonder, then, that there were escapes and attempts to escape when they could glimpse the promised land from their windows.

We were there to act as guards, not to question the reason for these people being under guard, but we did interfere in a small way. By the time of our transfer to Halifax, we had familiarized ourselves with some of the departmental requirements, and in several instances we were able to find sponsors or employment which led to the release of a few of the men. One I recall was a professional photographer. Employment was found for him in that field. The last time I heard of him – several years ago – he had married and was the leading photographer in his district. They gave us no trouble, and the work became a routine, eight-hour-a-day assignment. During working hours, it was possible to pick up a great deal of information regarding the customs, systems, and ways of life in various parts of Europe. During the evenings, several of us made the most of our private rooms by taking correspondence courses.

We were transferred back to N Division in Ottawa in the spring. The division had returned to Landsdowne Park for the winter and was housed in another building, this one even less comfortable or satisfactory than the first. The training routine was about the same with probably a little more attention being paid to lectures on the Government, the role of the police and federal statutes, particularly the recently enacted Opium and Narcotic Drug Act. The Force had been given some work in that field. Criticism was still being levelled at the Government for maintaining riot police, but the critics were not yet in full cry. That was to come a year or two later, when conditions throughout the country had improved to a point where there was little likelihood of the critics being left out on a limb.

Again, in the spring, Landsdowne Park had to be vacated to make room for the exhibition. This time the division moved to what was then an army rifle range in Rockcliffe. It is now the site of the Eastern Training Division of the Force and of the headquarters of the RCMP Air Division and of a police laboratory. In 1921, there were no buildings there. The summer passed pleasantly enough, but the routine was becoming monotonous and to some extent meaningless, without a clearly defined future. Then, in September, to my great joy, I was transferred to Montreal where, I was told by the Officer Commanding, I would be employed on police work.

5

-»»->»->»->»«-««-««-««

Booze, Brothels,
and Drugs

Montreal was a graft-ridden city in the early twenties. The rot of bribery and corruption had crept into branches at all levels of Government and had spread to undermine law enforcement and to tilt, if not upset, the city's scales of justice. Hold-ups, robberies, crimes of violence, every offence in the calendar of crime occurred with what should have been regarded as alarming frequency, but the local authorities were not disturbed enough to take positive action.

Brothels operated openly in a red-light district that covered more than a dozen blocks. While not licensed, the houses paid taxes under an indirect and smoothly organized system. By arrangement, raids were carried out during which it was required that a "madam" and a specified number of girls and "found-ins" would be available for arrest. The frequency and timing of the raids and the number of arrests required were worked out in accordance with the size, location, class, and business potential of each establishment. Regular patrons, having been warned, stayed away during these brief interruptions, while the madam and her girls went visiting for an hour or so before resuming business as usual. Their places were taken by "stand-ins," derelicts recruited from the flophouses and hang-outs of the area for a set fee of two dollars. Each plea of guilty brought fines that followed a fixed scale. The fines were paid forthwith by representatives of the organization that controlled the brothels.

Gambling houses and bookies carried on business under a somewhat similar system of indirect taxation. Even the pick-pockets were organized. In return for a percentage of their take, paid regularly as insurance, the

34

organization provided bail and the services of a leading defence counsel.

Occasionally a few interested and indignant citizens banded together as a reform committee, but apart from attracting a smattering of news and editorial comment, these committees accomplished little. Their statements that crime was organized and protected were easily refuted by the production of statistics showing large numbers of arrests.

The public had become too inured and apathetic to be much interested in reforms. There was even pride and relish in Montreal's reputation as a wide-open, pleasure-loving city, and many persons outside the underworld had direct profit motives for hoping that Montreal's reputation would not be improved or purified. It brought millions of dollars of tourist trade from other parts of Canada and the United States which were, at least legally, still dry under the experiments with prohibition.

Basic responsibility for law enforcement rested with the municipal and provincial authorities, but having established protection, the criminal organizations had, inevitably, expanded into new fields. Some of these — such as counterfeiting, trafficking in narcotic drugs, and smuggling — were of interest to and partly the responsibility of the federal Government. In a not-too-positive move toward meeting its responsibilities, the Government authorized the Force to open a detachment in Montreal in 1920. The fact that a strength of only ten men was authorized indicated either a lack of appreciation of the situation or supreme and optimistic confidence in the ability of the Force.

It soon became very apparent that to make even a small dent in the crime front more men would be needed. After some delay, authority was granted to increase the strength to nineteen. My transfer to Montreal was part of this move toward reinforcing the detachment. The new establishment could scarcely be regarded as excessive, since the nineteen included a superintendent, administrative staff, and even a cook. At the most, only ten men were available for investigational duties, and a great deal of their time was taken up with inquiries in non-criminal matters. Certainly my new posting offered great opportunities for experience and training in police work.

The offices and barracks were located in an old but very comfortable building on Sherbrooke Street, directly opposite the main gates of McGill University. The Officer Commanding, Superintendent Wilcox, a tall, quiet, reserved man, had had a great deal of experience in the Yukon and Northwest Territories and on the prairies, but the problems of those areas, while important and frequently hazardous, had been direct and open. Organized crime was something new and appalling to him, as were the many indications of corruption in the administration of justice. While determined to do everything within his power toward improving the situation, he was fully aware of his lack of familiarity with the complications of police work in a large and corrupt city. Therefore, he concentrated his efforts on administration and on trying to secure more manpower and equipment and support for his detachment. For the actual carrying out of police work, he leaned very heavily on his senior NCO, Staff Sergeant Salt.

Salt – stocky, fast moving, fast thinking, decisive – was an extremely able NCO. He possessed a photographic memory, unlimited courage, and an amazing ability to come up with the right hunches at the right times. He had an abiding hatred for professional criminals and would go to great lengths in trying to keep youngsters and first offenders from heading into the ranks of organized crime. A driving taskmaster who worked long hours, he would not suffer fools or laggards. Salt was not cut out for the diplomatic service. His blunt, head-on methods ruffled many feathers in Montreal's officialdom, but the situation called for direct, positive action.

My transition from parade square to active police work was astonishingly rapid. I left Ottawa in mid-morning. By nightfall, I was hanging about restaurants on St. Lawrence Main trying to locate narcotic drug pedlars. Salt did not believe in wasting time. I was unpacking my gear in the room which had been assigned to me when word came to report to his office. He had obviously read my service file which was on the desk in front of him. No time was wasted on the "let's-get-acquainted" type of questions. A rapid-fire summary of conditions in Montreal was followed by a brief review of the difficulties of keeping abreast of the load with the ten men, including himself, available for field work. Of these, the six most experienced members formed a Criminal Investigation Branch squad. The other four – and I was one of these – were detailed to inquiries of a routine nature, such as verifying the details and references supplied by applicants for naturalization. He warned, however, that such division of work was only nominal.

"The CIB require help when they are carrying out searches, or stakeouts, or arrests. When they do, everyone is on call – including the cook – and help may be needed any hour of the day or night. Don't count on free time. If you do go out in the evening, make sure we know where to get you in a hurry. That won't bother you for a few weeks, because you are going to spend your evenings hanging around the 'Main.' The drug traffic is still fairly wide open. You're not known, and you look too young to be a policeman. One of the CIB boys will show you the hangouts and teach you some of their jargon. Every morning you will put in a detailed diary before going about your naturalization job. Every evening you'll be trying to make contacts among the pedlars. If you need help or information, talk to the CIB chaps. Understand?"

I said, "Yes, sir," with more assurance than I felt.

"Good. Just one more thing. There are so few of us here that we can work as a closely knit team. There must be complete trust among members of the team. If I get the slightest indication that a man can't fit, I'll have him transferred. If you make honest mistakes, and you will, I'll back you right up the line. If you make any other sort, I'll crucify you. Trust everyone on the team. Trust nobody – and I mean just that – trust nobody outside, until we have had a little more time to feel our way here. That's all."

One of the CIB men told me something of the workings of the narcotic traffic and took me for a brief ride down the Main and through the surrounding red-light district and Chinatown. As we drove, he kept up a running commentary on the areas through which we had passed, pointing out the places frequented by addicts, homosexuals, gamblers, fences, pimps, and prostitutes. He pointed out the better-known brothels, special "exhibition" houses, and "blind pigs." Occasionally he drew my attention to individuals.

"The man in the flashy, grey suit on the corner there is Charley White. He collects for the bookies and runs a string of about half a dozen hustlers on the side. The droopy blonde talking to him is his woman, Edith. She hustles too, and turns the take over to him. Most of the street-walkers around here are too old and worn-out for jobs in the houses, and most of them are on drugs. The fat, greasy little guy is Maxie. He runs a book in the cigar store right behind him. We think he pushes junk too." The fund of knowledge possessed by my guide was astonishing, as were the facts he supplied.

Back at the office, he had a few words of advice. "Don't hurry it. Just hang around the cafes for a few evenings, until they get used to seeing you. Laugh off anybody who approaches you – and try to act as though you know what it's all about. And, for God's sake, stop walking as though you're still on the drill square. Keep your hat on. That short hair-cut is a give-away, and get a pair of shoes. Those issue boots would be spotted a mile away."

And thus started my apprenticeship in Montreal. After two years in uniform, I felt uncomfortable in civilian clothes, particularly since I had grown since joining the Force and my old suit fitted like a bad buy from a second-hand store. At first I felt out of place and awkward in the blatant, noisome atmosphere of the "Main," and embarrassed by the approaches of the pimps and prostitutes. After a few evenings, the strangeness of these surroundings wore off, and I was able to concentrate on the job of locating sources of illicit drugs. It was not difficult. The Force had been active for only a short time, and the traffickers still did not believe that there was any serious threat to their rotten trade. Most of those arrested had been able to beat the charge, while the few convicted had been let off with small fines. Without too much to fear from the courts, they were actively seeking new customers.

The purchases were not the cautious, complicated "meets" of today.

Most of the petty "pushers" who frequented the cafes and cheap tawdry cabarets were addicts anxious to make sales, in order to increase their supply of the narcotics received as a salary. A request for a deck or two could usually be delivered on the spot. Larger amounts necessitated some delay, since the addict carried only a limited supply, not so much from fear of arrest as from lack of trust on the part of their suppliers. Prices were fantastically low by today's standards. A folded paper, or "deck," containing a grain of morphine or cocaine, cost fifty cents. Opium was thirty-five cents. All of the drugs were badly adulterated. Heroin had not yet reached the market.

I was fooled several times when the neat little "decks" I had purchased were found to contain epsom salts or milk powder, but I was able to establish contacts for the purchase of narcotics. The CIB then began to take an active interest. Each evening before leaving the office, arrangements would be made whereby I could be kept under observation during my visit to the "Main." I was told to attempt only one purchase a night, but to ask for several decks in the hope that the individual with whom I was dealing would have to go to his supplier. The plans did not call for searches or arrests, at least not in the early stages.

The illicit trafficking in narcotics had only recently been recognized as a vicious, serious threat in North America. Very little was known in Canada or the United States regarding the top men in the racket or their methods. Next to nothing was known regarding the international traffic or its leaders. A two-pronged attack was necessary. At the local level, efforts must be made to curb the spread of addiction through seizures and arrests. At the same time, a long-range plan had to be set up through the operation of which information would be gathered from every possible source – undercover work, informers, secret agents, surveillance – and then sifted and compiled for eventual use. My small efforts merely provided likely starting points for long, patient investigations which it was hoped would lead back through the addicts and their suppliers to the big traffickers – and, with luck and perseverance, to the importers.

After about a month, I was relieved of these nightly visits to the "Main," partly because of the increasing possibility that my daytime work would lead to my recognition as a member of the Force. It might lead, as Salt put it, "to getting your head lumped." He also had other duties for me. In the meantime, my routine daytime jobs, while lacking in excitement, provided good experience in meeting and dealing with the public and in learning my way about Montreal.

The other members of the detachment were as fine a group as one could wish to work with. The pressures of various duties left little time for outside interests. Even had this not been so, the low pay would have placed severe limits on social activities. Fortunately, everyone got along very well and, as Salt had said, formed a closely knit, keen, hard-working team. Except for the six members of the CIB squad, we were short in experience, but this was compensated for by eagerness and a desire to learn. The staff sergeant was the only married man in the group. He and his wife and children occupied an apartment in the barrack building, which made him available at all hours of the day and night. Most of his evenings were spent in his office, or in the small recreation room where he joined in discussions and in the swapping of experiences.

Morale was high, surprisingly so in the light of some of the circumstances. While our living conditions were quite comfortable, there was a woeful shortage of equipment and manpower. This, coupled with a cumbersome and too stringent control of expenses, added immeasurably to the difficulties of already difficult tasks. Authority had been granted to the Force to open investigational branches in several cities across Canada, but this had been done somewhat grudgingly, in order to offset growing public concern, particularly in the area of increasing traffic in narcotic drugs. In fact, it had taken demonstrations by irate parents on the West Coast over the distribution of cocaine to school children to bring about even limited action.

Only one automobile was provided in Montreal, an ancient dilapidated Buick touring car. There was no cell accommodation or fingerprinting or photographic equipment. For these services, we were dependent on the provincial or municipal forces, an arrangement which, in the light of the situation then existing in Montreal, caused many difficulties and frustrations. Authority to incur expenses for the purchase of drugs or counterfeit money during the course of an investigation had to be cleared with Ottawa in every instance, a ruling that imposed many obvious handicaps. All expenditures were controlled with parsimonious severity. As an example, members employed on night duties were allowed to purchase a "midnight lunch," worth not more than twenty cents, provided the duty lasted until two o'clock in the morning. The extremely high morale and devotion to duty developed in spite of, rather than because of, these conditions and regulations.

The loyalty and dedication of its members is, in my view, the most interesting and important feature of the Force. The reputation that the Force enjoys has developed more from that *esprit de corps* than from any other factor or combination of factors. Years later, as an Inspector, I was one of four officers appointed by Commissioner S. T. Wood to form a committee, the purpose of which was to discover how and why the Force was able to bring about and maintain such a high degree of loyalty in its members. It was the Commissioner's hope that the findings of the committee would provide a safeguard against changes that might upset the balance or offset the causes that engendered the most important and valuable asset of the Force. It seemed that it might even be possible to place greater emphasis on the controlling factors. Training schedules were examined, members at all levels were interviewed, discussions were had with personnel-management experts and with psychologists, but the findings of the committee were not very helpful or positive. Certainly the spirit of the Force had not stemmed from very considerate treatment or indulgence of its members. Analysis established that the pay had always been below the standards of the time. Since its inception, living conditions provided for the Force had left much to be desired. Only in recent years has serious consideration been given to pensions on retirement, or even for pensions to the widows and children of members killed on duty.

The committee did find a great pride in the uniform and in the traditions of the Force. We found, too, as we had known from our own experiences, that while members groused and grumbled among themselves because of the regulations, they were, nevertheless, extremely proud to belong to an organization that had a reputation for strict and tight discipline. The fact that a man was retained as a member of a Force known to act swiftly and sternly in dealing with breaches of discipline or incompetence brought personal satisfaction. The committee could only recommend that any moves toward relaxing discipline or changing the uniform should be made with the greatest caution. The all-important matter of loyalty and *esprit de corps* has caused me to digress. It is high time that I returned to the early days in Montreal.

The opium-smoking habit was spreading. While centred in Chinatown, it was by no means limited to that area or to persons of Chinese origin. A few arrests had been made, but the main effort had been against the traffic in the more dangerous white drugs, morphine and cocaine. These remained the chief target. However, Ottawa, disturbed by reports received from Montreal, Vancouver, Toronto, and other cities, instructed that a determined drive was to be made against the increasing traffic in opium.

It was not difficult to secure information regarding the location of the so-called opium joints. The main problem was the old one of manpower, of greatly increasing our work without disrupting developments in other fields. Salt's solution was typical. Since the opium joints were active during the night hours, all members would be in barracks, available for duty with the CIB men, six nights a week. During the daytime, members would carry on with their normal jobs. We were to have Sunday nights free – unless, of course, some emergency developed.

The searches started in Chinatown, where there was a concentration of opium joints. These were not the luxurious "opium dens" of the movies, wherein smokers sprawl in comfort on plush divans while scantily clad maidens flit across deep oriental rugs to serve their every want. These were rows of dirty, smelly little cubicles. The furnishings were simple: a wooden shelf covered with straw matting. Quite often the male smokers would be accompanied by a female companion – not scantily clad oriental maidens, but unclad prostitutes employed to loll about in the nude. Apparently the presence of a naked woman helped to form and lend some reality to the hallucinations of the smoker. I understand they served no other purpose at such times.

The premises used for smoking were usually on the upper floors of buildings, over shops, restaurants, or other business premises. Three or four of the larger and most frequented places were upstairs over gambling rooms. The first few raids took Chinatown by surprise. We were able to reach the opium joints before the alarm spread. Many arrests were made, and quantities of paraphernalia and opium were seized. The proprietors were, naturally, disturbed by these unexpected visits from the police. Several jumped to the conclusion that the searches were intended as "shakedowns" and offered bribes to have the whole thing called off. It took several weeks and many searches and arrests to convince them that we meant to put them out of business.

From then on the searches became increasingly difficult. Lookouts were posted, doors were barred, and a system developed whereby, in order to protect the proprietors, smokers were required to pick up their "decks" at some place other than the actual smoking premises.

Despite the pathetic and grim realities of the traffic, there were comic sidelights. The fad of students a few years ago to see how many bodies could be crammed into a motor car reminds me of the manner in which we used to crowd our ancient and dilapidated Buick. The appearance of the car in Chinatown set up an immediate hubbub, as the pedestrians watched to learn where we were going to search. As soon as the car stopped, a great clamour would arise as the onlookers shouted warnings. The clamour increased as we disembarked to race across the sidewalks, through the ground floor premises, and on up the stairs where there would be a great rushing of people trying to get away from the opium-smoking cubicles. Outside, in the meantime, there would be the sound of breaking glass, accompanied by a shower of opium pipes, lamps, and paraphernalia, as the smokers disposed of evidence.

After a few weeks, we discovered that our garage was being kept under observation, and that alarms were being telephoned to Chinatown whenever the old Buick started out. This, and the clamour that greeted our arrivals in Chinatown, was turned to some advantage. Several times each evening, when we were not otherwise occupied, some of us would pile into the old car and drive around the block; or, if the car chanced to be in the vicinity of Chinatown, a visit would be paid that area, during which two or three stops would be made. The resultant false alarms caused severe disruption of business in the opium joints and greatly upset the patrons. Probably this did as much toward breaking up their operations as the actual searches and arrests, since, in the early stages at least, the courts were extremely lenient.

The Chinese opium smokers were, almost invariably, peaceful and docile. Many of them were older citizens who had had the habit for years and could not quite understand why, suddenly, a fuss was being made. The non-Oriental addicts were younger people, some of them teenagers. Most were males, but there was a smattering of women, apart from the prostitutes engaged for decorative purposes. The majority were confirmed addicts, but many, particularly the younger ones, were still in the early stages, and they visited the opium joints only occasionally, to seek new thrills by "taking it on the hip." The fortunate among them would be disappointed by the squalid surroundings and discouraged by the physical suffering that followed their first experience with the opium pipe. But the majority, if left undisturbed, would increase the frequency of their visits, until before long they were firmly "hooked" and they too move on to the use of morphine.

As was to be expected, the opium traffickers resisted our efforts. There were many attempts at bribery, but these were quickly discouraged by the laying of charges wherever there was sufficient evidence. For a time they shifted to strong-arm methods, whereby hoodlums were employed to await our arrival. There were a few fairly rough sessions. Arrests were, of course, followed by sensational charges of police brutality which frequently resulted in acquittals. After the first encounters, the strong-arm men raised their prices, and this, added to the cost of lawyers, and the fact that our raids continued, brought an end to these attempts. Gradually the word spread that the "Horsemen," as we were nicknamed in the underworld, meant business. The reputation brought unexpected dividends. A considerable flow of information started to reach the office from responsible sources, and our efforts began to receive the active support of newspapers.

Our efforts were not confined to Chinatown. Opium joints were located and searched in other parts of the city. In some cases, it took many raids to discourage the patrons to the point where the place could no longer operate with a profit. Continued harassment, rather than the extremely lenient sentences handed down by the courts, brought about eventual closure of the dives.

Two of the most troublesome places were located in the heart of the red-light district. These were operated for the prostitutes of the area. Most of the girls were addicted to the white drugs, cocaine or morphine, but there were enough opium smokers among them to provide a very lucrative business for the two smoking houses. They believed that the smoking of opium prevented pregnancy. The two houses were active after four o'clock in the morning, the closing hour of the brothels. They were large, rambling places, with many rooms and cubbyholes on several floors. The searching of these houses was an experience not to be undertaken lightly, or easily forgotten.

The entrance doors were reinforced with strips of two-by-four lumber and were always barred until the proprietor satisfied himself regarding callers by use of a small peep-hole. We were able, at times, to enter by rushing in immediately after someone had been admitted, but more often it was necessary to break open the door, a procedure that gave ample warning to the occupants. Inside there would be bedlam, as thirty or forty partly clad or unclad women dashed about trying to dispose of opium and paraphernalia, trying to get out of the rooms in which smoking had been in progress. For these searches, we had located three or four reliable and necessarily husky matrons who always accompanied us. We were completely dependent on these matrons to bring about some semblance of order among the girls, a vastly unpleasant and difficult task. Eventually, and after frequent skirmishes, the girls would be secured in one or two rooms, under the watchful eyes of the matrons, while we searched the premises. If drugs were found, the operator or operators would be taken in and charged, but the girls were rarely arrested or charged, except in the cases of extreme and violent obstruction. More often than not, the operators were able to get off scot-free or, at most, by the payment of a small fine. Their business was too lucrative to give up easily. Again, it was continual pressure and harassment, rather than the sentences of the courts, that forced them eventually to close up.

It was during one of these searches that I had my first experience of being shot at. The proprietor of this particular place had some years before been a physical instructor with one of the local police forces. He became addicted to drugs and was discharged, and he drifted into the narcotic traffic. Unlike most drug addicts, he was an extremely violent man. On this occasion, we were forced to break down the door. As it crashed inward, the tall, still well-built proprietor was standing, spread-legged and wild-looking, in the entrance hall, with a drawn revolver. Salt – as always the case when he was with us – was the first man through the door. By chance, I was immediately behind him. The proprietor opened fire at once. Salt did not hesitate for a split second. Although armed, he made no attempt to draw his revolver but rushed forward to bring the still-firing man down with a well-executed flying tackle around the ankles. Fortunately, the man had not had much practice with firearms. None of us was hit.

6

-»»-»»-»»-»»-»»-«««-«««-«««-«««

Further Undercover
Work

Staff Sergeant Salt had been right in warning us that there would be little free time. In fact, there was scarcely time to get the required amount of sleep. At first, my part in these activities was limited to minor tasks, such as escorting prisoners, taking part in static surveillance, or guarding exits to prevent escape during searches. This changed after a few months, and I was gradually brought into the planning and the carrying out of investigations. A few months later, following the transfer of a member of the CIB squad, I was promoted to the rank of Detective and made a regular member of that squad. Apart from giving my ego a lift, the promotion brought some financial reward. Henceforth, the Force would pay me fifty cents a day toward the upkeep of civilian clothing. Fifty cents may not seem a munificent amount, but on a salary of two dollars, it was most welcome.

My new duties brought me into frequent contact with the courts as a witness and in the securing of warrants. The experience was interesting, educational, and at times disheartening and frustrating. Our lecturers had trained us in the belief that in the courts of Canada the judges, lawyers, both defence and prosecution, and the police were concerned only with the discovery of the truth in matters before the courts, and the impartial administration of justice. Some forty-four years in law-enforcement work has taught me that this is generally so. But in the early twenties, Montreal provided my first experience with exceptions to that general rule. It also provided ample proof of the deterioration and rot that sets in when public apathy permits wide-spread bribery and corruption.

Application for warrants were made to the courts through clerks working at a counter that ran the length of a long room. It was the duty of the clerks to fill out the necessary forms, which were then taken to the chambers of one of the judges, where they were sworn to and signed. Behind the counter there were several rows of desks and filing cabinets which obviously contained copies of documents of a confidential nature.

Members of our Force were not made welcome during the early days, and we were frequently ignored and kept waiting for lengthy periods. During my first such experience, one of the desks behind the counter was occupied by a nattily dressed, curly haired, pudgy little man who was busily engaged making notes from files taken from the cabinets. On subsequent visits to the courthouse, I saw him again, sometimes back at the desk going through documents, sometimes in the corridors talking with judges, court officials, lawyers, and policemen. He was clearly a man of considerable authority, and I decided that he must be the chief clerk, although his distinctive clothes, his flashing diamond rings, and his backslapping mannerisms did not seem to fit that role.

It was some weeks before I learned his identity. This was Little Tony, one of the most important if not the most important figure in the Montreal underworld. Little Tony had a direct interest in the brothels, bookies, and gaming houses, but his chief occupation was that of organizer and "fixer." It was widely rumoured and believed that he operated a sort of underworld consultant agency and insurance company, through the use of which – and in return for a percentage of their take – criminals secured technical and legal advice in the planning of their operations and in the securing of firearms and stolen cars. If things went wrong, the organization provided bail, counsel, and such pressures and contacts as could be supplied through Tony's wide net of bribery.

Certainly his easy and open access to confidential records, and the authority that he exercised around the courts, put him in an excellent position to carry out those fuctions. The ease and regularity of acquittals brought about on behalf of his clients readily established his ability at corruption. He was also in a position to check the police reports and court records to make sure that his customers were not holding out as to the amount of the take. Little Tony was to be an evil power around Montreal for another three years, until time ran out for him and three of his associates on the scaffold in the Yard of Bordeaux Jail. But until then his influence and that of his corrupt and criminal associates frequently seemed much stronger than the forces of decency and law and order. It was not surprising, in view of little Tony's access to court records, and his "early-warning system" for clients, that many of our searches proved futile.

This situation did not present much of a problem as regards the searching of opium joints, since the operators, even though they had been "tipped" that a search warrant had been issued, had no way of knowing when it would be executed. This left them the choice of remaining closed, which would have been highly desirable from our point of view, or of trying to outguess us as to the timing of the search. Further, the harassment of frequent searches was an effective weapon toward putting them out of business, whether or not the searches were in themselves successful. The situation was serious in other and more important cases. Months of patient investigation into the activities of suppliers of narcotics or counterfeit money could be – and were on many occasions – rendered ineffective by a tip-off just as we were about to close in.

For a time we found a partial answer in the willingness of one of the judges to sign warrants at his home during the evenings. This was helpful in urgent cases, when the search or searches could be carried out before the next opening of the courthouse. After that, the warrants were rendered almost useless by the fact that they had to be registered in the court records. Apart from the problems caused by tip-offs, there were other difficulties in the carrying out of searches.

Investigations do not often culminate in areas close to Courts, or in the vicinity of the homes of judges willing to be disturbed at any hour of the night. In many cases, circumstances place close limits on the time during which a search may effectively be carried out. This is particularly so with the traffic in narcotics. Inability to act speedily proved almost as great a handicap as the leakage of information regarding the issuance of warrants.

Eventually these problems were solved, insofar as narcotics were concerned, through the issuance of Writs of Assistance to a few carefully selected members of CIB staffs across Canada. In effect, these Writs are permanent search warrants, giving the authorized holder the authority to search anywhere at any time, provided he has reasonable grounds for believing that narcotics are on the premises. Such powers of search were by no means new, since they had been granted under other federal statutes, particularly the Customs and Excise Acts, for many years, but their use by the Force in combatting the narcotics drug traffic brought about loud cries from defence counsel. Despite objections, the Writs of Assistance have continued in use and have proven a most effective method of removing some of the protection and advantages enjoyed by traffickers and importers of narcotics. Objections against the placing of such wide powers of search in the hands of the police are still aired from time to time. As recently as last year, the matter was brought up in the House of Commons when several members decried the use of Writs as a threat to the liberty of the individual, and as a deplorable example of police-state methods. The critics ignored the fact that the holders of Writs are accountable to their superiors, to the courts, to the Minister of Justice, and ultimately to Parliament. In all the years that these Writs have been in use, and despite vigorous protests by defence lawyers, there has not been one instance of abuse of the authority they grant. Beyond question this authority has interfered with the liberty and freedom of many criminals.

The rather obvious lesson that the effectiveness of police work depends to a very considerable extent on the calibre of the prosecuting counsel was impressed upon me during my early experiences in Montreal. Until events proved the fallacy of such procedure under existing conditions, appointments were made by the federal Government from a long list of approved lawyers. Many of the appointments made it clear that in compiling the list at least as much attention had been given to rewarding the politically faithful as to ability, experience, or even character. Sometimes the appointees were able, interested men, capable of meeting high-priced defence counsel, but too often the Crown was represented by men known as incompetent or lacking in experience before the criminal courts, or worst of all, were known to be connected with underworld characters. There is no more certain way to dampen a policeman's interest in his work or to raise doubt as to the desire of the legislators to have the laws enforced than by appointing party hacks as prosecutors. Eventually circumstances compelled a change whereby several outstanding lawyers were appointed to represent the Force on a more-or-less permanent basis. Until that time, we were often out-manoeuvred, and sometimes sold out, in court.

While there were frustrations and disappointments, there were successes. Persistent pressures put the opium joints out of business. Drug pedlars were driven from the street corners. Drugs were no longer available to those who might experiment with their use. The easy spreading of addiction was curtailed. Step by slow step led to wholesale suppliers and importers of illicit drugs. Important seizures were made, and while it was difficult to secure convictions or adequate sentences, the seizures alone helped reduce the attractions of the traffic.

During the summer of 1922, a new series of counterfeit five, ten, and twenty dollar bills began to appear in Montreal and other eastern cities. The bills were excellent reproductions, printed from beautifully engraved plates on good quality paper. Investigation indicated that the counterfeits were originating in Montreal. However, weeks of investigation served only to bring about the arrest of a few unimportant passers, who were unable or unwilling to assist us in getting to the higher-ups. As the bills appeared in ever-increasing numbers, we were flooded with complaints from the business community. Quite rightly, the press started demanding action. Then, suddenly, we had a bit of luck.

A salesman of printers' supplies, Jack Grant, came forward with interesting information. An energetic, bouncy young man, who might well have been cast in James Cagney's roles, Grant told a very convincing story. Most of his friends and contacts were engaged in printing and stationery or allied trades. In recent weeks, his suspicions had been aroused by a sudden display of affluence on the part of two of his contacts. He had made a point of cultivating their friendship, and he had been successful to a point where they were now seeking his help in the securing of inks and paper suitable for use in counterfeiting. He was quite sure that these men were back of the recent flood of counterfeit money.

Grant was prepared to work with the police in return for fairly large sums of money. He was told that our headquarters' authority for the payments would be sought, and he agreed to continue his efforts to secure useful information. Several days later, Grant telephoned in great excitement. He claimed to have overheard a conversation between his two friends, which indicated that one hundred, five dollar counterfeit bills had been delivered to a small tobacconist whose address he gave us. A search squad discovered ninety-eight counterfeit five's. The tobacconist admitted having purchased one hundred bogus bills at twenty per cent of their face value.

During the next several weeks, we received a great deal of information from Grant. Twice he gave information regarding deliveries that were to be made on the street. Several times the information told of bills already delivered. On each occasion the information proved to be precise, too precise in fact. It seemed doubtful that a man in a situation such as he had described could secure such accurate and detailed information. There was another reason for suspicion too. Headquarters had been very slow in authorizing payment for the informant. When authority was received, it was for much less than the amounts he had asked for. Although he had stated that his only interest was money, he raised only the slightest objections to the greatly reduced payments.

Arrangements were made for an around-the-clock check on his activities. Results were not long delayed. On the second evening, he was followed to a point on the banks of the St. Lawrence River at the East End of Montreal Island. A motor boat from one of the small islands picked him up. An old farmhouse and a barn were the only buildings on the island, and the lights there remained on until three o'clock in the morning. Grant was brought back by the same motorboat at about eight in the morning. That afternoon he returned to the island and was seen to enter the farmhouse. In the late afternoon, he and two other men were observed carrying packages to the barn. Again the lights remained on, until about three o'clock. In the meantime, a warrant to search had been secured, and arrangements were made for water transportation. A squad of about ten men moved quietly out to the island shortly after the lights had gone out in the farmhouse.

The place was surrounded without a sound. To our great surprise, we found the front door unlocked. A flashlight revealed a switch near the door. A startling sight greeted us when the lights were turned on. Almost every inch of the wall was covered with twenty dollar bills. Crumpled bills were on the floor around a printing press that stood in the centre of the room. Even the hallway, which could be seen leading toward the rear of the house, was papered with twenties. Obviously the press had been used to print one side of a large batch of money which had been hung up to dry, in preparation for printing the other side. Grant and three men were found in a bedroom in the upper part of the house, and they surrendered without resistance.

Counterfeit money was everywhere: in cupboards and pantries, under the beds, and in neatly wrapped bundles. A search of the barn revealed tens of thousands of dollars of crumpled counterfeit five and ten dollar bills hidden between the boards in the stalls. At several places in the yard, it appeared that there had been recent digging. We un-covered a number of large cement pipes filled with crumpled bills – in order to give them a used, aged appearance. All of the plates were found.

Grant admitted that he was the leader of the gang and had organized the entire plan. Although he had outsmarted himself by approaching the police with too-precise information, his idea had been fairly clever. He had hoped that he would be able to gain our confidence to a point where we would ask him to assist in running down information that we might uncover. Thus he would have knowledge of our activities, and a warning if we were getting anywhere close to his organization. The two men whom he had named as suspects, and on whom we had spent a great deal of time in surveillance, were innocent of any connection with him. The persons whom we had found in possession of counterfeit as a result of his information were what he called "give-aways," little customers whom he had sacrificed in order to lend weight to his story. He was sentenced to four years in prison, ample time in which to realize that lies should never be very precise in detail.

There was no let-up in the volume of work. Usually several important cases would be in various stages of development against a background of more-or-less routine inquiries, searches, and arrests. Certainly better results would have been secured with more men and equipment but, as it was, the situation offered an excellent, high-pressure cram course in law-enforcement work, if one were as fortunate as I was to have the guidance of dedicated officers and NCO's. We had an added benefit after the appointment of permanent counsel in that several of the lawyers so appointed were interested in guiding and developing young policemen.

The work was not lacking in variety and experience. Thinking back to those rather crowded days of forty-odd years ago brings on an assortment of memories: some sad, some tragic, and some with an element of humour. There were the young people "hooked" on narcotics because the easy availability had allowed them to try drugs for "kicks." There were the parents pleading for the arrest of their youngsters in order that they might undergo such attempts at cures as jails offered drug addicts. There was the young prostitute lying naked and screaming on an opium-smoking bunk as she suffered through her first experience with the drug. And there was the searching of brothels for narcotics – brothels graduating from the luxurious houses where dalliance was expensive and the girls young and pretty, on down to the cheap tawdry places where intercourse was handled on a production-line basis whereby the girls carried tally cards punched by the matron each time the prostitute headed for the bedroom with a new customer, where it was not unusual to find from twenty to thirty punch marks on the card. In one case, a tally of forty-two marked a girl's efforts for a fourteen-hour day.

I have a very soft spot for a little man who I brought back from Cochrane, Ontario, on a warrant of commitment. Sleep had been in short supply before the trip, and the journey to Cochrane was hot and dusty. I spent most of the night locating the little man and securing the necessary signature of a local magistrate. We left Cochrane early the next morning, another hot, sultry day. The coach had few passengers so we occupied a double seat with the prisoner sitting next to the window. I bought two magazines, gave one to the prisoner, made myself comfortable by putting my feet up on the seat opposite. I was drowsy, but awareness that losing a prisoner carried an almost automatic penalty of six weeks in the guard room kept me awake for a time. Eventually, however, drowsiness and the heat won out. I went sound asleep, to awaken with a terrific start more than an hour later. There was no real cause for alarm. My little prisoner was sitting quietly by the window. When he saw that I was awake, he smiled apologetically. "I hope I didn't disturb you, sir. I had to go to the toilet. I was very careful in stepping over your legs." The little man may have influenced the history of the Force. Members who have served six weeks in the guard room are not likely candidates for the Commissioner's desk.

In the United States, the infamous but powerful crime syndicates, nourished by the experiment with prohibition, were in their heyday of power and prosperity. In their enterprises they had the willing co-operation of distilleries of many countries. The great bulk of liquor exports from those countries established beyond any reasonable doubt that this co-operation was extended with the knowledge, if not the open blessing, of their governments.

Canada was no exception. Many Canadian distilleries joined in the vastly profitable effort to slake the American thirst. Trainloads of liquor

entered the United States from Canada. At customs points on inland
waterways, small boats and motor launches, incapable of sea travel,
were solemnly given clearance for Mexico with cargoes of liquor, often
several times a day. Fleets of cars and trucks were employed to cross the
border at many points across the country. Quantities of liquor sufficient
to meet local requirements for hundreds of years – even should the
inhabitants take to bathing in the stuff – were cleared to islands off the
shores of Canada. Some distilleries operated plants with many times the
output required to meet the demands of the Canadian markets.

It was only after the repeal of the Volstead Act had put an end to
the traffic that a commission and subsequently a committee were set up
to find out what had been going on. The reports of these bodies indicated
that this belated interest was not occasioned by moral objections but by
concern that the Government had not received its full share of the profits
by way of taxes.

Contacts and connections bought and paid for by the mobsters in
arranging for laxity in the enforcement of some laws will inevitably be
used to provide protection in ever-expanding fields of crime. Further, as
with everything else, crime does not remain static. A letdown in standards
of law enforcement, whatever the cause, opens the door for all criminals,
whether members of the mobs or enthusiastic amateurs. Conditions
brought about by the traffic in alcohol gave rise to many crimes in other
fields. Narcotics, stolen cars, counterfeit money, high-grade gold, and
merchandise of all sorts crossed the border without much interference.
The direction of the traffic in the various commodities depended on the
market demands of the two countries.

Responsibility for enforcing the Customs and Excise Acts rested with
the investigation services of that department, but as conditions worsened,
the Force was brought into the picture. First it was in connection with
the traffic in narcotics, and later as a result of complaints made by
industry and business. These complaints were against the increasing
volume of unfair competition being met with at many points across
Canada through the flood of smuggled merchandise.

In the fall of 1922, silk could be purchased as cheaply in Montreal
as in New York City, despite a tax of some forty per cent. Dresses, too,
were available at prices that could not be met by honest merchants. Under
pressure from the business community, the Government decided that
corrective measures must be taken. The Force was instructed to start an
investigation. In the meantime, I had the great good fortune of promotion to the rank of Detective Corporal. I was given three men and told
to set forth on the job of discovering the details of the silk racket. To the
utter amazement of everyone in the office, the letter of instructions from
headquarters contained a note to the effect that the matter of expenses
was not to impede the carrying out of a complete inquiry.

We were successful in locating a man experienced in the textile trade who possessed a wide range of knowledge regarding persons in the silk business. He agreed to work with us in learning the identity of importers involved in the racket. Two of the members of the little squad were left to continue inquiries in Montreal, while I went to New York with the third member of the squad and the co-operative silk merchant. Our method there was quite simple, at least in the early stages. Each morning the three of us got together in Grand Central Station to meet the incoming trains from Montreal. As the disembarking passengers entered the station, our informant would point out the persons connected with the silk trade who, in his opinion, might be mixed up in illegal transactions. It was then our job to keep track of their activities.

New York is not an easy place in which to keep a person under observation. We lost our suspects at least as often as we were able to follow them, but we did gather some useful information without their becoming aware that they were being watched. Almost invariably, those of our suspects who were in fact in the racket patronized one of the better hotels, while at the same time they rented a room in a smaller, cheaper hotel on 29th Street. This second room was registered under a false name and was used for meetings with New York associates and for the storage of merchandise.

After a time, and through the co-operation of the hotel detective, we were in a position to maintain a close check on the merchandise delivered to their rooms in the cheaper hotel, and on most occasions we were able to get into the rooms to mark the tags on the merchandise for future identification. We were able, too, to learn the names of many of the persons with whom our suspects did business. Most of them had poor reputations, and several were suspected of dealing in silks stolen from the lofts in New York.

From New York, the silk was shipped, by express, usually in lots of from twenty to thirty rolls, to points near the Canadian border. Obviously the next step in our investigation was to find out the means by which the silk found its way from the border points to the Canadian market. It was arranged that the two members of the squad still in Montreal would move to points along the border in order to learn, discreetly, what transpired following the arrival of the shipments from New York. It was not considered advisable at this stage to take any open action that might alert the smugglers. Our first job was to secure all possible details regarding the smuggling organizations. The observations carried out at border points established that the silk was usually picked up by men known to be active in the hauling of liquor from Canada to the United States. It seemed clear that silk smuggling was a by-product of the illegal traffic in alcohol, and that the men who were running alcohol south across the border were increasing their profits by running silk north into Canada.

It was clear, too, that all the facilities of the liquor traffic would be at the disposal of the silk distributors – cars, transfer points, warning systems, and protection.

Our next step involved the securing of detailed information regarding the liquor racket. It was arranged that I would be replaced at the New York end of the inquiry in order that I might attempt undercover work along the border. In this effort, I would be accompanied by Constable Jack Barnes. We were to pose as smugglers and liquor runners in the hope that we might penetrate the ranks of the syndicate runners and thereby secure detailed information of illicit border operations – somewhat chancy occupation, since both Jack and I had become well-known to the underworld through investigations, arrests, and prosecutions in the Montreal area.

We were supplied with a second-hand car which, while on the ancient side, was of a make popular among the runners. Consideration of our forthcoming duties prompted us to point out that money came easily to bootleggers and that, in order to maintain our pose, it would be necessary to follow their notoriously free-spending habits. Ottawa agreed, somewhat to our surprise. That was the one and only occasion in the Force when I was told not to worry about expenses.

As a start, Jack and I took comfortable rooms in a hotel in Plattsburg, New York, one of the headquarters of the bootlegging fraternity. We made a point of staying in our rooms during the mornings and early afternoons and of patronizing local sports events and night spots. We also made a habit of leaving the hotel in the late night or early-morning hours and remaining away for ample time to allow for a border crossing. Actually, we used these hours to familiarize ourselves with every border road in the area, in order to acquire the knowledge that is an essential part of the equipment of the runner.

After a few days in Plattsburg, we shifted our location to Moores and then to Malone. For a time we alternated between these and other border points, making sure that our arrivals and departures were always during the early-morning hours. In the process, and partly as a result of making gifts of bottles of Canadian whisky, we made a number of acquaintances and were soon on a first-name basis with hotel men, garage, nightspot, and restaurant operators who might reasonably be expected to know something of the rackets. At the same time, we tried to establish a bit of a reputation as free spenders. Our attempts in that direction provided us with some amusement – as we contemplated the shocked reactions there would be to some of the items on our expense accounts.

Gradually our efforts began to bring results. The first break was an invitation extended by a hotel proprietor in Plattsburg to sit in on a poker game. The other players were men we had seen around the hotels and night spots. We played a little poker that first night, but the playing was not serious. There were an unusual number of interruptions, during which the boys chatted in a seemingly open fashion about border activities. Most of the chatter was directed toward us in a manner that invited information. Clearly this was more of a "try-out" session than a poker game. From the general conversation, it was easy to gather that, with the exception of our host, the other players were all from New York – all easy-money boys and all working under similar conditions and controls. When we got to know them better, we learned that they were runners for syndicates hauling liquor between stop-over points in Canada and the United States, usually for a fee of two hundred and fifty dollars a load. At this first meeting, we evaded answering questions by a show of extreme caution and by indicating that we would like to know them better before discussing any details of our business. Fortunately for us, competition between rival gangs was not too serious to allow enterprising locals from getting into the game in a small way; there was enough business to go around. An additional factor in our favour was that the criminal fraternity had been given little cause for concern by law-enforcement agencies.

We must have passed the test at the first meeting because other invitations followed. Our circle of acquaintances spread to include many of the runners and their friends and contacts, most of whom were connected in some way with the bootlegging and smuggling business. There was a surprising degree of camaraderie among the runners, whether they were employees of rival organizations or small independent operators. At times the situation became tense as the result of highjacking. During those times, runners who were not employed by the syndicates came under suspicion, occasionally with dire consequences. On the whole, however, the gang wars of the cities did not reach the border supply points. The markets could absorb as much as the runners could transport. Apart from an expected reticence about the times they would be crossing the border, and aside from details about their employers and customers, there was a free exchange of information on road conditions, police and customs activities, highjacking dangers, and warning systems.

In connection with warnings, we found that each group made its own arrangements but that a great deal of information was pooled in a loose but still effective way. Many persons were on the payroll of the smugglers, usually on a "value received" rather than a salary basis. People living close to customs or police posts kept a close watch, and passed the information on regarding activities, visitors, and licence numbers to an arranged contact. These were usually night-club, garage, and restaurant operators, and they made a good profit by selling the information to interested parties.

Most of the runners had helpers living close to the border whose job it was to patrol the road immediately before each crossing. The runners, as a rule, worked in pairs, with one man driving an empty car or "pilot" truck. A great deal of information received from these sources was made available to accepted members of the border-running brotherhood by keeping friendly hotel clerks, garage men, restaurant owners, and others advised. Once accepted – and when the word spread that we paid well – we were surprised by the ease with which we could pick up information regarding conditions on the border by dropping in for a friendly visit with persons known to be part of the network.

It would have been unwise to ask direct questions, but this was not necessary. The runners gave their information freely. The tipsters were always hopeful that their information would be worth a few dollars. We tested the speed and efficiency of the warnings by arranging with Montreal to have roads patrolled or to have questions asked by our men at border points. The bootleggers' telegraph really worked, and news of police activities was on the smugglers' net within an hour. On several occasions, we took advantage of the situation to improve our status among the smugglers by arranging for the setting up of road patrols and then feeding information regarding their locations into the network. The accuracy of our information was usually confirmed by other sources and served to indicate that we had excellent coverage along the border.

While we were thus employed, the undercover men in New York continued to check on the activities of Canadian importers and advise Montreal of shipments to border points. Attempts to keep these shipments under observation were called off temporarily because of the danger of alarming the smugglers, at a point that would interfere with our undercover work. From our end, we were able to learn the identity of runners who became active around the time that the shipments were due to be moved into Canada, and to gather information as to the routes used by them. In Montreal, information was being compiled regarding suspected merchants and their associates, the location of premises controlled by them, and details about their cars and trucks.

After the inquiry had been under way about six months, it was decided that enough information had been gathered to warrant the taking of direct action. The several weeks that followed were very busy ones for our men in Montreal – and somewhat apprehensive ones for Jack and me. We remained at our undercover posts, but the "heat" was on along the border and in Montreal, and the easy-going camaraderie gave way to hostility and suspicion. We were able to gather some information that assisted the search squads in countering the moves of the runners, but after a while Salt decided our game had become too risky. He ordered us back to Montreal.

A number of large seizures were made along the border and in Montreal. The inquiry had accomplished its purpose. The silk traffic had been stopped, at least for the time being. Jack Barnes and I enjoyed the fairly rare distinction of being mentioned in the Commissioner's Annual Report.

There was an amusing aftermath to our undercover activity along the border. During his first inspection at Montreal after these events, Commissioner Starnes, who had recently replaced Commissioner Perry, stopped in front of me to comment on the silk inquiry. Starnes was a short, stout, heavily moustachioed French-Canadian who had earned a tremendous reputation, particularly for his work in the North. He made a few complimentary remarks and ended by saying, "You played a lot of poker, Corporal, with the bootleggers."

I agreed, and added that this had been completely necessary as part of the investigation.

"Yes, I know all about that," he said. "But you are one hell of a poker player. I look at your expense accounts and always you lose. Our recruit training must be slipping."

At the request of the Department of Customs and Excise, the Force remained active in the enforcement of those acts, while an increasing number of requests for assistance were received from other departments, particularly the Department of Indian Affairs and the Secretary of State. While the strength of our detachment had been increased to twenty-seven, these added duties kept the staff working pretty much on a day-and-night basis. In addition to the normal investigational duties, we were occasionally called on to assist in the carrying out of special tasks, some-times in uniform. One of these special uniform tasks occurred in August of 1922, when several of us from Montreal were assigned to work with men from other divisions in escorting harvest trains from points in Eastern Canada to Winnipeg. A squad of four members was detailed to travel with each of the fifty-four trainloads of harvesters. The train on which I was to travel originated in Nova Scotia and carried about seven hundred passengers.

We boarded it in Eastern Quebec. The sight of the old crowded immigration coaches brought back memories of my trip West on the train just three years before. The passengers were in a holiday mood and, as was to be expected in the circumstances, a bit noisy and boisterous, but on the whole they made up a grand trainload. There were a few obvious hotheads, but these were vastly outnumbered by good, solid citizens bent only on working hard during the harvest on the prairies in order to earn badly needed dollars.

In accordance with the policy outlined in our instructions, we went through the train chatting with passengers and inquiring as to the cause of the troubles – some of them of riot proportions – that had erupted at some of the stopping points the previous year. We heard the same complaints that I had experienced: exorbitant increases in prices charged by merchants for groceries and supplies necessary to passengers.

In each car, one of us made a little speech outlining our plan and asking the co-operation of the harvesters. We requested that at each of the stopping places they remain on the station platform, until they received a signal from us. During these short intervals, we would approach the merchants and tell them that so long as reasonable prices were charged we would remain to keep the peace. In the event that they tried to take advantage of the harvesters' needs by charging outrageous prices, we would return to the train. The passengers were entreated to report excessive prices to us and to remain quiet and orderly at all times. This policy worked extremely well. The merchants seemed pleased that they were being offered some protection, and in almost all instances they kept their prices at a reasonable level.

At a few points we received complaints of overcharging, and a word to the storekeepers corrected the situation. At other times, some of the few troublemakers attempted to raise disturbances, but they were kept under control by the majority. At only one place, a small town in Northern Ontario, with one general store facing the railway station on the only street, was there a serious threat of trouble. The passengers were badly in need of supplies since in the last stopping place all stores had been closed and boarded up against the arrival of the special trains. The proprietor of the general store, probably aware that the harvesters were low in supplies, disregarded our advice and put the prices several times above normal. We tried to talk him into reason, but despite the fact that the mood of the people who had crowded into the store was getting ugly, and despite the fact that several hundred more passengers were waiting to get into the store, he insisted that it was his right to charge whatever prices he wanted.

Things were threatening to get out of hand. The passengers in the store were on the verge of starting real trouble, while the crowd outside began shouting and throwing rocks. Fortunately for us and the merchant, the train crew was alert. The engineer blew several long blasts on the whistle and the train started to move. The threat of rioting ended with the passengers racing to get aboard. The train stopped a few hundred yards down the track. My companions and I had another talk with the merchant who by this time was starting to worry that he might be left with the extra stuff that he had stocked in the hope of gouging the harvesters. He agreed to bring his prices down to a reasonable level. After a short talk to the passengers, the train was backed into the station. Needed supplies were available at fairly reasonable prices.

This same policy worked well on all other trains. There was not one really troublesome incident with the harvest trains that year. I have always hoped that the engineer of our train prospered and advanced in the company.

7

>>>->>>->>>->>>-<<<-<<<-<<<-<<<

Settling In

The work in Montreal was a very small part of the increasing volume and wide variety of duties being carried out across Canada. Following the extension of the jurisdiction of the Force in 1920, many departments of the federal Government developed the practice of calling for assistance. By 1923, work was being carried out under thirty-seven federal statutes, ranging from opium and narcotic drugs, shipping, immigration, customs, excise acts, to the laws governing the shipment and storage of explosives; from Indian, industrial disputes, and post-office acts to occasional assistance under the Leprosy Act.

As was the case in the provinces, the work of the Force in the Yukon and North West Territories had greatly increased. Long and difficult patrols to the few settlements scattered throughout the vast northland had been part of the work of the Force since the turn of the century, as had been the investigation of crime, but as more and more departments availed themselves of the services of the Force, many new duties were added. An extract from the annual report of the Officer Commanding the Yukon Territory for the year 1923 gives some indication of the multiplicity of work being performed in that territory:

> *Our coroner's work is performed by the officers, and also magisterial work at places other than the towns of Dawson and Whitehorse. Staff Sergeant Dempster performs the duties of coroner and magistrate for the Mayo district. Non-commissioned officers and constables on detachment act as postmaster, veterinary inspectors, immigration officers, cus-*

58

toms officers, collectors of royalties, etc. The Officer Commanding Whitehorse and district acts as sub-mining recorder, Crown timber and land agent, deputy sheriff. The Officer Commanding Division acts as immigration inspector and fisheries inspector for the Yukon Territory, registrar of vital statistics, and chief registrar of weights and measures. All members of the Force are game wardens, ex-officio. Besides enforcing federal and Yukon statutes and ordinances, we enforce the city bylaws, collect royalties on gold exported, issue permits for the export of fur, and issue licences to big-game hunters. Under the direction of the administrator, estates of persons dying from accidental, sudden, or violent death, and those of insane persons in outlying points, are looked after by us.

In addition to the duties being carried out in the police field, the Force had been given the responsibility of keeping the Government advised of the development and activities of the burgeoning Communist Party. The growth of the Party started under the guidance of paid agents sent from Moscow. Its dangerous potential for creating trouble, and the extremely secret operations of its underground apparatus posed many problems, but from the very beginning the Force met with success in penetrating the inner circles. The information thus secured served to keep the Government closely informed regarding the plotting, membership, and growth of the party, and of its complete adherence to the dictates of Moscow. These disturbing facts demanded an expansion in the security and counter-intelligence work of the Force in the way of increased manpower, additional equipment, special training, and improved system of records, better methods of analysis of information received, and closer supervision of this delicate and highly important work. The groundwork laid in those early years formed the foundation for the present security and intelligence branch of the Force, a service which, in my opinion, and in the opinion of professionals in other countries, must rate with the best and most experienced counter-intelligence organizations in the world.

Despite the constantly increasing responsibilities, and the carrying out of those responsibilities in an efficient and economical manner, there was still a considerable amount of opposition to the Force. Many persons held bitter memories of clashes with police during the recent disturbances. Others, who had not witnessed the riots and who knew little of the facts or causes, accepted the stories that were circulated regarding high-handed action and brutality by police. As memories of the actual conditions and circumstances faded into the background, the need for the maintenance of law and order to prevent chaos was forgotten; good work in other areas was overlooked or played down, and to some people the Force emerged as the villain of the piece. Much of the criticism came from sincere but misinformed and misguided persons. Publicity seekers, anixous to get their names into print, came forward with exaggerated and false stories that added to the clamour raised by the sincere critics. The situation was not lost on the Communists, and the party issued reams of circulars, news letters, and newspaper articles that screamed of the alleged brutality of the "Cossacks." The wave of criticism reached the floor of the House of Commons, and again there was talk of disbanding the Force. Recruiting was stopped, and for a time free discharge was offered to members. The future did not hold much promise.

In the meantime, a problem of my own had developed to a point that called for a decision. I was courting a charming girl and was very anxious to propose marriage. Under the circumstances of my employment with the Force, however, such a proposal was out of the question. Regulations permitted members to apply for permission to marry only after seven years of service. Permission might then be granted, at the discretion of the Commissioner, provided not more than fifty per cent of the members was married.

I was certainly not inclined to postpone marriage for a minimum of three years, nor was I inclined to attempt to support a wife on my very small income. Basic pay was still two dollars a day. If permission to marry was granted, in the distant future, the Force would pay me an additional one dollar and eighty-five cents a day "marriage allowance," hardly enough on which to support a wife in Montreal, even forty-odd years ago.

I was reluctant to leave the Force, but the condition imposed by its regulations left me no alternative. I left the service with deep regrets at the end of my fourth year. I remained out of the Force for eight years, during most of which time I was employed by the Better Business Bureau of Montreal. When, many years later, I became Commissioner, one of my first acts was to revise and make drastic changes in the marriage regulations.

While with the Force, I had subscribed to several correspondence courses, but barrack-room life and long working hours are not conducive to concentration. The regular schedule of the Better Business Bureau and my quiet, comfortable living accommodations provided welcome opportunities for study. After finishing the correspondence courses, I enrolled for a series of extension classes at McGill University and Sir George Williams College. The classes, which extended over several years, proved interesting and very helpful.

More important for my future happiness and well-being was the fact that I had time to pursue the main objective I had had in mind on leaving the Force – that of persuading a wonderful, petite, and lovely Canadian girl of Irish ancestry, Doris Helen Quinn, to marry me. She accepted my proposal, and we were married in 1926. Her constant help, encouragement, and companionship have brought a lifetime of happiness and good fortune. For me, Lady Luck will always have smiling Irish eyes.

I kept in touch with old friends in the Force. In fact, while my new occupation brought better working conditions, higher pay, and freedom from both the discipline and – at times – frustrating regulations, I missed the work and friendships of the Force. There is a great deal of truth in the adage that after a few years in the Force a man will remain a "Mountie" for the rest of his life.

As had been anticipated, the attitude of the Government toward the Force changed with returning prosperity, a consequent decrease of crime, and a reduction in the danger of violent demonstrations. The Coalition (or, as it was known, the Union Government) – which had increased the strength and expanded the jurisdiction of the federal police in order to secure the country against riots and threats of large-scale violence – had been succeeded by a Liberal Government led by William Lyon Mackenzie King.

While in opposition, King and some members of his party had been severely critical of the expansion of the Force. This criticism was carried into the election campaign and became one of its features. In office, Prime Minister King and his Government continued to hold that their predecessors had blundered in enlarging and expanding the Force, a position which the new Government could safely assume because of the changed conditions across the country.

A series of confused and confusing changes were made in affixing cabinet responsibilities for the Force. Control which for years had rested with the President of the Privy Council – usually the Prime Minister – was shifted to the Minister of Militia, a somewhat bewildering move by a Government that had expressed fears of a "police state." Later, an equally bewildering switch of control placed the Royal Canadian Mounted Police under the Department of National Defence, which combined the police with the army, the navy, and the air force. Biting attacks by the Opposition soon convinced the Government of the error of this move. Eventually the Force was placed under the control of the Minister of Justice. One wonders why it took so long to reach this obviously proper decision.

Debates in the House of Commons as to the disposition of the Force held little promise for its future. An Independent Member of Parliament, J. S. Woodsworth from Winnipeg, where the Force had been compelled to take decisive action, proposed a motion which would have banished the Force to the Yukon and Northwest Territories. An able, widely respected member, Woodsworth was constantly torn between his abhorrence of mob violence and his fear of a police state. His motion was defeated by a vote of one hundred and eight to forty-seven, but the debate was long and bitter.

While saved from the threat of banishment to the Arctic, the Force did suffer some severe curtailment. Recruiting was discontinued and free discharges were again offered all members. Within five years, the establishment had been reduced by half. Pay, office, and living accommodations were poor, and equipment was outmoded or non-existent. Despite the increasing demands for service to departments of the federal Government, a disturbing crime wave, and an active and growing Communist Party, the Force remained in the doldrums throughout the twenties.

Prime Minister Mackenzie King and his Liberal Party were defeated in an election held in 1930. The Conservatives under The Honourable R. B. Bennett took over the reins of Government. Members of the Force, trained to avoid political affiliation or entanglement, saw little cause for either enthusiasm or disappointment over the change. The federal police organization was understaffed, underpaid, and poorly equipped, but this had been so since the inception of the Force under Liberal, Conservative, and Coalition Governments.

There was nothing to indicate that the incumbent Government would have any more interest in a sound and realistic development of the federal law-enforcement agency than had been shown by the previous ones, but circumstances were combining to bring about some changes. The need was obvious and, politics apart, had been obvious for some years. As Government departments expanded with the growth of the country, there were increasing requirements for a large variety of services that the Force could not always meet expeditiously or efficiently because of the severe limits placed on its resources.

Prime Minister Bennett had practised law in Calgary, a city that had its beginning as a settlement built around one of the first outposts of the North West Mounted Police. He was familiar with the history and traditions of the Force. His legal practice had brought him into contact with members and had enabled him to study their methods, discipline, loyalty, and ability. His actions, after assuming office as Prime Minister, made it clear that he was determined that the Royal Canadian Mounted Police should be given the backing and financial support necessary to enable its reorganization into a modern, well-trained, well-equipped department able to meet the increasing and complex demands of the country.

Just a few months after the new Government came into office, Commissioner Courtland Starnes expressed a desire to be retired to pension. During his eight years as Commissioner, he had made many valiant attempts to bring about a reorganization that would have improved both efficiency and the lot of those under his command, but lack of interest or support by those in control frustrated most of his efforts. Now, after a record forty-five years of devoted service, he wanted to be relieved of the burdens of office. The wonder is that he had stuck it out for so long.

In order to carry out his plans for a complete reorganization and modernization of the Force, the Prime Minister had, as a first requirement, the appointment of a man known and respected as an able executive who, as Commissioner, would enjoy the confidence of Parliament, the public, and the officers and members of the Force. He offered the appointment to Major General James MacBrien, a selection that indicated the importance Mr. Bennett attached to his program for the Force.

General (later Sir) James MacBrien had an outstanding record. He was a former member of the Force, having enlisted as a Constable in 1900. He left after brief service in order to join the forces in the South African war. His military service had taken him from Private to General and to senior posting in the army – as Chief of the General Staff, a position from which he had resigned in order to follow his interests in the developing field of civil aviation. Despite his many accomplishments and enviable career, he was only sixty-two.

At first, MacBrien declined the appointment, principally on the grounds that promotion should be from within the Force and that an appointment from outside would have an adverse effect on morale. It was pointed out to him that the next senior officers in the Force were reaching retirement age and that other retirements were pending. It took a number of meetings with the Prime Minister before he was persuaded to accept the appointment. He agreed with the firm understanding that there would be no political interference in the operation of the Force. On August 1, 1931, he became the seventh Commissioner.

The combination of Government support and an able Commissioner, backed by the willing efforts of the officers, non-commissioned officers, and men, produced excellent results in an amazingly short time. Within a year, the Force had taken over the policing duties from municipal and provincial authorities in Alberta, Manitoba, New Brunswick, Nova Scotia, and Prince Edward Island. A similar contract with the Province of Saskatchewan had been in operation for seven years. Another important extension occurred in April of 1932, when the duties of the Preventive Service of the Department of National Revenue were absorbed.

The expansion of the Force necessitated a greatly increased strength which could not be fully met through the enlistment of men from the provincial forces. Recruiting was started, and word was spread that members who had left the Service during the doldrum period would be welcomed back, even though they had committed the hitherto unforgiveable sin of marrying. I applied for a re-engagement. Although she was sure, through experience during our early courtship, that it would mean irregular hours, frequent absence, and possible transfer to any point in Canada, my wife encouraged me in this. She knew, too, that any hopes or dreams of success in the way of wealth would end with my acceptance back into the Service. My application was approved, and on April 22, 1932, I re-engaged as a Constable for a five-year term.

8

-≫≫-≫≫-≫≫-≫≫-≪≪-≪≪-≪≪-≪≪-

Gypsum Queen
and
Other Matters

A tremendous change had come over the Force. There was an air of great activity, of eager excitement, of a purposeful rush to do the many things that required doing to keep up with all the new duties and responsibilities. Across the Force, there had been an increase in strength of sixty-four per cent. Many of the new members had come to the Mounted Police from provincial forces and the customs and excise services. Many of the others were re-engaged men. All required training or retraining to meet the changing requirements.

While training, administrative procedures, and promotional and posting systems were being altered to meet new conditions, the day-to-day work must be carried on – and carried on in a manner that would clearly demonstrate that the sudden burst of confidence being shown by the Government had not been misplaced. Old members and members recently acquired from other services worked with an enthusiasm and a confidence in the future. In a few months, the new Commissioner, enjoying as he did the confidence and support of Parliament, had rejuvenated the Force.

I was caught up in the new training program a few weeks after re-engagement, when instructions were received from headquarters that I was to attend a training course of three months' duration in Regina. The return to barrack-room life and to trumpeters who disturbed the peace at five-thirty in the morning, and blew calls demanding that lights go out at ten-thirty, was a bit of a shock, as were the first few encounters with the horses and riding and drill instructors. I had softened during the eight years of civilian and married life, and the instructors seemed united in their determination to get me back in shape.

The new order of things was apparent in the training schedule. Riding, drill, and physical training were still part of the daily routine, but they were now secondary to lectures and training on subjects directly connected with police work – in particular, with the new duties of the Force. The customs and excise acts, provincial statutes, criminal code, rules of evidence, mock trials, scenes of crime demonstrations, the making of plaster casts, fingerprinting, taking of statements, schemes designed to improve our powers of observation, lectures by experts in medical-legal work and in photography – all these were part of the three-months' training course. Certainly the Force was intent on going places in a hurry.

The members of the class had been drawn from all parts of Canada. Several had had no experience with military-type discipline, the drill square, or riding school; but to a man, they were determined that if membership required these discomforts, they were to be suffered quietly, if not enthusiastically, even if the riding caused the uninitiated to walk uncomfortably and bow-leggedly for days. Morale was too high to be affected by such trifles.

Back in Montreal, I was detailed to CIB duties as a member of the General Investigation Squad, a catch-all group which handled a wide variety of inquiries that did not fit into the work of the squads specializing in narcotics, customs and excise, counterfeiting, and Communist-activity investigations. I found that the contacts made and experience gained during my years in civilian life were of tremendous value in carrying out these new duties. Apparently my superiors found my work satisfactory. In October, I was promoted to my old rank of Detective Corporal.

A few days after my promotion, I was transferred to the narcotics squad. Conditions had changed greatly. The opium joints that had taken up so much of our time in the early twenties were gone, and with them had gone the easy availability of opium that had been spreading addiction. While there was still some small demand for opium and cocaine, the traffic was mostly in morphine and heroin.

Drugs were no longer being peddled on the street corners. The pedlars had gone underground, and police pressures kept them there. Even the sale of a capsule of drugs was surrounded with many precautionary measures. The spread of addiction to the so-called "white drugs" had been curtailed, and for several years the addict population had remained almost static. In most cities across Canada, arrangements had been entered into with the municipal police, whereby they kept the pressures on the "pushers" and addicts, while the Mounted Police concentrated on large and international traffickers. Excellent arrangements for liaison and co-operation had also been worked out with authorities in the United States, and a start had been made toward co-operation with forces overseas. As a result, a number of highly important investigations were brought to successful conclusions.

Among these were the related cases of Harry Davis and Pincus Brecher. Davis started his criminal career while still a newsboy on the streets of Montreal. He worked his way up – or down, depending on the point of view – from messenger boy for the underworld, to petty thief, to pimp, to narcotic pusher. Eventually he climbed – or clawed – his way to the top of the underworld dung heap, where he associated and worked with bank robbers, hold-up men, and narcotic traffickers. His underworld connections spread to the United States and Europe. The police knew this slim, well-dressed, rather good-looking man as a leader among criminals. He was both smart and lucky for a time; then his luck ran out.

Through the joint efforts of the newly formed United States Bureau of Narcotics and the members of the Montreal office of the RCMP, an exceptionally large quantity of drugs was seized. Intensive investigation developed evidence directly implicating Davis. He was arrested, tried, and convicted, principally on evidence supplied by one Charlie Feigenbaum, another underworld figure. Davis was sentenced to fourteen years in prison and twenty lashes. After serving most of his sentence, he was released and he immediately returned to his old haunts and associates, but he had lost his touch and power. He was shot to death by one of his own associates.

During the Davis investigation, information and later strong evidence was developed against a New Yorker, Pincus Brecher, a somewhat mysterious, shadowy figure, reputedly worth several millions, and long-suspected of being tied in with the international narcotics racket. His arrest in New York caused something of an international sensation. Extradition proceedings were started, and after months of long-drawn-out legal battles, he was brought to Canada to stand trial.

Charlie Feigenbaum, the man whose evidence had contributed to the conviction of Harry Davis, was slated to be one of the chief witnesses against Brecher, and rumour had it that several other underworld figures were scheduled to "sing" at the Brecher trial. On a bright summer afternoon, fat Charlie Feigenbaum waddled to his car, which was parked at the curb of a side street near busy Mount Royal Avenue. He was loading it with provisions for a holiday trip to the Laurentians. As he approached the car, a man sauntered slowly across the street, leaned on the front of Charlie's car to steady his aim, and pumped five shots into Charlie's stomach. Unhurriedly the murderer then rejoined a pal who had been waiting in a car with the engine running. They switched cars a few blocks away, where a third man was waiting for them.

Several of us from the Drug Squad joined detectives from the City Police at the scene of the crime, but there was very little to be learned. As is so often the case, eye witnesses gave conflicting descriptions of the murderer and the driver of the get-away car. An intensive joint investigation was carried out by all police forces in the Montreal area, but the results were inconclusive. We did learn, however, the identity of the man, a Canadian criminal, who had driven the second get-away car, and we learned that the other two men had been brought in from New York to execute Charlie for a fee of $250 each and expenses. However, there was not sufficient evidence to bring them to trial. The investigation was handicapped by the fact that many persons had had motives for removing Charlie. So far as the Brecher trial was concerned, the murderer did not silence Feigenbaum, since his evidence at the previous trial was available. The murderer did frighten other criminals who had been toying with the idea of giving evidence, and that may have been the reason back of the killing.

During his trial, Brecher had the services of outstanding defence counsel, but their best efforts could not break down the mass of evidence presented by the forty-two witnesses called. Brecher was found guilty and remanded for sentence. A very severe penalty seemed inevitable, but Brecher did not wait for the judgment of the Court. On his return to Bordeaux Jail, he brought the case to a dramatic climax. As the guards led him along the walkway of the third tier of cells, he plunged over the railing, to meet death on the steel plates below.

The breaking-up of an international gang of narcotic traffickers will always cause some disruption in the distribution of drugs, while realignments are worked out between the overseas suppliers and the traffickers in the United States and Canada. But as there are usually several international groups in operation, the traffic does not stop. So great are the profits, that any vacuum left, as the result of police action, is quickly filled. Very often the planning and financing are carried out by crime syndicates that are protected by corrupt hirelings, lawyers, and many echelons of underlings. The top men can rarely be reached by law-enforcement agencies. The breaking-up of one of their organizations simply amounts to the closing down of one of their branches. Another branch is opened as quickly as the necessary arrangements can be made. There is no let-up for the police in their work of combatting the traffic.

Unlike the United States, where use of this drug is a major problem, Canada has had little trouble with marijuana or Indian hemp. A few seizures have been made, but in almost all cases the offenders were members of "hot" musical bands or other performers who had imported the drug for their own use. This comparatively happy situation is all the more remarkable in that at one time marijuana grew wild in many parts of the country – particularly in the Province of Quebec where, it was said, early settlers cultivated the plant for use in the manufacturing of rope and twine.

With addiction to this drug spreading in the United States, particularly among juveniles, the Force and the Department of Health became concerned over the possibility that news stories and photographs regarding marijuana, which were appearing in the United States press, might lead to widespread recognition of the plant in Canada and to its subsequent use by addicts and experimentation by juveniles. It was decided that a campaign of eradication should be started. The Narcotic Drug Act and the Noxious Weeds Act provided the required authority.

In the Spring of 1933, several members of the drug squad and members of detachments across the Province of Quebec started scouring the countryside. It was found that the seed of the once-cultivated plants had spread far and wide. Many patches were discovered. As the chore of tearing the plants out by the roots required a greater labour force than could be supplied by the police, application was made for authority to employ the number of labourers required in the various areas, and for the hiring of trucks to cart the stuff away for burning. The plan was good, but its execution produced results that were directly opposite to those hoped for. Red tape delayed the granting of authority to cover the necessary expenditure until the plants had reached maturity and were laden with ripe seed-pods. The roots of the large plants were tough, and they covered a wide area. The act of tearing them up disturbed and, in effect, cultivated the soil. Into this cultivated soil dropped the ripe seeds shaken loose by the strenuous efforts of the workmen. A much larger crop of marijuana was assured for the next season. The whole job had to be done again the following year. Fortunately, authority was received in time to prevent the recurrence of the happenings that had provided much amusement for the farmers, most of whom had watched our efforts with knowing interest.

At the height of the campaign, two members of the drug squad, while driving between Montreal and Ottawa, spotted a small stand of marijuana in the corner of a well-kept garden surrounding an immaculately clean cottage. In accordance with instructions, they stopped their car and approached the cottage to talk with the owner. Their subsequent actions were scarcely in accordance with the "always-get-your-man (or woman)" motto which Hollywood has given the Force. The owner of the cottage was a tall, rather gaunt spinster of uncertain years, whose hobby was raising canaries. The policeman explained the reason for their call, read the sections of the Narcotic Drug and Noxious Weeds Acts bearing on the situation, and explained that it was their duty to destroy the marijuana plants. It developed that the lady grew them for the seed, which, when fed to the canaries, made them sing and sing.

On behalf of her happy birds, she took furious objection to any ridiculous law that would deny them their happiness. The constables expressed their regrets, explained that they had no alternative but to destroy the plants, and started for the garden. They were half-way to the marijuana patch when the door of the cottage burst open and the spinster, armed with a broom, and screaming, "Scat you brutes!" rushed forth to do battle. To their everlasting credit, the policemen decided that the situation called for discretion rather than valour. They beat a hasty retreat to their car and drove off. As far as I know, the lady continued to grow marijuana, and her birds continued to sing magnificently for the rest of her days.

In 1934, I was temporarily assigned to the *Gypsum Queen* inquiry, a case that went back to the alleged torpedoing of a Canadian schooner of that name off the coast of Ireland by a German submarine in 1915. Almost fifteen years later, the skipper, Captain Freeman Hatfield, a tough old sea-dog from Parrsboro, Nova Scotia, placed a claim for reimbursement before the War-Reparations Commission. In his claim, it was alleged that the schooner had been lost as a result of enemy action and that, therefore, he was entitled to compensation from the Government. In making his claim, he was represented by Senator Hance J. Logan, also from Parrsboro, Nova Scotia. The claim was successful and payment totalling over $71,000 was made to Hatfield in 1931.

One year later, information casting doubt on the story of the torpedo version of the loss of the schooner reached the Government. A Royal Commission, set up to inquire into the matter, discovered that the story of enemy action was a complete fraud. The vessel had actually foundered during a storm.

At the time of the hearings of the Royal Commission, Captain Hatfield had vanished, along with half of the $71,000. The other half had been left with the Senator, who claimed that he had kept the money in order to make investments for the Captain, and that he had received only the expenses incurred while acting for his old friend and fellow townsman. Everything else, according to the Senator's story, had been forwarded to the Captain.

Sporadic attempts were made by the Commission to locate Hatfield and the money, but the inquiries were not pressed too hard. It seemed that the matter had been shelved. In 1934, questions were asked in the House of Commons, and the Government decided further action should be taken. The Force was instructed to attempt to locate the missing skipper and the missing funds. It was known that he had purchased shares in Montreal, but the Royal Commission had been unable to discover the nature or the amounts or distribution of these investments. Montreal, therefore, was a logical point at which to start the new investigation. I was assigned to the case.

Luck was with me. I was able to discover details of the purchase of some forty-thousand dollars worth of the shares of a Montreal company. The shares had been purchased in the name of the Captain. From the company, I learned that dividend coupons from the shares were being received regularly from a bank in New York. A trip to New York established that the bank there had simply acted as a clearing house. At first, they were unable to supply information as to the source from which the coupons had been received. Fortunately, the cancellation stamps had been made with a rather peculiar shade of ink, which after some study the officials of the bank recognized as a colour used by a bank in New Jersey. In New Jersey, I found that the shares were being held on behalf of Hatfield and that the money received from the dividend coupons was being deposited in a sizeable account being maintained by the skipper. They had not seen him for over a year. The last withdrawal had been by way of several small cheques cashed by a bank in Jacksonville, Florida.

Through the office of the British Consul in New York, arrangements were made whereby action toward seizure of the stocks and the bank account would be started immediately following receipt of a wire from me saying I had located the missing skipper. The bank agreed to advise our lawyers in the event an attempt was made toward any large withdrawals.

From Jacksonville, the trail, still over a year old, led back to New York, then back to Florida, and again to New York, where the skipper had stayed a few weeks in a fleabag waterfront hotel owned by a well-known gangster. The desk clerk was not helpful. He had never heard of Hatfield, and was sure that no one by that name had ever been a guest, and the register covering the dates in which I was interested had been mislaid.

Through the willing co-operation of the Captain of the Old Slip Station of the New York City Police, I met the gangster owner of the hotel. After a brief discussion, he telephoned the hotel and the desk clerk suddenly regained his memory. He remembered Hatfield very well and even had a forwarding address – a boarding house in the Bronx.

In the Bronx, the landlady remembered Hatfield and added a new element: Hatfield had been accompanied by a plump middle-aged lady, a native of the Bronx, who was very cross-eyed. They had occupied a room for several months, during which the landlady had become quite friendly with Hatfield's companion. She had received a letter from her a few weeks after their departure. As far as she could recall, she had kept the letter, which had a forwarding address. It might turn up sometime, but she had her own troubles and was much too distraught to make any attempt to find it.

In conversation, it developed that the landlady's troubles were very real. Just that day she had been served a writ ordering her to vacate the premises, despite the fact that she had a lease. She was a widow with no income other than that derived from operating the boarding house. To add to her burdens, her son, who lived with her, had been arrested by the city police and was being held as the result of some alleged traffic violation. Certainly she could not be expected to show very much interest in searching for an old letter.

I took her to see the lawyers who were representing Canada in the Hatfield matter. They discovered that the lease covering the property she occupied was quite valid and that the landlord had been trying to bluff her. Having settled that problem, they arranged bail for the son and agreed to appear on his behalf when the case was brought before the courts. The landlady was greatly relieved and most anxious to do something to indicate her gratitude. After a great deal of searching, she located the missing letter.

It had been mailed from Manchester, New Hampshire. The letter mentioned that the couple were living on a farm "near New Boston." The trail was getting warm, and as I had no authority in the United States, I decided to seek aid of the United States marshal at Concord, the point closest to my new area of interest. The Marshal was most co-operative. Having discussed the case at some length, he detailed Deputy Marshal Walter Bean to work with me, an arrangement that, because of Deputy Marshal Bean's vast experience and knowledge of the countryside and his desire to be of assistance, proved most satisfactory.

Inquiries in Manchester produced no results. We then canvassed the New Boston area without success. Deputy Marshal Bean recalled that the name "New Boston Road" was at times applied to several of the roads in the area. Inquiries revealed that a fair number of the farms along these roads had new tenants, and we decided to visit each of these. We drew blanks on our first four calls. At the fifth farmhouse, I knocked on the door, and it was opened by a rather stout, middle-aged lady who was very cross-eyed. On a pretext of some sort, I inquired after her husband. "The Captain," she said, had gone into town but would be back in about an hour. I told her I would come back later.

We watched the house, and after a short time a car pulled into the driveway. The driver readily admitted that he was Captain Hatfield. Deputy Marshal Bean placed him under arrest. The old sea-dog took his arrest very calmly, almost as though he had always known that some day this would happen. He was a ruddy faced, raw-boned man of medium build with the rugged, weather-beaten look of an ancient mariner. There was scarcely any grey in his sandy hair, and he seemed a good ten years younger than his age of seventy-three. I could not help thinking that in his prime the Captain would have been a good man to have alongside one if the going got really rough.

In the car, on the way to Manchester, he asked me for details regarding his predicament and legal position. I advised him that he would be taken before a United States extradition commission at Manchester and that the details of the charges brought against him by the Canadian

Government would then be explained to him. He would have the choice of waving extradition proceedings and returning to Canada with me or of remaining in custody pending the outcome of the extradition hearing.

On our arrival in Manchester, I left Hatfield in the care of Deputy Marshal Bean while I located a telegraph office. Wires, advising of the arrest, were dispatched to my Officer Commanding in Montreal, and to the lawyers in New York in order that action might be started forthwith toward seizure of the shares and bank account in New Jersey.

On returning to the courthouse, I found it overrun with newspaper reporters and photographers. The case had all the ingredients of a good story. Schooners, submarines, a Canadian Senator, a wreck at sea, fraud, and the long pursuit of an old sea-dog up and down the Atlantic coast by a "Mountie." The papers made the most of it. The case was headlined internationally.

On his appearance before the United States Commissioner Charles V. Barnard, Captain Hatfield decided to fight the proceedings. Extradition is usually a long, drawn-out procedure. He remained in custody in the United States for seven months before being returned to Canada, where he was sentenced to four years' imprisonment. Beyond question he had defrauded the Government and deserved punishment, but somehow I have always been a little sorry that I did not run out of leads somewhere along the trail.

On my return to Montreal after the *Gypsum Queen* investigation, I was called before the Officer Commanding. He reminded me of an interview some months earlier during which he had questioned me regarding my opinion of the work being done to combat the huge illicit alcohol racket that was flooding the Quebec market. I had been critical of the work on grounds that while we knew the men back of the illicit operations, we had not been successful in bringing them to court. In general, seizures and arrests had been limited to retailers and to persons found on the premises of illicit stills. The "big names," the organizers who planned the operations and who derived most of the profits, had so far remained hidden behind their underlings and escaped punishment.

The Officer Commanding asked if during the interval I had changed my mind regarding the liquor squad or, as it was called, the "Preventive Service." It was, obviously, a leading question, and it was equally obvious that I was being jockeyed into a difficult position. The Officer Commanding, Assistant Commissioner F. J. Mead, a tall, lean career policeman who had come up through the ranks, was an alert, imaginative man who knew every angle of police work, including methods of getting the best efforts from his subordinates. One of these methods was to pick a man for a job, put him on a spot from which he had to deliver, or admit inability, and then give him all possible support in his efforts to successfully complete the task. I could not alter my previous stand. I repeated my criticism and added that I could not change my views as long as we were only catching the "small fry."

"I don't have much time for critics unless they know a way to do a better job," said the Officer Commanding. "Now we'll see if you can back up your criticism. I am transferring you from the Drug Squad to a special detail which will concentrate on getting to the top men in the liquor racket. Name any four men in the division, and they will be assigned to you, as will Police Car X. You will work independently and be responsible only to me. You have three months in which to convince me that you are able to do more than criticize."

The instructions were simple, "Put up or shut up," but the matter of bringing them to a successful conclusion offered many complications and difficulties. It was known in a very general way that the big "pots," stills capable of producing five hundred gallons of high quality alcohol a day, were being built and operated under the control of a Canadian organization closely tied in with an American syndicate. It was known too that the smaller stills, ranging up to two hundred gallons daily capacity and turning out alcohol of widely varying quality, were the results of efforts of several small Canadian groups to get a share of the very profitable bootleg racket, profits that ran from five to seven dollars a gallon.

Illicit "whisky blanc" or straight alcohol was also reaching the large Quebec market from St. Pierre and Miquelon, Newfoundland, and the United States. The alcohol from the islands, an aftermath of "Rum Row" of the days of the Volstead Act, was smuggled on shore in the maritimes or along the St. Lawrence River and trucked to the Quebec market. The traffic from the United States was for the most part the product of illicit stills being operated in that country by the syndicates.

The maritime divisions of the Force and the patrol boats of the recently acquired marine division had mounted a very active campaign to suppress the traffic from the islands. Their efforts had met with considerable success. Similarly, the border patrols had made a number of important seizures and had curtailed the flow of liquor reaching the Quebec market from the United States. In effect, these successes served to aid the still operators in Canada by reducing the competition from other sources. The quantities of illicit alcohol reaching the Quebec market had not decreased, rather the reverse. Only the sources had changed.

The four men for my little special squad were chosen with great care. I selected young men whose records and performance indicated a keen interest in their work and little regard for regular or limited hours. Loud protests from the several squad heads affected indicated that I was indeed getting good men. While the members of the squad were somewhat lacking in experience in liquor work, we had one great advantage over the members regularly employed on those duties. A great part of their time was taken up with the routine but necessary work of making small seizures and attending court and interviewing petty informers; whereas we were able to concentrate on the securing of information regarding the activities of the top men in the racket.

We had another advantage. The Officer Commanding had indicated that he was prepared to take an unusually liberal view in the matter of expenditures for the special squad. The four men of the squad were single men living in barracks. They were moved into an apartment in downtown Montreal, partly in order that the separation from other duties would be complete, and partly in order to impress them with the importance attached to their new duties. To men used to the extreme economy of the Force, the fact that the work rated the expense of renting an apartment was significant.

The apartment became the centre of our operations. As a starting point, we examined all files containing information regarding the liquor traffic and had lengthy interviews with the squad heads and more experienced members of the preventive squad. From the information gathered, we selected the names of four persons all of whom were indicated as the top men of the largest organization in the racket, the one organization said to be closely associated with the Detroit crime syndicate known as the Purple Gang. For several weeks we concentrated on following these men in order to learn their habits, associates, premises in which they appeared to have an interest, descriptions and licence numbers of automobiles or trucks used by them, or by people in contact with them. Then for several weeks we concentrated on finding out everything we could about the lesser lights, the persons whom we had established as part of the big organization.

In the meantime, we had secured a very useful addition to our scanty equipment. An ancient panel-bodied truck had been purchased to help in the job of maintaining a watch on our growing list of suspects. The old truck was garaged in a residential area, well removed from the haunts of the bootleggers. Neighbours must have wondered about the vehicle and the frequency with which it changed colour. Through the use of fast-drying lacquer, we could complete a paint job in a few hours and did this whenever we thought that it was time for a change. The old truck eventually collapsed – I suspect from the weight of paint – but during its service, it proved most valuable.

By the end of the three months' trial period that had been allowed, the special squad through surveillance and by studying seizures made by the regular liquor squads, and with some help from informers had put together a fairly detailed picture of the operations of the illicit liquor business. The really large stills were being built by a qualified engineer and workmen imported from the United States. Under arrangements with the syndicates, the Canadian organization paid a lump sum to the syndicate, salaries to the engineer and workmen, and guaranteed to continue the salaries and provide counsel in the event that the importees should be arrested. The Canadian group also agreed to pay any fines that might be imposed.

On the completion of a still, the American workmen remained in Canada for about a month to train a Canadian crew in the operation of the somewhat complicated apparatus. The Americans then withdrew from the operation except for a business agent who remained in Canada to make sure that the syndicate received an agreed-on part of the profits, usually about twenty per cent. The operators of the stills sold only in large wholesale lots with four or five groups handling all of the output. From there down, the distribution system fanned out to smaller distributors, until it reached the consumers through small dealers. The system of distribution was thorough, with bootleggers readily available in most neighbourhoods and in most factories and business houses.

Several of the large stills owned by the organization had been seized by the regular preventive squad, but prosecutions had been limited to the persons found on the premises whose fines had been paid by the organization. We learned, however, that the operators were becoming greatly concerned because the courts were imposing increasingly heavy fines. They were even more concerned because the Force, in consultation with excellent counsel provided by the Department of Justice, had adopted the practice of prosecuting on charges of conspiracy as well as on the substantive offences. To an increasing extent, the courts were giving jail sentences, which not only increased the costs to the operators, since they had to pay salaries to their jailed employees, but imprisonment also increased the threat of some of the employees talking to the police. Despite these fears, they added to the threat by starting to welch on some of the promised salaries and by employing less expensive counsel to defend the persons charged.

Apart from general knowledge regarding the operations of the racket at various levels, we had been successful in amassing a wealth of detail regarding premises, cars, trucks, and the part the various people played in the traffic. Armed with this, and assisted by the manpower of the preventive squad, we started to take definite action. A number of seizures of large quantities of alcohol were made, and these led in turn to the seizure of stills belonging to the "big four."

The first of these was concealed in a bakery building which operated under the name "Mother's Tasty Pies." The smell of yeast and baking bread helped to conceal the tell-tale odours of the still, always a major problem to the operators. Seven men were found on the premises and duly charged. Five drew jail sentences. We found out later that these men were unhappy because the amounts paid to their families were far below the figure that had been agreed to.

Another large still was discovered near Three Rivers, Quebec. Again the persons found on the premises were charged and all – in this case, five men and a female cook – were given jail sentences. Again the operators welched on their payments, and this brought us the services of another informer.

From time to time, the special squad, which had been increased to seven men, concentrated on keeping track of the actions of one of the "big four." By these means, we discovered that they had an interest in a factory building in the East End of Montreal. While none of the "big four" visited the factory, they did have meetings with a man known to us as their employee, and he, in turn, spent most of his time on the premises. The evasive tactics used during their meetings, and the extreme caution shown by the employee in trying to evade surveillance while going to the building, were sure indications that the building was going to be used for some purpose other than that indicated by a newly erected sign, which proclaimed it to be a toy-manufacturing company.

It was a three-storey brick structure with a large yard, surrounded by a high board fence, in a newly developing part of the city which was intended for industrial sites. Streets, sewers, and water supplies had been laid, but at the time there were few buildings, the closest being a biscuit factory in the next block. Inside the fence that enclosed the premises in which we were interested, piles of lumber had been stacked in a manner that effectively blocked the view of the yard that might otherwise have been had from the upper windows of the biscuit factory. This precaution would hardly have been necessary in the operation of a legitimate business. When we first viewed the premises, a new sixty-foot steel smokestack was under construction. Deliveries to the building were made by closed trucks which we were able to identify as belonging to the still organization. The drivers were known as employees. It looked as though another big "pot" was in the making, but the absence of odour and the fact that the smokestack was still under construction indicated that it was not yet in operation. We decided to keep it under observation and to intensify our efforts toward watching the movements of the "big four." We hoped that eventually we would be able to secure evidence which would enable us to connect them with the operation.

It was discovered that the top man of the organization was making fairly frequent calls at an apartment on Sherbrooke Street West. Again the evasive tactics used by him in going to the apartment indicated that his dealings with the occupants were not entirely above suspicion. Inquiries brought information that the occupant was an Italian-American from Detroit who claimed to be an "insurance executive." Through the co-operation of United States law-enforcement contacts, we were able to learn that he was, in fact, a member of the Purple Gang. We had discovered the syndicate's "payoff" man.

A few days later I received a call from the squad member who was keeping the "toy factory" under observation. Smoke was coming from the chimney for the first time. After consultation with the Officer Commanding, it was decided that we would search the place the following day. In so doing, we would have the assistance of about twenty men, most of them thoroughly experienced in liquor work.

At about ten o'clock the following morning, we attempted to open the gate but found it locked. Despite our loud knocking, there was no response, except that two men scaled the fence on the far side in an attempt to escape. One of our men had to climb the fence in order to remove the two-by-four bars that held the gate. The yard was deserted. Inside the building we found five men. There were a few outmoded woodworking machines on each of the floors, but these had not been installed. Incongruously, a start had been made toward the manufacture of papier-mâché dress display dummies. Disjointed arms, legs, torsos, and hairless heads were strewn about. There was no odour of alcohol or "mash," the brew from which alcohol is distilled. Nor did an intensive search that lasted over two hours disclose the slightest indication of a still. I questioned the two men who had attempted to escape as to their reasons for trying to run away. Their answers were vague and far from convincing. As to their employment, they said they had been hired by the "boss," whose name they did not know, as sweepers. Each of the five men found in the building also claimed to have been employed by some unknown man to work as a sweeper. Four of the men were Canadians; three were Americans.

Although a still of five-hundred-gallon capacity is hardly an item easily concealed, all the circumstances indicated that, despite our fruitless search, there must be one hidden somewhere on the premises. I instructed our men to start the search all over again. An old railway-engine boiler had been mounted on concrete saddles in the boiler room, ostensibly to supply steam for the operation of the woodworking factory. Although the machinery was not in operation, the boiler had a fair head of steam. I was in the boiler room pondering this point when one of the searchers called me over to a small clothes closet in one corner which, probably for the want of something better to do, he had been examining with meticulous care. The concrete floor in the cupboard had a covering of wooden slats. When pushed, through the slats, the concrete seemed to move a little.

We quickly removed the floorboards and found that the concrete did, indeed, give about half an inch when pressure was applied. A sledge-hammer made short work of the concrete slab which we found was hinged to open downward. We also found that the slab was controlled by a mechanism that could be activated by shoving a nail in a small hole in one of the uprights of the clothes cupboard.

A ladder led down into a passageway about six feet wide and seven feet high. On each side of the passageway, which was about a hundred feet long, were banks of vats for the aging of the mash. At the end of the passageway was a large room containing a huge, modern, carefully engineered still. Off this room were other vats. Beyond the still, a short passage led to a point where the city sewage pipe had been broken open in order that the mash could be disposed of after distillation.

To dispose of the fumes, a five-foot suction fan had been installed to draw the fumes into the ventilating pipe that ran the length of the entrance passageway. Then it ran through the ceiling and through one of the concrete saddles into the smoke box of the engine and on up the sixty-foot chimney. The passageway, the still room, and the mash tanks were all well constructed of concrete. An oil tank truck in the garage, which adjoined the boiler room, was to have been used for the transportation of the alcohol, which would be piped to the garage from the still after passing through a gasoline-pump-type measuring gauge.

The still was capable of a daily output of five hundred gallons of alcohol of excellent quality. The problem of odour had been mastered, as had the usually tricky problem of disposing of about five thousand gallons of run-off mash a day. There was just one flaw in the planning. I am not at all sure that we would have continued beyond the first search had the woodworking factory been in full operation.

The seven men found on the premises were arrested, charged, found guilty, and given jail sentences. Again, the "big four" failed to live up to their promises that they would provide efficient counsel, arrange bail, and pay the salaries of their employees while they were in jail. And, again, their welching brought us informers. We now concentrated on tying together all the bits and pieces of evidence implicating the "big four" that we had been able to secure during the several months of investigation.

In all, the seven stills which belonged to the organization had been seized. Every scrap of evidence or possible evidence was carefully reviewed and correlated. Property rentals, ownership of cars, meetings by members of the "big four" with various persons, purchases of plumbing supplies, molasses, sugar, and hardware for the erection and operation of the still – all these were investigated. In almost every instance, a "go-between" had been used; but we were now in a position to produce the evidence of some of these people, several of whom had given complete statements. Two of these men had been so close to the inner workings of the organization that they requested, and were being afforded, protective custody.

The briefs of evidence which we drew up were quite impressive, as was the separate brief prepared in connection with the American payoff man. Our lawyers were convinced that the evidence was sufficiently strong to justify the laying of charges against the "big four." They and their American contact were arrested. The four Canadians were released on bail, but the American contact man was not so fortunate. At the request of the prosecution, he was held without bail.

I interviewed him in Bordeaux Jail a few days after his arraignment, and after warning him that anything he might say could be used in evidence, I asked him if he wished to make a statement. He was scornful of the suggestion and supremely confident that his friends in Detroit would "fix" the whole matter. He would be free in a few days.

It was several months before the cases came up for trial. In the meantime, we were successful in securing some additional evidence, but the case was far from air-tight. The "big four" had employed the very best of counsel for their own defence. The American, who was still being held without bail, because of the possibility that he would escape to the United States, was not represented by counsel, a fact that we found odd and interesting.

On the afternoon of the day before the trials were to begin, I received word from the governor of Bordeaux Jail that the man from Detroit wanted to see me as soon as possible. The Detroit gangster was a changed man. Used to living in luxury, he had found the jail cell and the strict regimen of jail life hard to take. Gone was the cocky, self-assurance of the successful hoodlum who was certain that the backing of the syndicate would protect him. Gone, too, was the neat, carefully groomed appearance that had marked the stockily built Detroiter on our first meeting. Lack of expensive barbers, manicurists, and valet service had removed the gloss, and with it his confidence and arrogance, and had reduced him to a very ordinary and frightened mobster who saw a long jail term ahead.

He started the conversation by asking what sort of a "deal" we could make if he decided to give evidence for the prosecution. I repeated the usual police warning and went on to point out that there could be no question of a deal. If he gave evidence, the court would be aware of his action and might take that into consideration. Beyond that he could expect nothing.

He was not convinced and returned to his attempt to secure a promise of leniency in return for his evidence. He was quite frank in his attempt to impress me with the importance of the story he could tell, and he reviewed in detail the part that he had played in the organization and the position in that organization of each of the members of the "big four." All of this he was willing to repeat from the witness box if we would give him a break. I could only say that we could not and would not make deals or give promises. The matter was in the hands of the court, and there it must remain.

He was silent for some time, before breaking into a torrent of abuse of his fellow accused. They had double-crossed him. Contrary to their agreement, a lawyer had not been appointed to defend him, nor had his wife been paid her weekly salary according to arrangement. They had bungled everything, and their stupidity had led to the arrests. Now they were leaving him to rot in jail, probably for a long time. All right, deal or no deal, he would show the "bastards." He would play it their way.

He was thoughtful while he reviewed the situation and then said, "I'll plead guilty tomorrow morning, and you can put me in the witness box whenever you like. I'll tell the court everything I have told you and hope the judge will give me a break, but there is one condition to which you must agree. I am willing to talk as far as these bastards are concerned; but before I can do that, I must get the o.k. from my boss in Detroit. If he says talk, I'll talk my head off; but you know what will happen to me if I sing without getting the go-ahead?"

He gave me the telephone number of a hotel in Detroit and the name of the man he wanted to speak to, a man well known as the head of the Purple Gang. I put the call through for him in the governor's office and listened in on an extention. He outlined the situation to the boss and detailed the double-cross that had been given him by the Canadian organization. It was apparent from the conversation that the head mobster was aware of the situation and that he had strong words with the "big four." He pointed out, however, that "action" which would have been possible in the United States could not be taken in Canada because of the risk involved and because of the reputation of the Canadian courts for handing out stiff sentences. He was reluctant to authorize the prisoner to talk, but after some coaxing he gave his consent.

The following morning there was some consternation in court among the other accused and their lawyers when the Detroit gangster pleaded guilty and was forthwith called to the witness stand. With his evidence, the outcome was almost a foregone conclusion. The "big four" were found guilty and sentenced to lengthy prison terms. They fought all the way to the Supreme Court of Canada, but the sentences were upheld.

The man from Detroit was sentenced to two years in prison, but a question arose as to his citizenship. The United States held for some time that he had not acquired American citizenship and that, therefore, they would not accept him on his release from the Canadian prison. It took many months to straighten out the matter, and during that time the man remained in confinement in Canada. In all he served more than three years.

With the big organization out of business, the smaller operators had the field to themselves and started to expand, but their prosperity was short-lived. They did not have the resources, skill, or protection that had been enjoyed by the "big four." They did not survive for long the efforts that could now be directed against them.

In 1963, a public furore was raised over the suggestion that the United States syndicates were active in this country. Several prominent persons – judges, lawyers, politicians – expressed doubts that the American gangsters were reaching into Canada. Some were even inclined to ridicule any suggestion that organized crime of any sort, American or Canadian, existed in Canada, despite the many clear and obvious signs. The widespread publicity given these somewhat futile discussions recalled to my mind the fact that almost thirty years ago an American gangster was so fearful of the discipline of his mob that he considered it necessary to secure their permission before giving evidence in a Canadian court. It would take supreme optimism – coupled with an utter lack of knowledge or a disregard of crime in Canada – to come to the conclusion that the syndicates were so easily discouraged that they abandoned their efforts to invade such a prosperous target.

Increasing police pressures called for greater ingenuity on the part of the bootleggers. One small organization, which included a chemist, thought that they had discovered a way around those difficulties when they developed a method whereby commercial alcohol, on which there is very little excise tax, could be made potable by redistillation. They set up a hole-in-the-wall office which purported to be that of a company engaged in the manufacture and sale of perfume and shaving lotions. Through this office, they purchased large quantities of perfumed commercial alcohol. The alcohol was transported to a barn near St. Thérèse, from where, after distillation, it was sold in the Montreal market.

Their process did, in fact, remove the poisonous chemicals, and the product was quite drinkable, although somewhat scented. Unfortunately for them, the purchase of hundreds of gallons of perfumed commercial alcohol aroused the suspicions of officers of the Excise Department which brought the matter to our attention. A discreet visit to their business premises convinced us that there was something very wrong with the entire set-up.

They were kept under observation for a few days, during which we discovered the location of the barn in which their distilling operations had been installed. About one o'clock one morning, ten members of the liquor squad descended on the barn and found the still in full operation. The barn reeked of rose water, eau de cologne, and the scent of lilac. It took several hours to draw the fire off the furnace, drain the mash, load the alcohol into the police truck, and take the necessary police photographs. During all this time, the police were working in an atmosphere heavy with cheap perfumes. The heavy scent penetrated and clung to their clothing. It was rumoured that several members had difficulty convincing their wives that they had in fact been engaged in police business during the night.

In the late fall of 1937, I was promoted to the rank of Detective Sergeant and given the direction of the Narcotic Drug, Liquor, and Counterfeiting Squads – a task that kept me pretty well confined to an office, which I shared with another Sergeant. Apart from our duties in connection with the squads, we were called on to receive visitors seeking information or advice, and this we found cut heavily into our working hours.

As in any police office, a fair percentage of visitors were unfortunate people suffering from some sort of mental disturbance and seeking police help in order to free themselves from whatever troubles they imagined were plaguing them. Among our visitors – and for what reasons I will never know – a fair number of middle-aged ladies, started to appear all of whom, oddly enough, told almost the same story. They would start, hesitatingly, doubting that their story would be believed. They would go on to say that they were being bothered and threatened by "a gang" that had them under partial control by radio.

At times, the radio-control voice would awaken them during the night and compel them to dress and go to some specific point in the city, or the voice would order them to go without food for days and would tell them to shun certain old friends and insult others. These visitors demanded that the police take immediate action toward breaking up "the gang." Even the most delicately formed suggestion that they should see a psychiatrist usually brought a storm of abuse. We abandoned that tactic and tried suggesting that they should take their troubles to a lawyer or to some close family friend. Sometimes this approach worked temporarily, at least to the point of getting them to leave the office; but they would return later to tell us that the radio voice had forbidden them to follow the proposed course of action. Having received a sympathetic hearing, they would return to our office again and again, and it became increasingly difficult to terminate the interviews. We had almost decided that in order to get on with our other duties it would be necessary to refuse to see these people, when my office-mate came up with a bright idea based on the proposition that reason is of little use against unreason.

From then on we adopted new tactics. Having listened very patiently to the tales of radio control by "the gang," we would use our own brand of unreason. Certainly we believed their story. The police knew all about the operation of such radio gangs and had, in fact, broken up quite a number of them. We would then go on to state that the police laboratories employed scientists far superior to those engaged by the gangs, and that our scientists had worked out an almost unbelievably simple method of defeating the efforts of the radio gangs to control individuals. All that was required was that the victim carry a three-inch length of lead pipe at all times. This would ground the radio-control voice, and the gang would be unable to penetrate the protection thus afforded. It was explained that the piece of pipe must be kept within two feet of the body at all times. At night, it must be placed under the pillow. During the day, it should be carried in a pocket or in a purse, but at all times great care must be taken that the piece of pipe would never be more than two feet away from the body.

Having held forth on the success of this method of defeating the criminals, we would hand the unfortunate visitor a three-inch length of pipe, several of which we had had prepared in readiness by the garage mechanic. After repeating the warning about keeping the pipe within two feet of the body at all times, the visitors would be shown out. The idea worked, and not one of the troubled ladies appeared again at our office.

A few months after my promotion, I was required to take the usual refresher course at Regina, a course that lasted three months. This class proved excellent, with top-level lecturers drawn from many fields. Judges, lawyers, medico-legal experts, psychiatrists, accountants, photographers, fingerprint men, welfare workers, parole officers, and – for the first time in such classes – lectures on Communism.

The class comprised thirty-two senior NCO's and as is always the case, the evening "bull sessions" added greatly to the value of the course. The exchange of information and experience by members drawn from all divisions provided a great deal of useful information regarding changing patterns of crime and methods that had been developed in the different areas toward meeting such changes. Another beneficial effect of these "bull sessions" was that they brought about a realization of the wide diversity of duties being carried out by the Force, a variety that few, if any, law-enforcement agencies are called on to perform.

In the Northwest Territories and Yukon, members were patrolling thousands of miles by dogsled or canoe and were visiting Eskimo and Indian villages to carry out work assigned to the Force by federal Government departments or in the investigation of crime. On the Atlantic and Pacific coasts and on the St. Lawrence River and Great Lakes, the patrol boats of the Marine Division chased smugglers, performed rescue work, and assisted the land forces in their police duties. In the so-called contract provinces, the divisions covered the entire range of police work from murder, bank robbery, and cattle stealing, to the patrolling of small towns and the enforcement of such laws as the Migratory Birds Act. In the non-contract provinces, the work was very similar to that being done in Montreal, in the narcotics, liquor, and counterfeiting fields, and in connection with approximately forty other federal statutes.

Since reorganization, the Force had learned and kept abreast of its new responsibilities. Training had been vastly improved. Equipment, although still leaving much to be desired, had been improved, and more equipment would be forthcoming according to the men from head-quarters. There was talk of setting up scientific laboratories at Ottawa and Regina, the establishment of permanent liaison offices in Washing-ton and London, England. It was even rumoured that consideration was being given the use of a system of radio communication between division and, wonder of wonders, police cars were to be equipped with heaters.

I doubted the last rumour because a few months previously I had had the temerity to apply for heaters for the cars in Montreal. I used as an argument the rather obvious fact that in the wintertime an unheated car is a rather uncomfortable spot from which to carry out surveillance. A curt refusal from headquarters pointed out that for many years members of the Force had ridden horses across the prairies in sub-zero weather without benefit of heaters. But clearly the Force was changing. The transition from frontier policing to a modern law-enforcement body was well under way.

9

➤➤➤➤➤➤➤➤➤➤➤➤➤➤➤➤➤➤

Preparations for War

The Special Branch – that part of the Force responsible for the gathering of intelligence regarding subversion and espionage in order to keep the Government well informed – had, since 1917, concerned itself almost exclusively with the activities of the Communist Party of Canada. By 1936, it became apparent that an even greater and more imminent threat was being posed by budding Nazi, Fascist, and Canadian Fascist groups. To meet this problem, special branch sections across Canada were increased; administrative and co-ordinating staffs at headquarters were strengthened; contacts and liaisons were established with intelligence agencies in the United Kingdom and the United States; training courses were set up in Canada; and selected members were sent abroad for specialized training.

By 1938, the Force had successfully penetrated the Nazi, Fascist, and Canadian Fascist parties to the point where officials, memberships, and many of their plans were known. Copies of instructions and planning programs were reaching the Special Branches almost as quickly as they were being readied by the leaders of the espionage and subversive groups. Indeed, in many instances, the Special Branch was aware of the plans of the Fascists and Nazis before detailed instructions for members had been drawn up by their leaders. Even more important, the Force was aware of direct espionage activities being carried out in Canada by the German Nazi Party.

Apart from the German Nazi and Italian Fascist parties in Canada, the memberships of which were drawn mostly from former nationals of those countries, several Canadian Fascist parties sprang up across the country. In Montreal, the group was headed by Adrien Arcand, a tall, rather impressive-looking man with considerable oratorical ability. His fiery speeches placed great emphasis on abuses, real or imagined, that had been suffered by the people of Quebec at the hands of the English Canadians, Great Britain, and the United States. All of this, he claimed, would be quickly and easily corrected following a Nazi victory in Europe, when he would become the leader in Canada.

His spell-binding powers appealed to the lunatic fringe, and by 1938 he could claim a party membership of twelve thousand. Many of his meetings were held under swastika banners, with all of the trappings of Hilter's Nazis. His organization was closely tied in with the Silvershirt Organization in the United States, with Mosley's group in the United Kingdom, and with German, Italian, and South American Nazi and Fascist parties.

At one stage, Arcand's party printed and sold, at a discount, many thousands of dollars' worth of their own money which was to be redeemed at face value when the Nazis took power. The German State Railways, with offices in the Dominion Square Building in Montreal, provided cover for German espionage activities in Canada, and to some extent in the United States. Werner Haag, the head of the German State Railway office, specialized in activities which brought him into contact with leaders in Government, political, business, and financial circles.

His reports to his German masters were almost invariably accompanied by photographs of him taken with prominent Canadians, probably to convince the Nazi bosses of his ability as a "mixer." Another cover was provided by the Montreal office of a German sales agency that specialized in the sale and distribution of high-frequency equipment which, according to our technicians, could quickly be turned into powerful transmitters.

It was obvious that if war broke out great activity would be required on the part of the police if the carefully laid plans of the Nazis, Fascists, and Communists were to be disrupted. The staffs of the special branch were again enlarged to allow for the compiling of briefs. These would be studied by the Force and by appropriate Governmental departments so that detailed preparations might be made for the taking of the necessary steps.

During 1939, the Force was given the responsibility of surveying industrial plants, harbours, canals, and sites. It would secure detailed information upon which the Government could decide the relative importance of the various points. Later the Force was called on to set up a branch to advise industry and Government regarding precautionary and protective measures.

These entirely new and vastly important responsibilities did not bring with them additional staff; and further, since no one in Canada had had experience in these fields, it would have been impossible to recruit men for these purposes. Improvisation was called for.

As a starting point, business and professional men were approached and asked to sit on advisory committees to aid us in our work. Through the co-operation of such committees set up in several cities across Canada, and with the assistance of the engineers employed by the Force, selected members were able to learn something of the vulnerability of industry in the event of war, and of possible protective measures.

Squads were set up in each of the affected divisions, and a careful survey was made of every important industry, harbour installation, canal, or power site in Canada. Usually the police team was accompanied by professional men without whose assistance the work could not have been accomplished. By the end of the survey, the Force had amassed volumes of information regarding the vital points across Canada; in addition, it had developed members with sufficient training and knowledge to be able to offer advice regarding the setting up of guard systems and other precautionary and protective measures. Thanks to the tremendous interest and co-operation of business and industry, many of the suggested security arrangements were started forthwith; and all reasonable security measures had been taken insofar as industry was concerned well before the outbreak of war.

During October of 1938, I was called to headquarters at Ottawa to discuss several current investigations. I remained there most of the day and, having completed my business, I drove back to Montreal. On reaching my home, I was met by a very excited wife who told me that I had been promoted to the commissioned rank of Sub-Inspector. I could scarcely believe the news. There were only ninety-one Commissioned Officers in the entire Force, and it seemed unlikely that I had been chosen to join that select group. Further, I had just left headquarters and had received no word of the promotion there. Nevertheless, and in compliance with a request left with my wife, I telephoned the Officer Commanding. He confirmed the good news and congratulated me.

I learned later that just a few minutes after I had left headquarters in Ottawa, Commissioner Stuart Wood, who had been appointed to that office on the death of Sir James McBrien, received the Order in Council making me Sub-Inspector. He had tried to locate me, but I was on the way to Montreal. The break into commissioned rank is probably the most important advancement of a career in the Force. It called for a family celebration.

Within the Force a rather sharp line is drawn between commissioned officers and other ranks. For that reason a newly appointed officer is almost invariably transferred out of the division and away from members with whom he has served as Constable and NCO. There are many pleasant postings in Canada, but there are also areas that are regarded as "penance" transfers. Doris and I and our ten-year-old son Weston waited for the arrival of the instructions concerning my posting with hope and some trepidation.

To our utter surprise, the orders, when they did arrive, instructed that I was to remain in Montreal to assume command of the Criminal Investigation Branch, which included the Special Branch and the newly formed Civil Security Squad.

I was getting nicely settled into my new office when some interesting and fairly heavy duties were added. Advice was received that His Majesty King George VI and Queen Elizabeth would visit Canada in May of 1939. The Force had been given the responsibility of making the necessary policing and security arrangements. Instructions received from headquarters advised that Deputy Commissioner King and Assistant Commissioner V. A. M. Kemp had been appointed to direct the work of the divisions concerned and to co-ordinate our planning with that of other police forces and that of other Government departments. In the divisions, it would be the direct responsibility of the Officer Commanding and CIB officers to see that the detailed and precise planning required was carried out with meticulous care. Our Division was affected in that Their Majesties were scheduled to arrive by ship at Wolfe's Cove in Quebec City and that they would attend various functions in that city before proceeding to Montreal and other points in the Province of Quebec.

During the next few months, a great part of our time was taken up with the careful planning required in preparation for the Royal Visit. Meetings were held with provincial and municipal forces and with numerous committees that had been set up by all levels of Government. Trial "runs" were made over the routes to be followed by Their Majesties in order that timing might be estimated to the minute. Buildings, hotels, railway cars, railroad tracks, and the areas in which the various planned functions would take place required careful study for reasons of security. Passes had to be arranged for guests at the functions, and the police-press liaison had to be worked out.

Every possible eventuality required study, and the setting up of alternative arrangements so that any possible contingency might be met. Traffic jams might occur to delay the cavalcade, the police, or the arrival of guests. Trains might be delayed, or Their Majesties might, through interest in some particular display, incident, or person, throw the proceedings off schedule; and, of course, there were the inevitable changes in the official program, which meant that some of the work had to be done over and over again. Fortunately, other police forces – and, indeed, everyone, whether directly concerned or not – pitched in with a will, and the program was completed ahead of schedule.

Apart from such obvious police responsibilities as the routing of traffic, timing of the cavalcade, traffic, crowd control, and the provision of escorts, there is always a heavy responsibility for the safety of the Royal Party and other personages. Their Majesties were immensely popular, and Canadians were looking forward to their visit with joy and eager anticipation. But there are always the fanatics and crackpots who might try to harm or embarrass the visitors.

One of the methods employed by the Force in attempting to cope with the lunatic fringe during Royal Visits, or the visits of important heads of state, is the compiling of a book listing the names, descriptions, and peculiarities of all known persons who, in the opinion of the police, might attempt to make a scence. Well in advance of the arrival of important visitors, all police forces across the country are asked to submit information regarding such persons in their community. The information received is compiled and printed with copies of the book going forward to all police forces. When the arrival of important visitors draws near, the police in the communities concerned pay particular attention to the persons referred to in the book and report any unusual activities. This method has proven its value on many occasions.

In the book compiled for the 1939 visit of King George and Queen Elizabeth, there appeared the name and description of a little old lady, a widow with some considerable financial means, who lived in a town in Northern Ontario. Under "peculiarities," it was stated that the lady believed that she was Queen Victoria and had stated publicly on several occasions that she intended to travel to Quebec City in order to meet "the children" on their arrival at Wolfe's Cove.

Shortly after the distribution of the book, the police of her town advised us that the little lady had left for Toronto with the announced purpose of purchasing a new wardrobe. From our people in Toronto it was learned that she had visited a dressmaker and ordered three dresses which, to the wonderment of the seamstress, were to be made from old patterns that had been provided – patterns from the Victorian era.

Having arranged for her wardrobe, she visited an art gallery where she purchased two oil paintings for three hundred dollars. These, she announced, were to be small gifts for "George and Elizabeth." She then returned to her hometown, where she purchased railway tickets to Quebec City, arranged for rooms on the ground floor of the Chateau St. Louis, in Quebec, and busied herself packing in preparation for the journey.

Two days before the scheduled arrival of Their Majesties, the little lady travelled to Quebec surrounded by old-fashioned luggage, with the two oil paintings sharing her seat. Her appearance did not arouse a great deal of curiosity since she had chosen to travel incognito and was wearing a dress of fairly modern design. At the hotel in Quebec, she hung the oil paintings out of one of the windows of her ground-floor suite. Neatly written little cards were attached announcing that the oils would be presented "to Their Majesties, my great grandchildren," and signed, simply "Victoria."

I had been detailed to take a troop of twenty-five men to Quebec to carry out policing duties at the arrival ceremonies. From then on we were to "leap-frog" ahead of the Royal Couple to assist in the policing of all functions in the province. The *Empress*, on which Their Majesties were sailing, was delayed two days by fog and icebergs, which necessitated some hasty rearrangements at the Ottawa level, but did not upset the plans for the Province of Quebec too much, in that the details of the program were not altered except for the dates. "Victoria" remained at the Chateau St. Louis and continued to display the oil paintings outside her window.

The *Empress* was due at eight o'clock in the morning. I arrived at Wolfe's Cove with my troop at about five. The docking area had been roped off. At one end stood a newly erected dais on which a number of dignitaries were to be presented to Their Majesties. Leading from the dais, a red carpet stretched across the enclosure to the far end, where His Majesty was to inspect a Guard of Honour of the Royal Twenty-Second Regiment. Another red carpet ran at right angles to the dockside, where Their Majesties would disembark and be greeted by the Governor General, the Prime Minister, and several other persons of high office. The decorations were magnificent. Everything was in readiness for the arrival of troops detailed for the ceremony – military bands, guests, and the public in preparation for the pomp and ceremony that would welcome the first reigning British Monarchs to visit Canadian shores.

About an hour after our arrival, a taxi made its way from upper town down to Wolfe's Cove. The cab stopped a little distance from the rope barrier, and the driver rushed to open the door. Slowly and majestically, "Queen Victoria" alighted. After a brief conversation with the driver, he took a folding chair and the oil paintings from the cab and followed the "Queen" to the rope barrier, which he lifted to allow her entrance into the enclosure. After carefully surveying her surroundings, she selected a spot at the end of the red carpet, at the precise point where His Majesty would inspect the Guard of Honour. The folding chair was placed in the desired position by the driver, who then put the oil paintings against the side of the chair, gave a rather smart salute, and started back to the cab. At the rope he turned towards me, smiled somewhat sheepishly, shrugged his shoulders, and took off.

Along with the other policemen on duty, I had been somewhat taken aback by the early-morning arrival of "Queen Victoria." A plainclothes man had been detailed to keep her under surveillance just to make sure that she did not cause embarrassment or create a scene, but apparently she had left the hotel before the start of his tour of duty.

For the occasion, the little widow was wearing a black dress with the wide sleeves and voluminous skirts of the Victorian Era. As a headdress, she wore a small round hat of the style worn by Queen Victoria in several of her portraits. A purple sash, sparkling with several "orders," completed her ensemble.

Having recovered from my initial surprise, I took stock of the situation. Certainly the lady had to be moved – but gently. There was no threat to security here. Just an elderly woman who wished Their Majesties all the good in the world.

I walked along the red carpet, and after saluting, presented myself to "Her Majesty." With her permission, graciously given, I explained that there had been a most regrettable error on the part of the planning staff in that they had neglected to advise her regarding last-minute changes in seating arrangements – changes that had been brought about by the King's desire to inspect the Guard of Honour. Her reservation had been changed to a place immediately behind the rope.

She was most kind and understanding. I escorted her to a spot behind the barrier from which she would have a good view of the proceedings, got her comfortably seated, placed the oil painting beside her, and saluted. She thanked me for advising her of the change in plans and, quite regally, gave me permission to leave. Queen, or no Queen, she was a marvellous little person.

Assistant Commissioner H. Royal-Gagnon, who had succeeded Meade as Officer Commanding the division, arrived a short time later. I drew his attention to "Queen Victoria" and gave him the details of the incident. A kindly, understanding man, he was greatly impressed by the story – so much so that he in turn presented himself to "Her Majesty."

The arrival of King George and Queen Elizabeth was a scene that I shall not soon forget; but somehow the gracious little lady dressed in black and wearing a purple sash and "orders," seated just behind the rope, will always be an important part of that scene. I had detailed a man to stand behind her to guard against the possibility that she might attempt to interfere with the ceremonies, but I need not have bothered. A Queen does not create scenes in public.

For the duration of the Royal Visit I was quite busy with policing duties. Later, Royal-Gagnon told me that he had related the story of "Queen Victoria" to one of the Ladies-in-Waiting who repeated it to their Majesties. They were so charmed and touched by the tale that they had arrangements made whereby the little lady from Northern Ontario was received by them at a private audience, during which they accepted the oil paintings.

We were not allowed much time to ponder the success of the Royal Visit or to discuss the many memorable occassions or interesting incidents that it had brought about. The threat of war hung over the land – and, indeed, over the world. Hope that war could be averted was fading. Time seemed to be running out, and there was much to do. All departments of Government that might be directly affected by the outbreak of hostilities were under extreme pressures to work toward complete readiness, and the Force, charged with the responsibility for internal security, was deeply involved.

Normal policing duties continued, but as the pressures mounted, work in the criminal field had to give way to the demands of intelligence and security. The Nazi, Fascist, and Canadian Fascist parties were growing in membership and becoming increasingly active and bold in their overt activities. Underground, they were carefully planning action designed to disrupt the Canadian effort in the event of war. Clearly, if war came, it would be vitally necessary to move quickly to forestall their planning. At the headquarters and Government level, it was decided that preparations must be made whereby the leaders of these enemy and subversive groups could be quickly arrested and interned if war came to dictate the need for such action.

The Communist Party of Canada was in a somewhat different category. For several years, their chief party line had been the "united front against Fascism," but their propaganda carried an undertone of criticism of "imperalist war," and their record warned that the party might do a complete sommersault if a shift occurred in the policies of Moscow and the Comintern.

During their twenty-two years in Canada the Communists had built a rather formidable underground which, as was established years later during the several espionage trials, penetrated many departments of Government and many branches of industry. On the surface and for the time being, they seemed to be on the side of Canada, but their direction came from Moscow. It would have been foolhardy to gamble that Moscow might not shake its head against a Canadian war effort. The police had to be fully prepared to meet such an eventuality.

The Government was properly and deeply disturbed by the thought of widespread mass arrests across Canada and concerned itself with setting up safeguards that would hold such arrests to the minimum dictated by circumstances. The outcome of the deliberations of the Cabinet was the setting up of screening committees comprising officials of the Department of Justice, acting with judges and lawyers especially appointed for the task. The police were required to submit evidence before these committees. It was their responsibility to decide which individuals should be arrested or organizations should be banned, if worsening conditions made such action necessary.

The drawing up of briefs showing the set-up and ramifications of enemy and subversive organizations and their affiliated and front groups, and the submission to the screening committee of briefs, on the hundreds of individuals connected with those organizations, required the full time of many members in all divisions of the Force. In the early stages, some slight difficulty and delay was occasioned by demands made by some of the committee men for more detailed and positive proof than police could provide; but as the committee men studied the files of the organizations under review, they came to realize that the rules of evidence governing the hearing of criminal cases could not be fully applied in assessing the potential danger from enemy groups. Even the most amateurish subversive and espionage agents surround their actions with some degree of secrecy – and we were not dealing with amateurs, at least insofar as the leaders were concerned. It is rare, indeed, that conspirators in espionage hold open meetings or keep exact records of their plotting; and, therefore, it is not entirely reasonable to expect the police to produce the proof positive that is rightly required in criminal cases.

There were pressures, too, in connection with preparations for the protection of installations vital to our war effort. As the threat of war deepened, more and more industries and installations were added to the "vital" list. The Force was called on to carry out an increasing number of surveys and to work closely with industry in the setting up of protective facilities and guard staffs. In July of 1939, we were instructed that we must be prepared to take over the guarding of a lengthy list of harbours, canals, and other properties in several of the provinces.

A number of the points to be guarded were in the Province of Quebec. The planning in this regard called for the use of experienced officers and NCO's who would supervise special constables to be employed for guard duty. In Quebec, as in most other provinces, the problem of arranging for "stand-by" groups of special constables ready to take over guarding duties at a moment's notice was solved by approaching the Canadian Legion and other veterans' organizations, all of whom were eager to help in any way open to them. While the manpower problem for this particular phase was quickly solved, there remained the work of surveying the areas to be guarded, deciding as to the strength required at each point, making tentative arrangements for food, quarters, clothing, and transportation. It was necessary to detail several members of our already hard-pressed staff to complete this part of preparatory planning.

As arrangements developed, the divisions began to receive, through headquarters, the results of the screening committees and the Government's decisions based on the recommendations of those committees. It had been decided that immediately following the outbreak of war with Germany, the top men of the Nazi Party's headquarters and branches and affiliated groups were to be apprehended, together with sub-leaders and those Nazis considered capable of and most likely to provide replacement leadership. The persons apprehended were to be brought before internment courts that would study the available evidence and decide, in the case of each individual, if internment should be continued. The same course was to be followed in the event of Italy entering the war. As regards the Communist Party of Canada, a wait-and-see policy was adopted. No direct action was to be taken, at least in the early stages, against the Canadian Fascist groups. It was hoped that the views and loyalties of many of the members of such groups might change radically in the face of an immediate and direct threat to Canada.

German espionage agents active in Canada were to be apprehended only after the declaration of war. This decision was not very practicable in view of our knowledge that the German agents had been sent to Canada to gather information and to set up espionage networks within the local Nazi groups, which networks were to take over at the start of hostilities. The German agents expected to receive warnings that would enable them to flee the country immediately prior to war. Our division was directly and heavily affected by these decisions. More than two hundred and fifty members of the German Nazi groups in the Province of Quebec were listed for internment pending hearings before Courts that would be set up for that purpose. Almost as many arrests were to be made among members of the Italian Fascist party.

While the wait-and-see policy adopted in connection with the Communist and Canadian Fascist Parties did not call for direct action, it did not offer any great relief for the police since inherent in that policy was the fact that the Force would be held responsible for the "seeing." The total strength of C Division, Province of Quebec, was at the time one hundred and sixty-four officers, non-commissioned officers, and men. Of that total strength, almost one hundred members were employed in manning the twenty-seven detachments throughout the province. Only seventy-three members were stationed in Montreal. We had been understaffed for some time, and our resources were already being stretched as far as possible. There was some hope of securing a few additional men, but this did not promise much relief in that the manpower pinch was being felt throughout the Force. Nor did the future hold much promise in the matter of manpower. We were aware that the Force would not compete with the armed services for recruits in wartime.

The Officer Commanding, Royal-Gagnon, made a number of trips to Ottawa and held many meetings with his officers and tried to devise ways and means by which the increasing manpower problems could be solved. Clearly the strength of the division was not sufficient to carry out the many duties that would come with war. It became equally clear that relief could not come from within the Force. It followed that outside assistance must be found, and since no funds had been provided, the assistance would have to be secured from volunteers.

Several business and professional men with military backgrounds were approached. Their co-operation was immediate and whole-hearted. Within a few weeks, we had located three hundred men of high standing in the community and of undoubted loyalty who were willing and eager to help. Lecture classes were arranged during which the volunteers were given such details as we were free to supply regarding what would be expected of them if war broke out. Detailed plans were drawn up, whereby the volunteers would work in groups under the guidance and supervision of experienced members of the Force. Our manpower problems were partially solved.

IO

-⟫-⟫-⟫-⟫-⟪-⟪-⟪-⟪-

Duties during Wartime

By the end of August, 1939, the lingering hope that some miracle would intervene to ward off the impending holocaust had been abandoned. Newspapers and magazines were filled with reports of rapidly deteriorating conditions in Europe. Radio programs were being interrupted every few minutes to bring special bulletins announcing the latest moves in the inexorable march toward war. The only question remaining was how soon hostilities would start, and it seemed clear that the estimates must be in hours, not days. The Cabinet was in almost constant session. All departments of Government were working on around-the-clock schedules to reach a state of complete readiness, a task made more difficult by inevitable and inescapable changes in Government decisions and policies.

For our part, we were busily engaged on last-minute reviews of arrangements for the mass arrests of Nazi agents, spys, and sympathizers, and for the searching of their homes, meeting places, and offices. Final arrangements were being made, too, for the rapid recruitment of special constables for the taking over of guard duties at those vital points for the protection of which the Force had been made responsible.

Apart from administrative preparation, there was the task of attempting to keep Nazi leaders and suspected premises under constant observation. For this purpose, a few of the business and professional men of our volunteer group had been called in, and these, along with every available member of the CIB, were engaged in surveillance work so that we would know the exact location of the Nazi leaders and be in a position to apprehend them immediately following the receipt of instructions from

97

headquarters. And a new duty was added. Already we were being besieged by visitors and phone calls volunteering information regarding alleged spies, most of which stemmed from the overwrought imaginations of the callers, but all of which required careful checking.

During the last few days before World War II, we received information from our surveillance teams that indicated that there was indeed need for urgency in our preparations. The Germans who had been sent into Canada to organize espionage and sabotage among their Canadian supporters were hurriedly leaving the country. In the tense atmosphere that prevailed on the last day of August, an incident occured which, while serious from many points of view, provided a fair measure of comic relief. During the late afternoon of that day, I received a telephone call from the Collector of Customs in Montreal advising me that just a few minutes earlier the officers of a German freighter moored at Sorel, about fifty miles east of Montreal, on seeing the approach of Custom officers, had chopped through hawsers to free the vessel which then proceeded downstream at full speed. The freighter belonged to a German line that had been frequently mentioned in intelligence reports overseas. It was alleged that many of the vessels of that line had been built to specifications provided by the German Government which included armour plating and other details of construction that would enable their speedy conversion into auxiliary cruisers.

The intelligence reports were hurriedly checked. The freighter that had broken away from Sorel was included in the list of these specially built vessels. It appeared that an auxiliary cruiser was escaping down the St. Lawrence. The Officer Commanding was away, and, in his absence I telephoned headquarters at Ottawa to report the affair and ask for instructions. A minor offence had been committed in that the freighter had left port without the required customs clearance, but that infraction alone would not justify precipitant action of the sort that might become necessary under the circumstances. We were not yet at war.

Headquarters was duly concerned, particularly in view of the tense international situation. I was told to await the receipt of further instructions which would be issued as soon as the matter could be taken up with the appropriate ministers. Headquarters moved speedily, and a few minutes later I was instructed that no action was to be taken by the Force as the freighter would be intercepted by naval vessels.

Within a few minutes, I received another call from Ottawa. There were no naval vessels in the St. Lawrence River or the Gulf. Those on the Atlantic Coast were committed to another assignment and could not be spared. We were to take such action as was possible toward stopping the freighter. The most logical place for such action seemed to be Quebec City, and it was suggested by Ottawa that arrangements might be made

with the Army to fire a shot or two across the bows of the vessel if demands to "heave to" were ignored.

These instructions were passed on to our detachment at Quebec City.
The required arrangements were underway when Ottawa called again to
countermand all previous instruction; no action was to be taken. Within
a few minutes that order was cancelled, and I was told that the freighter
must be stopped, but that there was to be no gunfire.

From then until the close of the incident some hours later, there was
an almost continuous stream of cancellations and changes. In the meantime, the press and radio had got hold of the story. Reporters were
dispatched to observe and report on the progress of the freighter by
following the roads that paralled the St. Lawrence River. The public was
kept advised of developments by frequent news flashes which interrupted
radio programs across the country. As the vessel came abreast of Three
Rivers, a launch filled with Customs officers entered the channel. Their
orders to stop were ignored, and, according to the broadcasts, they came
perilously close to being run down by the speeding freighter.

At Quebec City, Staff Sergeant Devallet, a thoroughly experienced,
capable, and practical old-timer, was in temporary command. Arrangements had been made for the rental of a tugboat, which would carry
Devallet and several Constables to a position in the river from which
he could hail the freighter and order her to "heave to" or suffer the consequences. The possible "consequences" were not clear, but it was hoped
that the captain would be in some fear of artillery fire from the old
fortifications on the embankment.

Ottawa had approved the proposed action. But as the vessel neared
Quebec, someone had an alarming thought. What if the freighter stopped,
allowed the policemen aboard, and then made them prisoners and proceeded on her way? Contemplation of such a ridiculous situation brought
another change of orders. No action was to be taken. This was relayed
to Devallet, who, by this time, was beginning to share my impatience
with the "on-again, off-again" instructions. We had scarcely ended our
conversation when another call was received from Ottawa – another
change of orders. "Operation Tugboat" was to be carried out. During the
subsequent relaying of these instructions, I made it very clear to Devallet
that in the event of being forced to call him again, I would be disappointed
if I was able to reach him.

Ottawa phoned again. There had been another change in policy. All
previous instructions were cancelled. No action was to be taken toward
stopping the freighter. I advised headquarters that I thought our men
might have boarded the tug, and that in the absence of radio equipment,
it would be impossible to cancel the previous instructions. A call to the
Quebec detachment brought the rather expected reply that Devallet had

left the building and could not be located. There was nothing to do but await the outcome.

Devallet and three constables, resplendent in full "review" order, and armed with a loud hailer and forty-five calibre revolvers, boarded the tug and were carried to midstream from where, in due course, they ordered the Captain to "heave to," or whatever it is that is required of a Captain under such circumstances. Probably the Captain feared action from shore batteries, or he may have had a change of instructions from his German masters, but, whatever the cause, he obeyed the orders shouted to him from the tug. The freighter was "captured" and taken in charge by a police-boarding party. It was subsequently discovered that the overseas intelligence report had erred in including the vessel in the list of potential auxiliary cruisers. She was just what she purported to be – a German freighter. The captain offered no explanation regarding his sudden departure from Sorel, and it was taken for granted that he had been following instructions from Germany.

One sidelight afforded us a few chuckles after the affair was finished. Staff Sergeant Devallet, a stockily built, courageous man, had one weakness. He did not like boats, and even the sight of one made him very seasick.

The Montreal headquarters of C Division had long since outgrown the accommodations provided by the ancient residential building that had served since 1919, but it took the immediacy of war to bring about a change. In August of 1939, we were authorized to move to the top two floors of the old post office building on Place D'Armes, but the move was to be delayed until extensive alterations had been completed in accordance with plans and blueprints drawn up in Ottawa. Arrangements were being made with the appropriate Government department whereby contractors would be employed to complete the renovations required to transform the long, unused, and rather dilapidated space into premises suitable for use as police offices and barracks.

By the first of September, the situation as regards working space had become intolerable. Royal-Gagnon and I visited the old post-office building. There was ample space to provide for the expansion that would follow the start of hostilities. However, nothing had been done toward preparing the place for police occupancy. The long, unused storage floors were deep with dirt and grime; plumbing facilities were inadequate; such partitions as existed had little more than a nuisance value. There were not even any telephones.

The urgency of the situation left little choice. Royal-Gagnon instructed that I would move into the new quarters the next day with the intelligence, security, and other branches that would be directly affected by the outbreak of war. He would remain with the administrative staff and normal police-duty squads at the old Sherbrooke Street building, which would also serve as barracks for single members until improvement could be brought about in the new location.

Through the speedy co-operation of the Bell Telephone Company, several telephones were installed that same day. Labourers were employed to shovel out the dirt and do a rough cleaning job, and arrangements were made with a moving company for vans to transfer office furniture, files, and such other equipment as would be required by what the members had labeled the "War Department." The move was made that night. September 2, 1939, was a bit of a madhouse as we tried to keep abreast of mounting pressures and at the same time settle into the new quarters.

Great Britain declared war on September 3, and similar action by the Canadian Government was expected momentarily. The entire staff was placed on "stand-to" alert, and arrangements were completed whereby the volunteers, who were to assist in the round-up of Nazi leaders, and the several hundred World War I veterans who would take over guard duties at vital points, would report for duty immediately following Canada's entry into the war.

Canada's formal declaration came on September 10. During the next forty-eight hours, more than two hundred leaders and sub-leaders of Nazi groups were arrested in the Province of Quebec, most of them in the Montreal area. Due to the surveillance work that had continued up to the last moment, all but two or three of the leaders were among those apprehended and they were arrested within the next few hours. Similar action was taken in all divisions across the country. Years of painstaking investigation that had at times brought severe criticism proved its value.

The internment of the Nazi leaders was, of course, aimed at disrupting the espionage and sabotage plans of the enemy, but it was some time before we learned how thoroughly that job had been done. Later, from captured enemy agents, we learned that the speedy arrests had completely wrecked the carefully built German espionage apparatus in Canada. This information was confirmed by the German High Command after the end of World War II. As further proof of the effectiveness of the anti-subversive work of the Force, there was the fact that not one case of enemy sabotage occurred in Canada during the war.

In the final stages, the arrest could not have been successfully carried out without the assistance of the civilian volunteers who, under the guidance of experienced members, did yeoman service. Nor could the work have been accomplished without the willing and excellent co-operation extended by the provincial and municipal forces.

Searches carried out at the homes of the persons arrested, at their offices and meeting places, and at the offices of German companies that were suspect – such as the German State Railways – unearthed vast quantities of evidence, all of which required careful examination and cataloguing, partly for later use before internment courts, and partly to round out our knowledge of the Nazi organizations. This evidence established the complicity of several leaders who had until then remained deep underground and unknown to us. They were quickly arrested.

According to prior arrangements, the prisoners were to be turned over to the Army, but understandably, the Army Detention Camp was not fully prepared for their reception. As a result, we were required to billet them in the old post-office building. Mattresses and blankets were borrowed from the army. The prisoners were bedded on the top floor. Meals, limited for the most part to sandwiches and coffee, were supplied by a catering company. The shortage of plumbing facilities caused some difficulty, as did the need for the provision of guards and escorts, but the situation cleared after three days when the prisoners were turned over to the army.

In the meantime, the Nazis appeared to be more appreciative than resentful of the slight hardships that they were called on to undergo for the Fuehrer. Many of them had seen service in the German Armed Forces, and the detention room was quickly organized along the lines of a German barrack room. They were extremely arrogant, and during interviews that I had with each prisoner, only three attempted to deny that they were Nazis. A number of them, on being brought to my office, gave me the Nazi salute and the "Heil Hitler" routine. Several boasted that they would be free within a month when, according to them, the war was scheduled to end with the complete victory for Hitler.

While the round-up of Nazi leaders had been taking place, Inspector Savoie, who had been placed in charge of the guarding of vital points, was, together with his NCO's and staff, busily engaged in signing on veterans and arranging their transportation to the various points for which the Force was responsible. While it took some days to complete arrangements for living accommodations, uniforms, duty rosters, and transportation facilities, guards were on duty within twelve hours of the start of hostilities. During the next twenty-four hours, over twelve hundred veterans were employed as special constables for these duties.

A few months later, Italy entered the war. Again, over two hundred leaders were apprehended in our division, and again similar action was taken in all other areas. The job was not so difficult this time, since the experience with the Nazis proved helpful in carrying out the mass searches and arrests, and the army was fully prepared to take the prisoners off our hands. The attitudes of the Fascist leaders was in marked contrast to that of the Nazis. There was no arrogance, and there was no Fascist salutes. Only three of the prisoners admitted support of the Fascist cause, and they even advanced many excuses.

Just a few days after the start of the war, some complications were added to our work through the invasion of hordes of workmen, carpenters, plumbers, painters, and telephone men, all intent on getting on with the job of remodelling and renovating the premises. In the end, their work proved most satisfactory and provided us with excellent accommodations; but for some weeks it was a little distracting for the staff to carry on with their work against background noises of trip-hammers cutting through concrete, old partitions being torn down, and new ones erected. Distractions were provided, too, by many skirmishes with the foreman in trying to decide on rights of possession of the various areas in the building.

During the searches carried out at the offices of suspected German-owned companies, the search parties had, in line with instructions, seized all available assets, including large quantities of office equipment and furnishings, some of which – particularly that seized from the offices of the German State Railways – was of excellent even luxurious quality. Pending the appointment of a Custodian of Enemy Property, temporary storage space was found in the old post-office building.

After a few weeks, a custodian was appointed. He was immediately contacted for instructions regarding the disposition of the seized furniture. No facilities had been provided along with his appointment. In the absence of storage space, he was at a loss to know what to do. Royal-Gagnon, who was carrying out the negotiations with him, advanced a very useful and practical suggestion. While the space used for the stored furniture was sorely needed to meet our constantly expanding requirements, we might be able to help out by keeping the furniture, if we could be allowed to make use of it in our offices. An additional argument was advanced that the equipment and furniture would be much less likely to suffer damage if placed in use rather than left stacked and crowded without adequate padding or other protection.

The Custodian was a most reasonable and perceptive man. Having visited the police offices, he knew that most of the furniture of the Force was well-classified by the troops as "Louis Riel period." He agreed that the seized articles should be put to use. A great change came over several of the offices, a change that during the several months that it lasted amazed officers visiting from other divisions. The Officer Commanding decided in favour of mahogany furnishings and a deep-piled, mulberry-coloured oriental rug with suitable oil paintings to add to the air of quiet dignity. My office and that of the secretary were magnificently furnished in oak with matching rugs and some very attractive original water colours. Several other offices benefitted from Royal-Gagnon's willingness to extend full co-operation to the Custodian.

For a few months, our offices equalled and probably surpassed anything that could be seen in the executive offices of our next-door neighbour, the head office of the Bank of Montreal. We were just becoming accustomed to our sumptuous surroundings when an inspection by

Commissioner Stuart Wood brought a quick end to our affluence. I am not sure what transpired between the Commissioner and Royal-Gagnon, but the seized furniture, the like of which had never been seen before, and has not been seen since in a police office, was shipped to the Chief Custodian of Enemy Property at Ottawa the next day. We returned to our "Louis Riel period" furnishings.

The appearance of counterfeit ration coupons necessitated many very lengthy investigations which resulted in the seizure of hundreds of thousands of fake books and in the prosecution of many counterfeiters and distributors. False National Registration certificates began to circulate in increasing numbers. Again widespread investigation was necessary and met with fair success. Cases of graft in the carrying out of government contracts were investigated and prosecuted in many places across the country.

The Force was made responsible for the arrests of delinquents who had failed to register as required by the National Registration Act. Later, the Force was given the task of arresting deserters from the Armed Services, a task that made very heavy drains on our resources. In the Province of Quebec, the number of delinquents and deserters totalled twenty-five thousand, a vastly disturbing figure when compared with our total strength of two hundred and fifty-eight regular members. In addition to constantly increasing new duties, there was, of course, the task of fulfilling our normal responsibilities in the police field and in our efforts to combat subversion and discover espionage. The latter responsibility – that is, work in the espionage field – was of obvious importance in that we were reasonably sure that the Germans would attempt to replace or rebuild their broken apparatus.

➤➤➤➤➤➤➤-➤➤➤-➤➤➤◄◄◄-◄◄◄-◄◄◄-◄◄◄-

The Spy Who Came
out
of the Sea

Late on the afternoon of November 10, 1942, word was received from the provincial police that their detachment at New Carlisle on the Bay Chaleur was holding a man who had been landed from a German submarine during the night. When arrested, the man was wearing civilian clothing; but on his insistence, he had been permitted to dig up a German naval uniform that he had buried at his point of landing, and to dress himself in that uniform. The man had been in possession of five thousand dollars in currency, one thousand dollars in gold pieces, a radio transmitter and receiving set, and a revolver. He was, according to the information received from the provincial police, insisting that he be placed in a prisoner of war camp under the provisions of the Geneva Conference.

After discussing this development with headquarters and requesting that arrangements be made for the close censorship of any news stories coming out of the Gaspé Peninsula, the Officer Commanding directed that I leave at once by car for New Carlisle. I was accompanied by Sergeant "Pete" Bordeleau (later Deputy Commissioner), and a German special constable, who was to act as interpreter.

This interpreter was a fabulous man who had served on German submarines during World War I and later joined the German Communist Party, in which he attained leadership. The rise of Hitler had forced his hurried departure for Moscow, where for some time he served as lecturer in one of the Soviet schools for the training of saboteurs. Subsequently, disillusioned by Communism as he witnessed it in Russia, he became an agent for the British Intelligence Service. His work for the British had been discovered during an assignment in South America. At that time, the Force had been requesting to provide asylum for him in Canada.

The trip to New Carlisle was made as rapidly as freezing rain and icy roads would permit. We arrived at the end of our four-hundred-mile journey early on the morning of the eleventh and immediately contacted the provincial police in order to secure further details regarding the arrest. The story did much credit to Earl Annett Jr. and his father Mr. Annett, the proprietor of a hotel, who was later decorated by the Government in recognition of his alertness and service in bringing about the arrest of a spy.

As told by Mr. Annett and the provincial police, the story started on the morning of November 10 when a stockily built man of medium height walked into the hotel carrying two suitcases and asked if he could be provided with a room in order that he could bathe and shave before lunch. New Carlisle is a small town, and the arrival of a total stranger would normally arouse some curiosity after the close of the summer season; and besides, Mr. Annett was well aware that the somewhat isolated and sheltered shores of the Bay Chaleur afforded excellent opportunities for the landing of spies from submarines.

He casually asked the visitor if he had arrived by bus. The stranger said that he had, which was his first mistake, since there had been no bus for several hours. Mr. Annett noted, too, that there was a strong and peculiar odour about the stranger which, while he did not recognize it, served to further arouse his suspicions. The odour was, in fact, the "submarine smell" which clings to the clothing of persons who have undergone long journeys by underwater craft.

The guest was given a room, and after bathing and shaving, he came downstairs for lunch. The proprietor immediately proceeded to search the room; and while he could not open the bags, he did discover in the wastebasket a discarded container that had held safety matches of a Belgium make. Such matches had been out of circulation in Canada since the beginning of the war. The visitor had said that he intended to take the afternoon train to Montreal. Therefore, Mr. Annett immediately dispatched his taxi-driver son to the office of the provincial police in order to alert them and to suggest that they await the arrival of the stranger at the railway station.

Having concluded lunch, the suspect proceeded to pay his bill; and in the process, used several Canadian bills of the old-style, large-size that had been withdrawn from circulation in Canada several years previously. Mr. Annett's suspicions seemed confirmed, and he immediately advised the provincial police of this recent development and told them that the stranger would be arriving at the railway station in a few minutes in the son's taxi.

A provincial police corporal boarded the train with the stranger and shared a seat with him. During the conversation that followed, the suspect claimed to be a radio salesman representing a Toronto manufacturer. The policeman noted the slight trace of a German accent, and this, together with the information that had been supplied by Mr. Annett, convinced him that the situation called for direct action. He identified himself and advised the stranger that he wished to examine his handbags. The suspect protested and produced a Canadian registration certificate made out in the name of Braunter and giving a Toronto address. This was another mistake on the part of the agent and indicated that the briefing given him in Germany had not been in line with the reputation of the German forces for methodical accuracy. The registration certificate was in English on one side and French on the other, the type of card used in the Province of Quebec. In other provinces, the registration certificates were printed in English only.

The Corporal insisted on examining the contents of the suspect's baggage, at which point the suspect announced, "I am a German naval officer. I landed from a submarine last night, and after landing, decided that I would desert. I, therefore, changed into civilian clothing and buried my naval uniform on the shore near the spot where I had landed. I insist on being allowed to recover my uniform and being given the treatment laid down for prisoners of war by the Geneva Convention."

Examination of the handbags revealed that one contained a radio receiver and transmitter, while the other held articles of civilian clothing, a revolver, about five thousand dollars in cash, some of which was in the old large-sized bills, and one thousand dollars in gold coins — hardly the equipment that one would expect to find in the baggage of a deserting naval officer.

The man was permitted to dig up and don his naval uniform and was then taken to Annett's hotel where he was placed under guard by the provincial police, to be held until such time as they received directions as to the disposition to be made of the prisoner. I requested that he be put back into the clothing that he had been wearing at the time of his arrest and then be placed in a cell in the local jail. Later in the morning I talked with the warden of the little jail who was delighted to have been given the custody of a German officer. The warden had served overseas during World War I and assured me that I need not worry about the safety of the prisoner, an assurance that was scarcely necessary.

The warden permitted me the use of his office, and I had the prisoner brought there a few minutes later. Corporal Bordeleau and a translator named Johnny were present. The prisoner entered the room in the best Nazi military manner, and after clicking his heels and giving me a curt bow, demanded that he be permitted to don his uniform and that he be treated as an officer and gentleman. My reply may not have been in the best military tradition, but at least it startled and served to deflate the prisoner. "Nuts. I believe you are a spy. Sit down and keep quiet until I speak to you."

At this stage, we needed to discover as quickly as possible if others had landed with him. We also wanted to explore the possibility of "turning him around," that is, of making him a "double agent."

The first thought of an intelligence agency following the capture of an enemy agent is not trial and punishment. The execution of a spy may reassure the public as to the alertness of the security services. In addition, it may add to the difficulties of the enemy in recruiting for their espionage nets. But the possibility of securing information and services of inestimable value is ended with the death of a spy. The first concern, therefore, is to secure the true story regarding the agent and his assignments and "targets," together with all information he may have regarding the enemy, and then to attempt to have him work as a double agent. An enemy agent thus "turned around" may be used to secure bits of information regarding enemy planning, interests, and activities; but even more important, he may be used to feed misinformation to the other side.

For a time the prisoner persisted in the claim that he was a deserting naval officer. Obviously, this was the "escape story" with which he had been supplied for use in the event of capture at the point of landing in the hope that it would secure for him the treatment of a prisoner of war. However, the story was soon upset by questions from Johnny, the interpreter, who had served in the German submarines during World War I. The prisoner could not answer even the most elementary questions regarding the procedures aboard a submarine.

Usually agents are given and rehearsed in a second escape story for use in the event of the first story being upset during interrogation. The prisoner proceeded to give us his second story. He now claimed to be a captain in the German army. According to this story, he had been stationed in Brussels where, a few months earlier, the Gestapo had discovered that he was living with a girl who was quarter-Jewish. Using this as a lever, he had been forced into the espionage service and had agreed to an assignment in Canada rather than face confinement in a concentration camp. He insisted that he had accepted the assignment under extreme duress and that it had never been his intention to carry out the assignment in Canada. He had hoped to get to Montreal and escape detection there until the end of the war. He was at a loss to explain why, if it had not been his intention to carry out espionage work, he had carried the radio receiver and transmitter with him.

During the interrogation, it was pointed out to the prisoner several times that in planning for his trip to Canada, his German matters had not been very thorough or efficient, nor had they shown any great concern for his safety. The old-style, large bills and the registration card had been dead give-aways, a fact which should have been known to German intelligence. It was also pointed out that the gold pieces with which he had been supplied would have proven extremely difficult to cash and would have undoubtedly led to a great many questions and probably to his arrest. His escape stories had been poorly planned and had offered him very little protection. Certainly not the sort of protection that should have been afforded by a competent organization really concerned with his welfare.

During this stage of the questioning, the good citizens of New Carlisle were holding commemorative services at the cenotaph in a park just outside the jail windows – it being November 11, Armistice Day. The prisoner was permitted to watch the services for a while and seemed deeply impressed by the rows of bemedalled veterans of World War I and the smart appearance of the detachments provided by the Armed Services. He was impressed, too, by the crowds that had turned out for the occasion and by the obvious loyalty, confidence, and quiet determination of all those who had gathered for the remembrance ceremonies. This was not in accordance with the propaganda that had been fed to the German people regarding the attitude of Canadians, particularly in the Province of Quebec, where we discovered later he had been told the people were on the verge of revolt.

Eventually he abandoned his escape story and admitted that, until the time of his arrest, he had had every intention of carrying out his espionage assignment. He had been landed alone from a submarine by a collapsible rubber boat during a rainstorm the previous night. His instructions were to make his way to Montreal and, once there, set up his radio equipment and contact his masters in Hamburg. Contact was to be made twice a day. Detailed instructions as to matters of interest to Germany would be relayed to him.

A second part of his assignment was to arrange for the arrival of other agents who, according to the very general information that had been given to him, would be low-level "expendable" saboteurs. He had not been supplied with the names of any contacts in Canada, but had been told that Adrien Arcand's Canadian Fascist Party was well organized and unquestionably loyal to the Nazi cause. He would be quite safe in contacting members of that party for assistance and information.

His background story, part of which was told to us then and part of which was learned during subsequent questioning, was interesting and remarkable. He had lived in Canada for several years before the war; and during that time, had married a Canadian widow who owned a business and was reasonably well-off. It had taken him only two years to go through the widow's money, when he hurriedly left Canada for Marseilles, where he joined the French Foreign Legion.

After five years of service in the Legion, he returned to Germany just before the outbreak of war. In Germany, he was a suspect because of his service in the Legion, and for a time was held in jail. His father, a man of some influence in the Nazi Party, was able to bring about his release and acceptance into the German Army. He had been assigned to a special school in Brandenburg for intensive training in sabotage.

Subsequently he was posted, along with a number of other trainees from the Brandenburg School, to the Dutch border where for some weeks they were given instructions, with the aid of models of the villages concerned, as to the carrying out of specific acts of sabotage within Holland. His group, wearing Dutch greatcoats over German uniforms, entered Holland ahead of the German invasion and carried out the planned acts of sabotage.

Later, the same groups, this time wearing Belgian uniforms, entered that country ahead of the invading forces and carried out acts of sabotage that had been assigned to them. Still later, these groups were posted at a point along the English channel where, for some months, they were trained into the parts they were to play in the first wave of the invasion of England. With the gradual disbandment of the troops gathered along the English Channel, he was reassigned to Brandenburg for further training and then posted to Brussels where he operated a counter-espionage group of civilians.

By that time he had been promoted to the rank of Captain, he had been decorated with the Iron Cross and had achieved a position of considerable authority. It was while in Brussels that the Gestapo discovered his association with a girl who was part-Jewish. He was immediately arrested and placed in a concentration camp for a few weeks where he underwent considerable hardship before being given the choice of "volunteering" for espionage duties abroad. After "volunteering," he spent several weeks in Hamburg undergoing training for his new duties. Later, when we were able to question him in detail about his training, we were somewhat relieved to learn that it had been of an extremely elementary nature and had not included "home-cooking" – the manufacturing of explosives from materials that could be secured in Canada without too much difficulty.

Having made a thoroughly clean breast of it, the prisoner requested that he be allowed to don the uniform that had been taken from him and that he be tried and executed without delay. I pointed out that he was in no way entitled to wear the uniform of a German naval officer, that he was a spy and would, therefore, be kept in civilian clothing. I also told him that, while a final decision would rest with whatever court heard his case, if a court found him guilty and sentenced him to death, it was extremely doubtful he would be executed by a firing squad. It was much more likely that if found guilty, he would be hanged. It was added, however, that there might be other ways out of the extreme difficulties in which he found himself. His reaction indicated that he knew precisely what I meant. Undoubtedly his German masters had told him that in the event of capture, efforts would be made to "turn him around."

At that point, I adjourned the questioning for a few hours. That evening we had another lengthy interview. During the securing of additional details of his story, I feigned considerable interest in the twenty-dollar bills found in his possession. On several occasions, while questioning him, I examined the bills minutely, ending each such examination with a question regarding enemies that he might have in Germany. He was obviously interested in and quite concerned about these questions and curious as to the reason back of them. He denied having any enemies in Germany, but I kept coming back to that point.

After a time, I handed one of the twenty-dollar bills to Bordeleau and suggested that he examine them. Since the bills were quite genuine, Bordeleau was at a loss to know what he was supposed to find or what he was supposed to say. But he took the bills to the window and went through all of the motions of a painstaking examination. He then slowly returned to the desk and handed me the bills. Shaking his head as though in wonder at some grave discovery, he said the only thing possible under the circumstances: "Tsk, tsk, tsk."

Curiosity and concern got the better of the prisoner. "What is this about the bills? Is there something wrong with them?"

"Why," I asked, "if, as you say, you have no enemies in Germany, would anybody have given you all these twenty-dollar counterfeit notes in addition to the old-style money?"

Whether he believed me, or whether he had approached the stage where he desired some salve for his conscience, I do not know. But his reaction was the one I had hoped for. He violently banged the desk and shouted, "Those God-damn Gestapo. The money was secured from them, and they have framed me. They wanted me caught and executed!"

He seemed to be on the verge of making an important decision, but hesitated before taking the plunge that would make him a traitor to old loyalties. He was obviously under great strain and fell silent for a few minutes before asking, "If I am executed, you think it will be by hanging?"

"Most probably," was my reply. He fell silent again for a time, and then broke down completely, sobbing and banging the desk while he repeated over and over again, "I will not be hanged, I will not be hanged." Again it was suggested that there might be other ways out of his difficulties. There was no need to go into further details. I added that we would be leaving early the following morning and that he must reach a firm decision before we left, as I was required to telephone my superiors to advise them of his attitude. He seemed ready to volunteer to act as a double agent, but I considered it advisable to give him time to consider the matter thoroughly and sent him back to his cell. Immediately after being brought to the office the following morning, the prisoner, without preliminaries or attempts to bargain as to the treatment that would be accorded him, announced that he was prepared to work as a double agent. I warned him that my superiors might not agree, but that if they did, there must be no reservation on his part. The turn-about must be complete. He assured me that his mind was made up, and again easing his conscience, ranted about the double-crossing Gestapo "swine."

I telephoned Royal-Gagnon to acquaint him with the developments and let him know that we would be leaving for Montreal at once. It was suggested that we have headquarters at Ottawa get in touch with the Chief Censor in order to get assurance that tight censorship would be continued. It should be mentioned here that several papers, having got wind of the story, had sent reporters to New Carlisle, where they had no difficulty in picking up details, since the townsfolk were agog over the capture of a spy. Although censorship had been imposed, it would have been fairly simple for the papers to have written a story to circumvent censorship regulations, or to have "leaked" the story to correspondents in the United States or other countries. The fact that not one line appeared until the lifting of censorship at the end of the war made it possible to continue our operation of this case, and reflects great credit on the press in general and, in particular, on those reporters who had the story.

The handling of a double agent is a tricky and complicated business. There is the overriding danger that the man might be a "triple agent" planted by the enemy, or that becoming a "double," he might relent and let his masters know that he had been captured and that his operations were being controlled, thereby becoming a "triple." A triple agent is of particular value to the enemy in that it gives them an opportunity to study the information supplied by the "controlled" source and compare it with information being received from other agents. In this way they are able to discover other agents who are working under enemy control.

The agent's "touch" on the key of his radio transmitter is of importance in that his style is well-known and recorded by his masters. Any variation can be easily recognized by experienced operators, and this, of course, gives ample opportunity to the spy to alter his style and thereby let his masters know that he is in the hands of the enemy. This point also raised concern regarding the agent's health. If he became unable to carry on with the operation, a stand-by operator must be used; and no matter how well the stand-by man might have watched and practised, he might never be able to exactly duplicate the sending style of the agent. Obviously the health and well-being of a "double" takes on great importance.

A major concern is that of replying to questions raised by the enemy. Answers must have the semblance of truth, while at the same time avoiding the giving of any information of value. To further complicate matters, misleading information must be handled with extreme delicacy and be of substance, it must be presented in a manner that will fit in with the information being supplied the enemy through other sources and other double agents.

On our arrival in Montreal, I found that Royal-Gagnon, working closely with Commissioner Stuart Wood and the Officers of headquarters intelligence staff, had anticipated the difficulties that we would have to meet. The Commissioner had already cabled the Intelligence Services in the United Kingdom requesting that one of their men be sent over to assist in co-ordinating our efforts with similar activities being carried out by them. Royal-Gagnon had enlisted the services of two members of our civilian volunteer group who were expert in the radio field. He had also made arrangements whereby the prisoner could be held in secrecy.

There followed several weeks of very detailed questioning of the spy. This was partly to elicit every scrap of information of value to the military or intelligence services and partly in order that his story might be thoroughly checked through the voluminous files of British Intelligence. During the early part of his questioning, the prisoner told us of several methods whereby it had been arranged that he could let his German masters know secretly that he was transmitting under control. This provided some indication that, at least, for the time being, he did not intend to work as a "triple." Subsequently we were advised by British Intelligence that his story had been checked as closely as possible, and that he was apparently telling us the truth. In the meantime we had, of course, checked his story regarding his previous trip to Canada and found that the details supplied were accurate.

It was then decided that an attempt should be made to have him communicate with his masters in Hamburg. This necessitated the setting up of a small team of code experts, radio experts, a stand-by operator who must be prepared to replace the spy in the event of illness, and a team of guards. It was also necessary to find suitable quarters from which the radio transmissions could be made and in which the prisoner would be reasonably comfortable and well-fed as a protection against ill health.

Johnny, the German chap who had acted as translater in New Carlisle, lived in one of the suburbs of Montreal where he owned his own home. His wife was a most excellent cook who specialized in German dishes. A three-roomed apartment was set up in Johnny's basement, and for several weeks attempts were made to contact Hamburg. Try as we would, however, his equipment was not equal to the task. It was clear that a much more powerful transmitter would be required and that a fifty-foot mast should be erected in Johnny's backyard.

Johnny spoke with a strong German accent, as did his wife; and they had been regarded with some suspicion by their neighbours since moving into the district. The neighbours were quick to notice strange goings and comings through Johnny's basement door. When these were followed by the erection of a radio tower, the neighbours felt sure that they had uncovered enemy plotting. Several of them visited our office to report their suspicions. Eventually, the Chief of Police of the Town of Mount Royal, the suburb in which Johnny's house was located, called at the office to repeat information that had reached him and to insist that some action be taken.

Because of the extreme secrecy which necessarily surrounded the operation, we were unable to tell the Chief the entire story. But we did assure him that we were aware of the activities and that, in fact, we had a hand in them. We went on to explain that the Canadian Government had asked the Force to carry out some experiments with a new type of radio which was being developed in deep secrecy and that our experiments were being carried out from Johnny's house. The Chief was asked to quietly pass this information on to people in the neighbourhood.

The equipment constructed by our radio experts worked beautifully – so well, in fact, that during our operations particular care had to be taken that our station would not boom through to Hamburg at times when atmospheric conditions would have made contact difficult. This would probably have aroused suspicions in the minds of the Hamburg operators.

We ran the station for about nine months during which Hamburg was contacted twice daily except for short periods during which the questions asked by the Germans were of a nature that would have given a spy a great deal of work and necessitated his absence from the set; or for periods of three to four days when excuses would be invented whereby operations could be discontinued in order to give us an opportunity to get a little rest.

Usually the schedule called for a meeting with Hamburg around noon and again at midnight. The work of deciding on answers to be transmitted, translating the answers into German, and then putting the messages into code, and, after the transmission, decoding and translating the message from Hamburg, was a lengthy process. Those of us who were performing other and more regular duties during the daytime found it necessary to arrange for an occasional break.

It was extremely interesting to learn, through the questions asked by Hamburg, the points of their interest in the Canadian war effort. Somewhat fortunately for us, the schedules called for just one transmission by Hamburg and one by the spy during each "meet." This afforded us an opportunity to study the questions and prepare well-considered replies. A committee had been set up in Ottawa composed of the chiefs of navy, army, and air force intelligence services, to handle questions of a military nature. Commissioner Wood fielded questions that had to do with non-

military matters. Meetings of the committee were attended by a repre-
sentative of British Intelligence, who made sure that the replies were
co-ordinated with activities being carried out by his service.

In the early stages, the operation produced information of some
considerable value; and the Germans displayed great interest in the
information supplied to them. Hamburg asked questions regarding the
numbers and types of Armed Service units stationed in the Montreal
area, and on one occasion instructed the agent to make a trip to Quebec
City and attempt to secure information regarding military units stationed
there, the number and type of vessels in Port, and all possible information
regarding submarine nets that might have been installed as a protection
against German submarines. Answers were provided after consultations
with the special committee.

At one stage the Hamburg station asked a number of questions about
National Registration Certificates and ration coupons. What were the
colours of the papers and ink used; what type face had been used in the
printing; what was the texture of the paper and of the cover of the ration
books? The information sought indicated the probability that the Germans were considering turning out counterfeit documents for future
agents.

Our "double" had only a layman's knowledge of the printing craft,
and the answers provided were held well within the limits that would
have handicapped a spy. Certainly the descriptions provided were not
sufficiently detailed to enable Germany to start a counterfeiting operation.
Germany kept pressing for more details, and in their anxiety for this
information we thought we saw an opportunity to secure information
regarding channels that might exist for sending documents to German
Intelligence; channels such as through another agent or through mailing
addresses in neutral countries.

In pursuance of this plan, the Germans were advised that their spy
had secured a ration book and a registration card. We did not follow the
information with a request for instructions regarding forwarding the
material, as such a direct question might have raised suspicions in the
minds of the spy masters. Our hope that they would transmit instructions
in this regard was not fulfilled. It was becoming apparent that the traffic
with Hamburg would be "one way," with the masters asking the questions
but avoiding the giving of information.

It was decided that an effort should be made to build Hamburg's
interest. They had already asked for information regarding the "Mosquito" bomber, which was still on the secret list, and we had supplied
only with such information as was known to the man on the street.
Through the air force member of the special committee, it was learned
that the "Mosquito" was to be taken off the secret list and that details
regarding the bomber were to be made public. Here was an opportunity

to display the ability of our spy. The public announcement regarding the aircraft was withheld for two months. In the meantime, we concocted a story regarding the "double" having been able to strike up a friendship with an air force officer from whom he had extracted details regarding the "Mosquito" bomber. The message to Hamburg ended with a listing of these details. Thus German Intelligence had all the information regarding the aircraft about two months before it was made public in Canada.

Hamburg expressed appreciation of the agent's efforts in a curt message, but the traffic continued to be "one way" in so far as the giving of information was concerned. Questions continued to come in. Shipbuilding yards, location of air fields, availability of food-stuffs and other supplies – all these provided some information as to the direction of their interests, but try as we would we could not get the slightest information regarding any other sources they might have in Canada, or other channels for the sending of information.

In the fall of 1943, a final effort was made to break through their wall of cautious silence. The spy had been in Canada for almost a year. Under normal cirmustances he would have been getting near the end of his financial resources, a situation highly disturbing to an agent in enemy territory.

His alleged worries over his financial plight were relayed to Hamburg. Questions on a variety of subjects continued to come in, but German Intelligence ignored his questions regarding a further supply of money. It may have been that they had no means by which to replenish his finances, or they might well have preferred to regard him as expendable rather than risk exposing other agents or channels. Whatever the reason, his pleas were ignored. It was clear that his Hamburg contact would not break the "one-way" rule.

After consultation with British Intelligence and with the Federal Bureau Intelligence which had been kept posted regarding our activities in this case and which had a direct interest in the co-ordination of information being supplied to Germany as part of an overall plan of deception, it was decided that there was no value in continuing the operation. I took the prisoner to London, England, where he was taken over by British Intelligence as an addition to their "library of information." The trip to London gave me an opportunity to work for some months with the British Intelligence services, a most interesting and profitable experience, and one that greatly increased my already considerable admiration for the know-how and quiet efficiency of the United Kingdom services.

It will be recalled that before leaving Germany the agent was told that on reaching Montreal he should try to contact members of the Canadian Fascist Party for assistance. These rather vague and risky instructions were of interest in that they indicated the extent to which the German espionage apparatus in Canada had been disrupted by the early arrest of its leaders, and they raised the possibility that other spies sent to Canada might be given the same instructions. As soon as the first rush of work that resulted from the setting up of the double-agent operation began to ease, some thought was given to the possibility of turning this piece of information to advantage. If a way could be discovered by which we could gain access to information reaching the inner circle of the Canadian Fascist Party, another link would be added to the counter-espionage network, and the likelihood of uncovering other enemy agents would be increased.

The Canadian Fascist Party had suffered some severe blows. Membership, according to Adrian Arcand's boast in 1939, numbered more than twelve thousand. But this had dwindled rapidly after the start of hostilities until only a small hard core remained, and even this hard core, alarmed by the internment of German and Italian leaders, remained quiet for awhile.

In the spring of 1940, emboldened by the fact that there had been no arrests among their members, the leaders started calling secret meetings. By June, their activities had increased to a point where, in the interest of the safety of the state, definite action had to be taken. Adrian Arcand and ten of his most active and valued cohorts were arrested. Documentary evidence produced at the preliminary hearing was so damning that the judge stopped proceedings and instructed that the exhibits be brought to the attention of the Attorney General. As a result, all of the accused were interned. New leaders attempted to hold the party together, but the arrest and internment of six of these men left the Canadian Fascists badly disorganized.

The Intelligence Branch had been successful in penetrating the party, but the penetration was not so deep as to guarantee that all of the party secrets would be known, particularly in view of the disorganization that followed the arrests. The few remaining die-hards were known, but their meetings and actions were surrounded with deep secrecy. The possibility that they might be approached to give aid to spies placed a new importance on them and on developing means by which better coverage of their activities might be achieved.

The spy we had "turned around" had been instructed to seek assistance from the Canadian Fascist Party. Why not have a substitute spy do just that? With proper handling and good luck, such a substitute might be able to so arrange matters that any information reaching the Fascists concerning spies would be channelled to him. We had the ideal substitute – Johnny, our erstwhile German interpreter. His long experience with underground and espionage work, his knowledge of the organization and methods of German intelligence, his courage and his quick mind, all fitted him for the job.

When the subject was broached to him, he was willing and eager to get on with it. After a great deal of discussion, it was decided that Johnny's new role should be upgraded. He would not pose as a rather low-level spy begging assistance; rather he would be a top-flight agent sent to Canada to repair the damage suffered by the Canadian Nazi and Fascist groups. He would demand rather than ask for help. He would insist that the Fascists work under his orders, lest some ill-advised action by them should interfere with his overall plan for reorganization.

If the leaders of the Fascist Party could be brought to accept his story – and, consequently, the leadership of a supposed Nazi agent – the resultant situation would be useful. A steady flow of information would reach us regarding their membership. They could be controlled and assigned tasks that would keep them busy and out of mischief, and any approach by newly arrived spies seeking assistance would be quickly brought to the attention of their leader, Johnny.

There seemed very little possibility that the Fascists would have means by which they would be able to check the story with Germany. Had any such arrangement existed, the spy would have been given more specific instructions regarding the making of contact. It was decided to go ahead with the plan.

The plan worked well. Within a few weeks Johnny, posing as a somewhat arrogant and overbearing Nazi agent, had overcome the initial doubts, and he established himself as leader in the minds of the group of six men who had been called together by the first man contacted. Johnny insisted that his identity be known only to this group, but that they pass word on to a small circle of tried and trusted supporters that a leader had arrived. Johnny harangued the little committee regarding the stupidity that had led to the breakdown of the Nazi and Fascist apparatus in Canada, which, he held, had been due to failure to follow the plans that had been laid down. There would be no more of that. He had been sent with definite instructions for the reorganization of the Party, and his orders must be obeyed without question.

From then until the end of the war, the Force, through Johnny, controlled the activities of the Fascist Party in the Province of Quebec. In order that control might be as absolute as possible, active membership was greatly reduced on the grounds that a small tightly disciplined group operating in deep secrecy would best meet existing requirements. Members not included in this small group were told that they must remain quiet until contacted by the party, unless information of outstanding importance reached them, in which case the information was to be turned in through arranged channels.

Members of the "active" group were given various assignments, such as submitting reports regarding the work being done at their places of employment, checking on freighter traffic in the St. Lawrence, and listing shoulder-flashes worn by servicemen seen on the streets of Montreal. Their reports, Johnny told them, were being sent to Germany; but he would not, for obvious reasons of secrecy and his own safety, let them know the location of his transmitter. Some of their reports were most interesting and would have been of value to the enemy.

The Fascists were content for a while, but by early 1944, they were becoming restless and impatient for action. There were increasing demands that they be permitted to carry out acts of sabotage, and increasing resistance to Johnny's tight control developed. It became obvious that measures would have to be taken to strengthen Johnny's hand.

We were aware that O Division, with headquarters at Toronto, had the custody of a German agent who had been captured some time previously and who was willingly assisting that Division in its counter-espionage work. We also knew that this man was a tall, blond autocratic-looking individual who had held fairly high positions in the Nazi Party in Germany. He would be able to put on a masterful act as a Nazi leader.

With the permission of the Commissioner and the Headquarters Intelligence Officers, a meeting was arranged with Assistant Commissioner V. A. M. Kemp, the Officer Commanding the Division, and his CIB officer, Inspector George B. McClellan. They readily agreed to have their agent brought to Montreal for a day or two so that we might make use of his services.

Johnny made an important announcement to the members of his Fascist committee. The top spy master for North America was going to pay a visit to Montreal and had consented to meet three members of the committee. He provided some highly interesting and entirely fictitious details regarding the background of the spy master. He concluded by saying that the selection of this man to head the Nazi apparatus in North America had been made by Hitler himself. A date for the meeting with the great man was arranged, and the three committee men selected for the task were told to remain by their telephones on that date and that they would receive detailed instructions.

The meeting took place in a small suite which Johnny had reserved in the Windsor Hotel. The committee men were kept waiting almost an hour for the arrival. Actually, since the agent was in custody, he was being held in an adjoining room and was escorted to the door of the suite and kept under observation until Johnny admitted him. He put on a masterful performance. After a round of "Heil Hitlers," he thanked the committee, rather curtly, for the work done on behalf of the Fatherland; all of which had been reported to him, and to Germany, by Johnny.

Having disposed of these preliminaries, he got down to the business of the moment. "I am told that you and your associates are eager to get on with the business of sabotage. This is nonsense. We are not playing a game of fireworks. We are fighting a war, and you will follow orders just as soldiers in the field must follow orders. I want no more of your idiotic talk about sabotage. When the time comes, you will get your orders. Until then there must be no nonsense."

He then condescended a little to explain, "Through the incredible stupidity of your leaders, and – I must admit – of the leaders we sent to Canada, our apparatus was wrecked."

"The Canadian police are content with their work and are now sound asleep. One act of sabotage will awaken them, and our months of planning will be upset. When the day comes, sabotage will occur across Canada and the United States – all on the same day. Until then, only fools and idiots would think of sabotage; and such fools and idiots would answer for their actions after the victory."

There were no questions or objections. The magnificent performance of the phoney feuhrer had overawed the committee men. He did not risk overplaying his hand by remaining for niceties or small talk. On leaving, the spurious leader warned that no one must leave the room for at least half an hour after his departure. There was another round of heel clicking, "Heil Hitlers." Then he strolled haughtily from the room and down the hall to where our guards were waiting. Budding revolt had been crushed. There was no more talk of sabotage by Canadian Fascists.

Another spy was landed by submarine on the East Coast, this time on the shores of New Brunswick. Again the agent had been forced into espionage service. Having arrived in Canada, he had no intention of risking his neck on behalf of the Fatherland. He buried his radio equipment and any other articles that might have aroused suspicion, went quietly to the nearest town, and boarded a train for Montreal.

In Montreal, he went to a brothel which was raided by the police during his visit. He was arrested with the other "found-ins" and taken to the central police station of the municipal force for "booking." Although, understandably, under great strain when brought before the Desk Sergeant, he had enough presence of mind to pose as a married man and express fervent hope that his wife would not learn of his arrest.

The Desk Sergeant was a friendly soul to whom the business of booking "found-ins" had become a matter of daily routine. He reassured the very agitated man before him that there was no reason why his wife should know of his predicament. He explained that many people appearing before him gave false names on such minor charges and then posted the nominal bail required. If they did not turn up the following morning, the bail, which was in the amount usually levied as a fine, would be confiscated, and no more would be said about the matter.

The spy paid the required twenty-five-dollar deposit and left the police station, and Montreal, very hurriedly. He went to Ottawa and secured a room in a reasonably priced rooming house. Although he had been supplied with a forged Canadian national registration card before leaving Germany, he was afraid to apply for employment. He made a point of leaving his rooming house in the early morning and returning at a regular hour at the end of each day in order to give the impression that he was gainfully employed. Most of his time was spent in moving-picture threatres or pool rooms, but he did spend many hours sitting in the visitors' gallery in the Parliament Buildings listening to the debates of members of Parliament.

The money, which he had been supplied before leaving Germany, lasted a little over a year. When it was exhausted, he walked quietly to the headquarters of the Force and surrendered. His radio set and other equipment were later recovered from the spot where he had buried them on the New Brunswick shores. This spy's effort for the Fatherland amounted to a holiday in Canada. At the end of the war he was returned to Germany, where he served as interpreter in refugee camps.

In the years leading up to the war, there had been a great deal of apprehension regarding the vaunted German Fifth Column and the supermen of the German Intelligence services. Certainly both proved effective in Europe. Probably they were too preoccupied to pay much attention to their Fifth Column in Canada, or to send their best men here; but, whatever the cause, it was quickly learned, to our great relief, that their organizations were vulnerable and that their agents were unwilling workers who had been forced into the espionage service and sent abroad without proper training, planning, equipment, or support.

The circumstances surrounding the capture by the Federal Bureau of Investigation of German spies landed from a submarine on the New Jersey coast served to further encourage us in the opinion that we were not, in fact, dealing with masterminds or supermen. The New Jersey spies brought with them, from the submarine, a load of explosives, which they buried in the sand at the point of landing. Spies and saboteurs unskilled in the manufacturing of explosives from materials easily obtainable in enemy territory face serious problems of supply, a problem that indicates lack of training. In the New Jersey case, too, the spy in charge of the group had been forced into the espionage service. Before landing from the submarine, he had determined not to risk his neck for the Fatherland – a decision that proved of tremendous importance in the capture of this group.

12

>>>->>>->>>->>>-<<<-<<<-<<<-<<<

Protecting Canada
from Itself

Counter-espionage and counter-sabotage responsibilities were important and time-consuming, but they by no means monopolized the services of the Force. Normal policing duties had to be continued, and to these were added innumerable new duties stemming from wartime legislation and regulations.

Many commodities had been rationed by the Wartime Prices and Trades Board. While the rationing regulations were an essential part of our war effort, and the controls imposed proved reasonably effective, they did open the way for unscrupulous and disloyal persons to make many dishonest dollars. Counterfeit ration coupons appeared by the thousands, particularly in the Province of Ontario and Quebec. Despite many prosecutions and convictions, the counterfeiting continued until the end of the war.

Trouble was experienced, too, as regards genuine coupons, in that a ready and profitable market raised great temptations for the employees of printing companies engaged in this work and persons employed in the transportation, storage, or distribution of the valuable little bits of paper. The sale of stolen coupons necessitated many investigations, some of which were quite complicated, and long-drawn-out before the culprits could be brought before the courts.

The printing of fake National Registration Certificates took up the time of the Force's Criminal Investigation Branch staffs. The flood of fake certificates became so great that for a time they could be purchased, without difficulty, for twenty-five cents. This problem was brought under reasonable control through the conviction of several printers and distributors; but, in the meantime, thousands of the false certificates had been put into circulation. This, in turn, complicated work in other fields, in that the counterfeit certificates provided false identification for deserters from the armed services, delinquents who had failed to register, and for other persons trying to establish false identities or evade the police.

Usually the rationing of commodities that are in short supply brings about the side-effect of black-marketing, and Canada was no exception. Huge profits could be made for black-market items, such as gasoline, tires, sugar, cloth, and a wide variety of food-stuffs. While the great majority of Canadians realized the need for rationing and were content to do their part by complying with the regulations, there were many people, from householders to businessmen, who were willing to participate in black-market operations, either to avoid the inconvenience of shortages or to make a profit at the expense of more loyal citizens.

The Foreign Exchange Regulations, the enforcement of which were of vital importance, gave rise to many and varied schemes, some of which were international conspiracies involving very large sums of money and necessitating lengthy investigations. Fortunately, there existed the closest possible co-operation between officials of the Foreign Exchange Control Board, the Customs Department, the Force, and the United States Secret Service, Customs, and the Federal Bureau of Investigation. Through the joint efforts of those agencies, a number of highly important investigations were brought to successful conclusions and illegal transactions were kept to a minimum.

Japan's entry into World War II brought pressures on the Force in British Columbia, where most of the Japanese Canadians were concentrated. Alarm, well mixed with hysteria, brought about demands for the removal of almost twenty-thousand Japanese citizens from the coastal areas; and, subsequently, for the dispersal of the Japanese fishing fleet and the seizure of Japanese-Canadian owned property in the "protected area." The Force was called on to assist in the evacuation and relocation inland, and in the protection of the fishing fleet and other properties, pending disposal by a committee set up for that purpose.

Since the end of the war, the action taken in dispersing the Japanese Canadians has been the subject of severe criticism levelled at the federal and provincial Governments and, indirectly, at the Force and the committees and groups connected with the operation. Criticism has been levelled also at the amount of reimbursement received by the Japanese Canadians. I am not sufficiently familiar with the background or details to know if the evacuation was really necessary, or justified, or handled in the best possible manner; or if the amounts eventually given as compensation for their material losses were fair or just.

The matter has been mentioned here simply to demonstrate another of the many duties that the Force was called on to perform. It may be that over the years the removal of the Japanese Canadians from the West Coast, and the hardships suffered by them, will bring large benefits to Canada. Indeed, some of these benefits are already apparent. The wartime evacuation broke up their concentration on the West Coast and eventually brought about the dispersal of the Japanese Canadians across the country. The nation has already profited through the spread of their industry, culture, and good citizenship.

On the East Coast, wartime conditions had reduced the old problem of smuggling to a mere trickle; but new duties had brought other and heavier pressures. Naval installations, the movement of troops destined for overseas, and the arrival and departure of convoys – these necessitated the placing of great emphasis on secrecy and, therefore, on close and active co-operation with the censorship authorities.

There was need, too, for the paying of particular attention to the protection of vital points, such as the harbours of Halifax and St. John. In the busy port of Halifax, a senior officer of the Force, Assistant Commissioner Alex Eames, was appointed by the Government as Security Control Officer, an appointment that carried with it the responsibility for making sure that all possible steps were taken toward the protection of that tremendously important port. There was need also to assist in the safeguarding of convoys by stopping – or at least curtailing – leakages of information. The carrying out of these responsibilities occupied the full time of a large number of members of the Force.

There was an extreme shortage of narcotic drugs; and while this greatly reduced the activities of traffickers and pedlars, it also brought about conditions that made more difficult the work of the drug squads in the major cities. Since the addicts could no longer secure drugs from the street-corner pedlars, they took to breaking into hospitals and clinics and doctors' homes.

There were changes also in the pattern followed by offenders under the Excise Act. Since the sales of sugar and molasses were strictly controlled by the rationing regulations, supplies could not be secured from the usual sources; but whisky was also in short supply and severely rationed, and the prices for bootleg liquor had soared to an all-time high. The temptations of this situation were too much for some of the illicit liquor operators, and they embarked on many schemes to secure needed supplies. Some of these involved crooked transactions with wholesale houses; others followed the more direct method of breaking and entering warehouses. While the output of illicit alcohol had been greatly reduced, the changed patterns would not allow for any sizable reduction in the strength of the liquor squads.

During the war years, the Force worked without the benefit of the

Marine Division or the small Air Division of four planes that had been in existence at the start of hostilities. The forty patrol boats and the planes were turned over to the armed services on the outbreak of war, and with them had gone ninety-eight per cent of the men of the two divisions who had volunteered for duty with the armed services. That total would have been one hundred per cent but for the advancing years of some of the members. These men served with distinction – some lost their lives, many were decorated for bravery, and a gratifying number were promoted to commissioned ranks in the services.

Overseas service was not limited to volunteers from the Marine and Air Divisions. On the outbreak of war, there was a very general desire among members to enlist in the armed services; but the desire was curbed by a ruling that members were performing essential services and must, therefore, fulfill their terms of engagement with the Force. While this ruling interfered with the wishes of the majority of officers and men, it was obviously based on sound, practical considerations. Apart from the need for good law enforcement, members had been trained and gained experience in many duties that had direct bearing and importance on Canada's wartime activities, particularly in the counter-espionage and security fields. Suitable replacements were not available.

Possibly in arriving at their decision, the ministers and the Commissioner had in mind the experience of World War I when wholesale enlistments so reduced the strength of the Force as to severely reduce its effectiveness and, therefore, threaten its future. While there was understanding and acceptance of the need for the ruling, the Commissioner felt that some exceptions should be made in order that the Force might be directly represented on the battlefronts, as it had been in all wars in which Canada had participated since Confederation. The Guidon, or Regimental Colours, carries battle honours from the Riel Rebellion, the South African War, and World War I, and the Siberian Campaign. The Commissioner's view that despite the pressures of other duties the proud tradition of participation in active service should be continued was shared by all ranks. This was clearly established by the flood of applications that followed a call for volunteers.

The First Provost Company RCMP was formed from these volunteers; and the services of the company were offered to the Department of National Defence. The offer was quickly accepted, and the unit was on active duty overseas with the First Division of the Canadian Army early in 1940. More than two hundred men from the Force saw service. Many were decorated, and fifty-nine earned promotions to Commissioned Ranks. Most of these men returned to the Force and to their old ranks when the war ended.

No account of the work of the Intelligence Branch during the early war years would be complete without mention of the Communist Party.

Trained and experienced in conspiracy and intrigue in Canada since 1917, and thoroughly dedicated to the "follow-the-leader" policies laid down by the Comintern, they were called on to perform convolutions that would have destroyed less fanatical and disciplined organizations.

For several years prior to the war, one of their main "open" activities had been promoting their international "united front against Fascism." The cause was a worthy one with wide appeal to Communist and non-Communist alike. The Party set up many fronts in the process, through groups aimed at attracting non-Communists. University groups, religious bodies, scientific associations, women's groups, business men, and wealthy patrons – eager in their desire to fight Fascism, but naïve in choosing their method and their company – extended moral and a great deal of financial support through these front groups, whose names and slogans made great play on the words "peace," "democracy," and "freedom."

Then came the signing of the non-aggression pact between Hitler and Stalin, the pact that opened the door for World War II. The Communist Party in Canada was taken by surprise. There had been no advance warning that the masters in Moscow, who had directed the international "united front against Fascism," would bring an abrupt reversal by making a compact with the enemy. Canadian party leaders were dumbfounded. Unable to attempt an explanation, even to the Party faithful, let alone to the front groups, where the sudden about-face was creating havoc among the innocents and parlour pinks, they went into hiding for a few days to await some guidance from Moscow.

Many of the people who had been sucked into front groups came to a sudden and belated realization that they had been duped. Membership dropped, prominent persons who had allowed their names and prestige to be used hurriedly backed away from the movement. Others, who had preferred to remain anonymous while giving financial aid to the party, withdrew their support.

Only a few of the inner circle of the party proper found that they could not accept this latest somersault; but most of the hard core of the party – and as shown later during the Gouzenko case, a few of those recruited during the "united-front" campaign – found it possible to perform the mental gymnastics necessary to adjust to the new order. The fight against Nazism and Fascism was out as far as the Communist were concerned. Now their efforts must be directed against the war effort, the "Imperialist War" that had been brought on by the capitalist and colonial powers. After some delay, the faithful were provided with a new party line – or, rather, a refurbished line to rationalize Stalin's pact with Hitler. Their wily leader had manoeuvred into a position from which he and the world Communist movement could watch from the sidelines while the great powers destroyed one another. After a period of confusion, the

Party, in support of the new line, embarked on a new campaign, "fight against the Imperialist War."

Their campaign started slowly because the leaders believed that they were in imminent danger of internment and that the party would be banned. For some reason the Government hesitated, and in the face of this dalliance the anti-war campaign became increasingly open, vicious, and widespread. Anti-war propaganda was circulated by way of pamphlets, mimeographed news sheets, and the party press. Criticism was levelled at every action of the Government. Half truths and untruths were built up in an attempt to spread dissatisfaction. Letters aimed at creating disloyalty and unrest were mailed to members of the armed services and to university students. Rationing, national legislation, security, censorship, and, of course, the "Gestapo methods" of the police were attacked. Vicious rumours were spread. In the Province of Quebec, the party, aware that there was a strong feeling against conscription, made propaganda capital by distributing pamphlets and rumours indicating that full conscription was imminent, while in other parts of Canada the Government was accused of bowing to the wishes of the Province of Quebec.

Eventually, decisive action was taken by the Government by way of the internment of a few leaders and the banning of the party. Then came the Nazi invasion of Russia, and the need for another *volte-face* by the party in Canada. Again there was confusion. For a few days Communist groups in some provinces continued to circulate propoganda against "Imperialist War" while others came out with a new party line demanding a greater effort on the part of Canada in the "war to save democracy." The confusion was not as deep or lasting as the one caused by the previous about-face. The new line was clear. The Communists must work toward a greater war effort not because of a sudden upsurge of loyalty toward Canada or sympathy in the Allied cause, but because the Soviet Union – and, therefore, Communism – was threatened.

The new direction of Red activity in Canada did not ease the burden of the Intelligence Branch of the Force. The Communists were not slow to take advantage of the fact that their new position made them much more acceptable to the public. While on the surface they fought vigorously for a greater war effort, and particularly for a Second Front to ease the pressures on the Soviet Union, their underground apparatus was busily engaged recruiting new members and setting up new front groups which were used largely for the breaking down of opposition to Communist ideology, but also for the screening and recruitment of agents into their espionage network. Their efforts met with considerable success. The Communist leaders who had been interned were let out, while those who had gone into hiding surrendered and were released forthwith. They were even successful in having one of their leaders elected to the federal Parliament from which position he was able to circulate a great deal of Communist propaganda at the expense of the Government.

Their efforts in the recruitment of espionage agents were also successful. The report of the Royal Commission in 1947 established that many well-placed and valuable agents were drawn in during this period and continued in the service of the Communists after the war. Some of them were under the direct control of the Communist Member of Parliament, Fred Rose, who was eventually jailed along with a number of other spies.

An unusual and rather difficult situation developed in Montreal, when information reached the Force that the Mayor, short, bulgy, caricature-like, Camillien Houde, intended to force the Government to intern him. Houde, much given to draping his ungainly form in cutaway coat and striped trousers, complete with top hat, pearly grey spats, carnation, and cane, had long been a centre of controversy in municipal and provincial politics. He was a shrewd, unfettered politician, whose opponents persistently accused him of almost everything, except honesty and a high sense of morality. For his part, he made no great effort to offset the rumours of wrong-doing and even less effort to claim virtue for himself.

He was tremendous on the hustings, with a style somewhat reminiscent of W. C. Fields at his best. His speeches were masterpieces of seemingly disarming frankness and sharp, topical humour. Huge crowds turned out to hear him; and despite the accusations and scandals; despite his frequent avowals that he did not intend to keep election promises; and despite the fact that few would admit having voted for him – he had remained as Mayor of Montreal through several elections. But another election was growing near, and he believed that the tide had turned against him.

To a small group of friends, he reasoned that he could not meet the very heavy costs that would be involved in setting up the sort of election machine required. Further, sources of income that had been open to him during previous terms in office had been lost to others; as a result, he was heavily in debt and some of his debts were of an exceedingly embarrassing nature.

So, he reasoned, the future looked black – so black that he must choose a new course in order to save himself from failure, bankruptcy, and possibly jail. He would get himself interned. An internment camp was certainly preferable to jail; and, with luck, he would emerge in an excellent position to re-enter politics. If the Allies won the war, it would be followed by a depression, and he would be able to pose as a martyr who had been interned because of his efforts to warn "my people." In the unlikely event of a victory for Germany, he could assume a slightly different martyr's role and would be sought after by the victors.

A report advising of Houde's intentions was forwarded to Ottawa where it received a somewhat sceptical reception. Houde quickly dispelled any doubt as to the accuracy of our information. He gave several inflammatory speeches, any one of which would have justified internment. But for good reason the Government hesitated. The arrest and internment of a mayor of a Canadian metropolis was not a matter to be lightly undertaken, particularly when that internment was being deliberately sought. Further, Houde's popularity, coupled with the tensions that existed in the Province of Quebec, gave cause for deep deliberation.

Houde was a very determined man. When action did not result from his first few speeches, he openly advocated defiance of the National Registration Act. The Government had no choice. We were instructed to arrest the Mayor and transport him forthwith to the internment camp. The arrest was made in the City Hall by Inspector J. L. Lemieux (later Deputy-Commissioner). Houde was brought to the offices, where he appeared happy and smiling, complete with cutaway coat, striped trousers, spats, and cane. He was in the best of good humour as the escort took him away to begin his trip to Petawawa.

Events proved that his planning, if not admirable, was far sighted. He took off quite a lot of weight in camp and emerged at the end of the war, healthy, well-rested, and ready to re-enter the political fray. The carefully planned martyrdom paid off. He won several elections and again became a power to be reckoned with in municipal and provincial politics.

13

⤛⤛⤛⤛⤛⤜⤜⤜⤜⤜

Visitors, Conferences,
Prisoners of War

In December of 1941, I had the great good fortune and privilege of meeting the Right Honourable Winston S. Churchill. The occasion was his visit to Ottawa following a Conference in Washington with President Roosevelt and the Canadian Prime Minister, Mackenzie King.

I had been detailed to board the special train with several Constables at the international border, to take over protection duties from the United States Secret Service. The special train arrived at the border crossing-point at about midnight and stopped just long enough for us to board the second-to-last coach which was occupied by Churchill. The last coach on the train was that of the Canadian Prime Minister. Having relieved the Secret Service men, and having posted men as required, I lost no time in getting in touch with Scotland Yard's Inspector Kelly, Mr. Churchill's personal bodyguard. It is always helpful to know something of the peculiarities, the likes and dislikes, of prominent persons when one is being held responsible for their safety.

Inspector Kelly was most helpful and willing in supplying details regarding Mr. Churchill, but his information was not comforting from a security point of view. The grand old warrior loved crowds and frequently disregarded all security arrangements in order to get close to, and sometimes lost in, the pressing, cheering throngs of admirers. At such times, he would permit Kelly to remain at his side, but took serious objection to any effort on the part of the police to form a tight, protective cordon around him. When good and ready to make his way out of the crowd, he appreciated some assistance from the police in clearing a way;

but this must be done as unobtrusively as circumstances would permit. Kelly's final advice was: "Watch him every minute if there's a crowd about. He can be gone in a flash."

The night passed without incident. Both Prime Ministers had retired early, as had most of their staffs and newspaper men who occupied the other eight coaches. They had had several strenuous days in the United States and were resting up in preparation for the Ottawa visit. The train was scheduled to arrive in Ottawa at nine o'clock in the morning. At about seven-thirty, we were given some indication that Mr. Churchill was in good health and that the tremendous strains and responsibilities of office were not having any great effect on his appetite. While passing through the lounge that we were occupying in Mr. Churchill's coach, a steward paused to display a tray that carried the huge breakfast that the Prime Minister had ordered. Certainly, the contents of the tray offered a great deal of fortification against the Canadian winter weather and the burdens of the forthcoming visit.

Members of the Cabinet, the Senate, leaders of the Opposition, and other Canadian dignitaries were to meet Mr. Churchill on the railway-station platform, and in order that the reception might be held close to the station and at the point where he would disembark, arrangements had been made whereby the train would be backed into the station.

About half an hour before arrival time, I went to the salon in Mackenzie King's car at the rear of the train. While awaiting the arrival of both Prime Ministers, I was deeply conscious of the tremendous burdens they carried. I wondered if anything in their attitudes or demeanours might give some hint of the outcome of the Conference, or indicate that the future was not as dark as it seemed by the news that reached the public from the war fronts.

The Canadian Prime Minister was the first to reach the salon. The Right Honourable Mackenzie King had ruled the Canadian parliamentary scene for some twenty years, an achievement that demonstrated his ability as a master politician and administrator, since he possessed few of the outward characteristics usually considered essential in a political leader and vote-getter. Unimpressive in appearance, quiet, and reserved in manner, his public image lacked the slightest hint of warmth or outgoing personality.

He entered the salon slowly and seemingly lost in deep and worrisome thought. After a few words of greeting, he sat in a straight-backed chair, knees together, hands folded in his lap, and head bowed, a rather prim and proper picture of dejection. If his appearance was a true reflection of the outcome of the Conference, we were in bad shape, indeed. A few minutes later, Mr. Churchill entered; and, at that moment, doubt and foreboding gave way to hope and optimism. His appearance, his tremendously forceful personality, his every move, exuded determination and confidence. In his presence, there could be no room for doubt. Victory would be ours! After chatting for a few minutes with Mr. King, Mr. Churchill crossed to join me at the exit door that led to the observation platform.

As I saluted, Mr. Churchill held out his hand and, as we shook hands, asked my name.

"Harvison, sir."

"Harvison – Harvison. That is an Old Country name."

"Yes, sir. My father came from Lincolnshire – my mother from the United States."

This brought a Churchillian "Hrmmph" and then, "American mother, eh?"

Up to that point, the brief conversation had been of routine small talk, used to fill in time, but the information that I, too, had an American mother seemed to catch his interest. He asked a few more questions regarding my family and service. He then made several very favourable comments regarding the Force, during which he displayed a gratifying and surprising knowledge of its work. Churchill made particular reference to the work of the RCMP Provost Corps overseas, and to the fact that the personnel, planes, and boats of our Air and Marine Divisions were on active duty with the armed services for the duration of the war. I was amazed that he had heard of and retained these details. While we were speaking, the train backed slowly around the curve leading to the station. In the distance, the station platform, crowded with dignitaries waiting to be presented to Churchill, came into view. At the far end of the platform, a temporary stage had been built to accommodate reporters, photographers, and radio announcers. Beyond them, through the glass partitions, we could glimpse the tremendous crowd that filled the rotunda.

The sight acted like a trumpet to an old cavalry charger. Churchill quickly signalled to an aid, who had been standing by with an overcoat, heavy muffler, and black Homburg. Despite my warning that it was very cold outside, he took time only to don his hat before stepping out into the icy blast. I stood with him at the rail of the observation platform. The train had stopped, and the crowds were still too far away to respond to his "V" for Victory signals. After a few minutes in the chill wind, he muttered, "Too bloody cold out here," and headed back into the coach.

A short time later, the train started to move slowly, and again the old warrior started for the door, but this time he paused long enough to don the overcoat and muffler. He then discarded the ordinary-sized cigar that he had been smoking, and from an inner pocket he drew forth and lighted a "torpedo" fully ten inches long. I opened the door for him, and as he passed through, he paused, momentarily, to deliberately hunch his shoulders into the well-remembered Churchill pose.

Now we were drawing close to the crowd, and as he appeared, hand raised in his famous "V" sign, a cheer went up from the waiting dignitaries, newsmen, and a small group of railway workers watching from a far platform. The cheer was taken up by those in the rotunda. The grand old war horse, who had been through a thousand receptions, most of them much larger than this, seemed moved and vastly pleased by the greeting and eager to get closer to the people.

While the Prime Minister was meeting the group that had gathered to welcome him, I sent a Constable to carry a message to Inspector Wilson, who was to take over responsibilities for security outside the station. My message repeated the warning I had received from Churchill's Security Officer, Inspector Kelly, regarding the Prime Minister's propensity to dodge security men and immerse himself in crowds. As we left the station, I saw that Inspector Wilson had taken heed of my warning. City, provincial, and RCMP men stood shoulder-to-shoulder forming a lane to the open door of a waiting limousine.

At the sight of Churchill and his "V" signal and waving cigar, a tremendous and continuous cheer went up from the thousands of people jamming the square. The Prime Minister paused for a moment, and then with shoulders hunched and jaw set in the old bull-dog look, he walked determinedly between the lines of policemen as though to enter the car. But at the end of the line, he suddenly veered left, squeezing between the last policeman and the limousine, and trotted out into the crowd. We lost him in the happy, cheering throng for about fifteen minutes. Inspector Kelly was at his side, and a few of us tried to ease the pressures a little, but it was clear that he was enjoying every moment of it. I noticed, also, that when the crowd pressed him too hard, he did not hesitate to make good use of his elbows.

When he had had enough, Churchill started working his way back to the car. The way was eased for him through the pressing crowd, and, after a series of stops while he set everyone to cheering by waving the still-huge cigar, we got him again to the start of the police lines.

The crowd had surged forward, and the police were having a hard time keeping the path open to the car. Camera men were being jostled about by the crowd and in their eagerness to get shots of Churchill, and because of the crush, they missed another subject that would have made an extraordinary and newsworthy photograph. Mackenzie King, usually pictured as sedate, aloof, and a little stuffy, had linked hands with the police in the centre of one of the lines and was pushing back manfully in an effort to clear a path. Grinning broadly, he seemed to be enjoying the experience and sharing the excitement and delight over Churchill's welcome to Canada. It has been widely reported that Winston Churchill was a very emotional man, and this is probably so. Certainly, he had the power to stir very strong and deep emotions in others.

His visit to Canada provided a surge of hope and determination toward victory in an already determined nation. He made two more visits to Canada during the war. In 1942 and again in 1943, the President of the United States and the Prime Ministers of Canada and Great Britain met at Quebec City, together with their Cabinets, military leaders, and advisors to plan global strategy in the pursuit of victory. The gatherings of the leaders of three nations posed security problems that, while small by comparison with the work of the Conference, were nevertheless of awesome size and importance. There have been few occasions in history when so many leaders have been brought together during wartime. An examination of the list of those attending the Conference was enough to shake even the most experienced security men.

Mackenzie King was attended by most of the members of his Cabinet and by the Chiefs of Staff. Prime Minister Churchill's party included the Foreign Secretary, Anthony Eden; Admiral of the Fleet, Sir Dudley Pound; Field Marshal, Sir Alan Brooks; Chief of the General Staff, Marshal of the Royal Air Force, Sir Charles Portal; and Admiral Lord Louis Mountbatten. Among President Roosevelt's advisors were such renowned wartime leaders as General George C. Marshall, General "Hap" Arnold, Admiral Leahy, and Admiral King.

The Force was fully conscious of the heavy responsibilities involved in providing security for each of these leaders and for assuring that their deliberation could be carried out in secrecy. The setting up of guard and pass systems, protection of documents, guarding against intrusion devices or interference with telephone circuits, and the supplying of escorts as conferees moved from place to place – all these called for expert planning of every detail with extreme care. An added difficulty was the requirement that security arrangements should be as unobtrusive as the situation would allow.

The Force had a man ideally suited for the task – Assistant Commissioner V. A. M. Kemp, a career policeman, whose ability had taken him from the humble rank of Special Constable Stenographer to one of the highest posts in the Force. He had had a wealth of experience in the planning and security field, and was known throughout the Force for his meticulous methods in planning operations. In his book *Without Fear, Favour, or Affection,* Kemp says of the Quebec Conference: "Perhaps those of us from the Mounted Police who were permitted to play our role could be forgiven a feeling of pride that we had been privileged to be on hand in even a humble capacity. It was not unnatural that we should sense the significance of the occasion. We realized that history was here, in the making, that a thousand years hence the citizens of the era might be taught the important decisions that were arrived at in Quebec."

He planned well and working with a carefully chosen staff made sure that the plans were carried out to the letter. The leaders went about their tremendous tasks with a minimum of inconvenience caused by security measures, although those measures were as close to being "air-tight" as they could be made. The fact that there were no incidents of an unwarranted nature during the Conference indicates that the safety of the galaxy of leaders was given adequate care. Even more important, there has never developed the slightest indication through friendly intelligence sources or from defectors, or from the files of the enemy, that there was the slightest leakage of information, or that security at the Quebec Conference was penetrated in any way.

In his planning, Kemp faced the usual problems of manpower, particularly during the 1943 Quebec Conference, when a number of extraordinary duties were making heavy demands on the resources of the Force. In meeting this problem, Kemp resorted to a solution that was used many times and in many ways during the war, the RCMP Reserve. I have already mentioned the very ready and welcome assistance extended by a group of business and professional men in Montreal on the outbreak of war. With the progress of war, and the increasing pressures of work, one hundred and fifty of those men were recruited, trained, and sworn in as members of the Reserve in Montreal.

In selecting men for this unit from among several hundred volunteers, particular attention was paid to the recruitment of members who were in a position to leave their normal employment on short notice to work with the Force. Attention was also paid to the selection of personnel whose occupation or profession gave them specialized knowledge that might – and, indeed, did – on many occasions, prove of value in our work. The men selected readily volunteered to undergo training, three evenings a week, for six months. At the end of that time, they were, if still considered suitable, sworn in and issued with the brown "patrol" uniform of the Force. Similar Reserve groups were set up in Toronto, Winnipeg, and Vancouver.

The eagerness of these men to serve is amply demonstrated by the remuneration granted them. There was no pay during the training period and, thereafter, whenever called out for duty, they were paid at the going, and low, rate for Constables. Certainly, it was not the pay that attracted the lawyers, doctors, chemists, and businessmen who formed the Reserve; but across Canada, several hundred men of high calibre were readily available to help in any emergency. Kemp made full use of these Reserves to supplement the regular members at the Quebec Conference and, as always, they carried out their duties in an exemplary manner.

An amusing incident involving one of the Reserves developed during the 1943 Quebec Conference. One of their members had been detailed for the "graveyard" (midnight to eight shift) to remain in one of the conference rooms to make sure that no unauthorized person entered. It was a dreary hum-drum chore, and in the very early morning hours, the

Reserve Constable, a somewhat portly gentleman, who had seen service as a Colonel in the Imperial Army during World War I, and who, when not serving with the Reserve, was the president of a large corporation, decided to make himself comfortable by loosening his tie and unbuttoning his tunic.

A few minutes later, the Sergeant Major entered the room on inspection rounds to find the Reserve Constable comfortably seated with his feet up on a desk. The Sergeant Major had been drawn from the training depot and was accustomed to dealing with and disciplining recruits, in which enterprise he had developed a suitably outstanding vocabulary. This he unleashed on the erring Reserve Constable. Having achieved the desired results by getting that member on his feet and properly buttoned up, the disciplinarian delivered a short, sharp warning as to the dire consequences of any future laxity and stormed from the room.

Just before lunch the following morning, the same Sergeant Major received word of changes in the program of Churchill. The Prime Minister would be having lunch with a friend in one of the small private dining-rooms. Guard postings were quickly altered to meet the change. To make sure there would be no slip-ups, the Sergeant Major took up a position in one of the corridors leading to the dining-room. It was a somewhat shaken Sergeant Major who saluted as Churchill and his friend walked by. The Prime Minister's luncheon companion was the Reserve Constable who had been so thoroughly dressed down during the night. It developed that he was an old school chum of Churchill's.

The Reserves performed yeomen service in a wide variety of emergencies. They manned the cars and carried out patrols along the lower St. Lawrence River during the months that German submarine sightings were being frequently reported. They served on various squads and particularly in assistance to the work of the security and intelligence branches. Detachments were reinforced by Reserves. They turned out to a man to assist regular members in policing the city of Montreal for a brief period when the municipal police went on strike. Whatever the emergency, a telephone relay system would bring at least two-thirds of their number into the barracks within an hour. An excellent spirit of camaraderie grew between the Regulars and the Reserves, and the Reserves became an accepted, welcome, and respected part of the Force.

While the work was heavy, there was time for the occasional bit of fun. One of these occurred as the result of an old and routine task carried out annually on behalf of the department of Government whose particular concern was the preservation of wild life. During the winter of each year, the Force received a plentiful supply of lengthy and detailed forms which detachment members were required to complete in order that the Department might gain knowledge of the snow-shoe rabbit population.

The Department did not suspend its interest in the habits and love-life of snow-shoe rabbits during the war, and in 1943, the usual batch of forms was received. These were given normal distribution, but, in addition, I sent copies to one of the Reserve Constables with a covering letter in which he was curtly instructed to complete the form after making a survey in the Laurentian Mountains. I rather expected a "what-the-hell" type of phone inquiry, but several weeks went by before there was a reaction. Eventually, the incompleted form was returned with a report which read: "Sir, I have the honour to report that during the last two weekends, I have made several lengthy patrols out of resorts located in the Laurentian Mountains. I can not complete the attached form since I saw no rabbits on snow-shoes. However, I did see many wolves on skis; and they seemed to have the same sort of thing in mind."

The Reserves gave invaluable assistance to regular members in an almost unbelievable episode that centered on a prisoner of war camp at Grand-Ligne, about thirty miles south of Montreal. The case necessitated the use of a large number of men for several months, and while the end result did not turn out as desired, the work of the several services concerned did defeat an utterly fantastic plot on the part of the Germans.

Prisoner of war camps were set up in Canada early in the war to receive prisoners taken overseas and thus relieve the strain on England. The guarding of the camps was the responsibility of the army, a function that they performed admirably, for there were very few escapes, and most escapees were quickly recaptured. Several of the camps were located in deep bush country in the northern parts of the provinces. At those sites, the remoteness, lack of roads, and hordes of mosquitoes in the summer months, and severe weather in winter discouraged escape attempts to a point where guard duties were not particularly heavy. However, there were prisoner of war camps located close to highways and large cities where it was necessary to maintain maximum-security precautions. Grand-Ligne was one of these.

Within the camp, the prisoners lived under the immediate control and discipline of their own senior officers and under conditions laid down by the army in accordance with the Geneva Convention. The camps were designated as white, gray, or black, and an attempt was made to separate prisoners into these categories and camps according to their character and record. The black camps contained officers and prisoners judged most likely to cause trouble or try to escape. Grand-Ligne, although in a thickly populated area, close to large centres, was a "black" camp. It housed about two hundred officers and four hundred other ranks. Overall security for camps in the military district was under the control of veteran Army Officer Major Ray Fairweather, a strict and able administrator. The Grand Ligne camp had a reputation as one of the best-guarded in the country.

In the summer of 1943, Naval Intelligence Officers approached the Commissioner with a very strange but true story. Their Service had succeeded in breaking a code being used by Germany to channel messages into Grand-Ligne. The messages had been discovered in the bindings of books, sent from Germany by the Red Cross, along with maps, Canadian and American currency, Canadian National Registration Certificates, and very detailed plans for the escape of some important prisoners.

Included among the Grand-Ligne prisoners were seven of Germany's leading experts in the engineering and building of submarines. These men had been captured in the North Sea by the Royal Navy during the trial run of a new design of German submarine. Their loss was a severe blow to Germany's submarine-building program. The High Command was willing to go to any lengths to secure their return.

The coded messages found in the book bindings instructed the German officers in command within the Grand-Ligne camp to concentrate on an effort to arrange the escape of nineteen of the prisoners, which was to include the seven submarine experts. The other twelve escapees were to run interference for the engineers by causing confusion among the pursuers. The engineers were to make their way to a point on the shores of New Brunswick where they would be picked up by a submarine. The instructions detailed the signal that would bring the submarine inshore, and it was clear from the secret orders that the map indicated the precise point at which the submarine would be waiting. But in the early stages, this particular point of the plan had not been decoded or discovered.

To this fantastic story, Naval Intelligence, during the first meeting with the Commissioner on this subject, added an almost equally incredible request. They had very compelling reasons for wanting to capture the German submarine, reasons that went far beyond the normal desire to make such a catch. Accordingly they requested that the nineteen men be allowed to escape and that the Force then arrange to "shadow" the escapees to the then-unknown point on the coast.

I was summoned to Ottawa to a conference that included the Commissioner and other officers together with representatives of Naval Intelligence. At this first meeting, we reached the rather obvious conclusion that any thought of "shadowing" escapees for some six hundred miles must be ruled out as totally impracticable. The decoded messages indicated that there had been previous instructions and that a start had been made within the camp toward preparing for a mass escape. It was also decided that the maps, currency, and other documents should receive further intensive examination in an attempt to discover the exact spot on the coast to which the escapees were to proceed. Following such study and the photographing of the documents, they would be replaced in the book bindings and delivered to the camp through normal channels.

We knew that other coded messages about the escape plan had already reached the prisoners.

In the meantime, there were two definite probabilities. First, the most likely plan for escape would be by way of tunnelling from the central building to a point beyond the perimeter of security fencing. Second, the work of tunnelling would already be underway.

I was instructed to make a survey of the camp in an attempt to learn if tunnelling was, in fact, in progress, without taking any action that might indicate to the prisoners that the plot had been discovered. Shortly after returning to Montreal, I paid a visit to Major Fairweather and, with him, went over the blueprints of the camp. The central building was an old stone, three-storey structure that had served as a boys' school. Several temporary frame buildings had been erected as additional sleeping quarters for the prisoners and as cook houses and dining and recreation rooms. The entire establishment was surrounded by a high, barbed-wire fence. At the front of the property, an eight-foot wooden fence had been put up outside the barbed wire in order to obstruct the view from a public road that paralleled the camp area. Between the fence and the road, there was a six-foot ditch, and beyond the road were open fields. If tunnelling was planned, it seemed likely that it would be from the central building, which housed most of the prisoners, toward the ditch, which would offer some cover during the escapes.

The following night, by arrangement with Major Fairweather, a technician and I crawled along the lip of earth between the fence and the ditch working with a microphone attached to a long probe which we pushed into the ground every few yards. We soon found that tunnelling was indeed underway. Judging from the sounds that reached us over the microphone, the tunnel already extended a considerable distance from the main building toward the centre of the wooden fence. We could clearly hear sounds of digging – long drawn-out scraping noises, as the receptacles containing loose earth were dragged back along the tunnel. At times, we could hear voices. The sounds were distant and muffled but unmistakable.

Escape plans and attempts are part of the normal and expected occupations of prisoners of war, and the possibility existed that the tunnelling that we heard was not connected with the plot to bring about the escape of the submarine experts. However, most attempts are carried out under the control, and with the assistance of camp "escape committees." It seemed most unlikely that the committee would sanction such an ambitious attempt as the digging of a three-hundred-foot tunnel as a separate operation at a time when they were working on a major break under directions received from the German High Command.

The following day we learned from Ottawa that there had been an important development there. A member of the Intelligence Branch,

Corporal (later Inspector) C. Bayfield, had been successful in discovering the secret of the map taken from the book binding. We now knew the exact point on the New Brunswick coast where, according to German planners, a submarine would pick up the escapees.

In the light of these developments, a new plan was worked out. During escape attempts, the method usually employed is to have a prisoner, not a member of the escape group, at each end of the tunnel. Signals between the men are transmitted by means of a cord. On the receipt of the "all-clear" message from the outside lookout, an escapee crawls through the tunnel and disappears into the night. An interval of several minutes is usually allowed between the "all-clear" signals, presumably to give each escapee time to get clear of the environs of the camp. Another advantage of this intermittent system is that the discovery and capture of one escapee does not necessarily lead to the capture of all who had passed through the tunnel, and those waiting their turn would quickly disperse within the camp on the receipt of an alarm signal from outside.

Since the mass break-out planned by the Germans involved the escape of nineteen prisoners, it was clear that if they followed usual procedures it would take from two to three hours to complete the operation. It was important to our plan that all nineteen be permitted to escape; there should be no disturbance to indicate to the prisoners in the camp that their scheme had gone wrong; and we should secure all documents in the possession of the escapees, particularly those carried by the seven submarine experts as a means of identification to the submarine Captain.

To meet these requirements, it was arranged that every evening immediately after nightfall a semi-circle of our men, a quarter of a mile deep, would form in the fields of the farms opposite the front of the camp and across the road from the deep ditch toward which the tunnel was being directed. The semi-circle was divided into sections, each of which was equipped with a walkie-talkie. The men forming the circle would be alerted that the actual escape was underway by a signal from an observation point overlooking the ditch. It would then be their job to wait until each escapee had reached the perimeter of the semi-circle and then make the capture as silently and quickly as possible. The plan was filled with "if's" and "but's," but it was the best we could devise under the circumstances.

In the event of success in the first phase of the operation, the second phase would be the release to news media of information regarding the mass break, but nothing about the capture of the escapees. We were aware that German submarines in the St. Lawrence and off the East Coast listened to Canadian radio broadcasts, and it seemed altogether probable that they would have been alerted to expect news of the escape.

From then on the intention was to simulate the German plans. From time to time announcements would be released regarding the capture of one or two of the escapees. These announcements would be in some detail regarding documents carried by the prisoners and would include the names of the individuals, but the seven submarine men would not be among those reported as captured. These reports of alleged captures would be made from points coming closer to the New Brunswick coast line, to the point where the submarine would be waiting.

The third phase in this strange plan — and, in fact, the reason for the whole operation – was to capture the submarine intact. The chances of success were infinitesimal, but the importance of the objective aboard the submarine made the gamble worthwhile, even in the face of tremendous odds. Seven German-speaking volunteers, among them our "Johnny" who had been active in the case of the "double-agent" spy case and who had served in German subs during World War I, were to be given special training by the Navy. It would be their job, when the time was right, to take up a position in an abandoned fish shed that stood on the shore at the point where the submarine would be waiting. After the exchange of the prearranged signal, which we had learned from the decoded messages, the seven volunteers were to board a lobster boat which, for the benefit of advance observation from the submarine, would have been placed on the wharf of the fish shed. The seven volunteers were then to row out to the submarine and attempt to bring about its capture.

In that dangerous and improbable venture, they could hope for some assistance and reinforcements from "Fairmile" speedboats which would remain concealed along the shore until the moment for action arrived. I think it was extremely fortunate for the volunteers that the plot did not come off. Submarine skippers are an extremely alert and touchy breed, particularly when they have brought their craft close to shoreline dangers. The volunteers were brave men training for an heroic endeavour, but the chances were that, had the plot come off, they would have been dead but unsuccessful heroes.

As an operational centre, we rented a vacant and isolated farmhouse about five miles from the Grand-Ligne Camp. Into this tumble-down structure, which was promptly named "Bleak House" by the men, we crowded about fifty regular and reserve members, together with a cook and cooking utensils. Each evening, as soon as darkness had fallen, the men were transported to the side-road close to the camp but out of sight, and from there they made their way quietly to their appointed positions in the semi-circle. Since the fields were in view of the upper windows of the main building, the movements of the police had to be carried out with considerable stealth.

Having taken up their positions, the men were required to remain quiet until just before dawn when they crept out of the fields to assemble at the pick-up point for transportation back to the slim and sketchy hospitality of "Bleak House." The operation continued for a little more than two months and called for a considerable degree of fortitude on the part of the members involved, particularly the Reserves, some of whom were getting on in years, and all of whom were working on an entirely voluntary basis. The weather was not kind, and during many of the nights there was a steady downpour of cold Autumn rain. When rain was not falling, clouds of mosquitoes of the twin-motored, dive-bomber variety made life miserable. These tiny marauders could not be driven off by cigarette smoke, since lighted cigarettes could have been seen from the upper floors of the camp building.

At least once each night use was made of the microphone probe and, as time went on, the sounds of scraping, digging, and occasionally of voices, came closer, until toward the end the sounds were quite distinct and clear, as though within a few feet of the probe. Digging started at about nine each evening and continued until just before morning roll-call at six o'clock. While tunnelling is slow business, the sounds indicated that the Germans were making progress and might make the break-through any night.

Frequent meetings were held with Major Fairweather, whose home was immediately adjacent to the camp. Nearing the end of the second month, during one of these meetings, he advised me that his men felt that there was unusual tension among the prisoners. The guards believed that there was something unusual afoot. We were discussing the probabilities when an NCO arrived in some haste to advise the major that a prisoner had been found hiding in some bushes in an "out-of-bounds" area just inside the barbed-wire fence at the side of the camp.

While it seemed unlikely that this incident was connected with the wholesale break that concerned us, I was anxious to see the point where the man had been found. Fairweather and I hurriedly left his home and followed the patrol path that paralleled the fence. We had reached about the half-way point when, suddenly, two figures broke from some bushes and started to race away. Fairweather fired a warning shot at which the racing figures hit the dirt and remained prone until ordered to get up. They were marched to the guard room and thoroughly searched. Both men were wearing bulky hoods of the type often used by the Germans in escape attempts, partly to cover the whiteness of their faces, which might reveal them to pursuers, and partly as a protection against the hordes of mosquitoes.

The prisoners' clothing contained several packets of bread, and each of the prisoners carried a knife that had been stolen from the kitchen; but there were no documents of the sort manufactured and supplied by escape committees to help escapees establish an identity if their attempt proved successful. It was clear that this break had been made without the sanction or assistance of the camp's escape committee.

It may be that their abortive attempt discouraged the other prisoners or brought about a delay in the planning for the escape of the nineteen men. Probably by some undiscovered means, the German officers in the camp received orders to discontinue their plot. Whatever the cause, the tunnelling work ceased that night. We continued the operation for two or three weeks, but the microphone was quiet.

It was decided to put an end to our activities and those of the prisoners by searching the camp. Earth, from the tunnel, the conceal-ment of which is always a major problem for prisoners, was found hidden in cupboards, under floor boards, and in partitions that had been carefully opened. The tunnel was a bit of a masterpiece in engineering, and it led from the foundation of the central building to within a few feet of the ditch outside the fence, a distance of about three hundred feet. Had the tunnelling continued without interruption, the semi-circle of guards would not have waited much longer for action. At it turned out, what might have been a vastly interesting and possibly productive operation ended in an anti-climax.

The tight rationing of liquor during the war years brought about a resumption in the traffic of illicit alcohol, but it did not reach anything like pre-war proportions. Some of the former experts and conspirators were still serving jail terms, while most of the others had found more lucrative rackets in such fields as trafficking in counterfeit or stolen ration coupons and registration cards, smuggling of high-grade gold, and taking part in black-market and foreign-exchange schemes. The illicit alcohol business was therefore largely in the hands of enthusiastic amateurs.

During a search for one of these amateurs, an incident occurred which might have proven serious if it had not been comical. Information had been received that a still was being operated by one of small com-munity farmers on the outskirts of Montreal, most of whom were of Polish descent. The information was not definite as to the exact location of the culprit's farm.

Late one night, I accompanied a small group of members of the Liquor Squad, one of whom spoke Polish, to the suspected area. It was our hope that, by quietly approaching each of the farms, the tell-tale odour of mash would reveal the location of the still. Two farms were visited in this surreptitious manner without incident or indication of illegal operation. At the third farm, as we moved slowly toward the darkened house, a dog started to bark, and a light went on in the kitchen. A few moments later, the back door opened, and a man stepped out. We crouched in the deep grass, hoping that he would not see us.

Suddenly there was a flash, and a terrific blast as he loosed a charge from a shotgun in our direction. The Polish-speaking chap was next to me, and I whispered to him to call out, in Polish, to advise the farmer that we were policemen. His shouted message brought no response for a few moments. Then came the reply, "You're a liar. Policemen don't speak Polish." This was immediately followed by a blast from the second barrel. Fortunately nobody was hit.

After a time we succeeded in convincing the farmer that we were indeed policemen. He had been well within his rights in taking pot shots at midnight prowlers and had every reason to resent and resist our presence. However, when the reason for our visit was explained, he proved most understanding and forgiving. Not only did he excuse the intrusion, he directed us to a farm operated by a non-Polish farmer where a fairly large still was found in operation.

An interesting facet of the public's reaction to news accounts of the progress of war was brought to our attention whenever the newspapers and radio carried information of a set-back or defeat. At such times, the office would be flooded by telephone calls, letters, and visitors volunteering information regarding alleged espionage or subversive activities. When France fell, when Hong Kong was lost, and again when the Canadian troops suffered heavy losses at Dieppe, the flood became so heavy as to require the setting up of a large, special staff to receive visitors and to handle mail and telephone calls.

Almost always, the information was the result of overwrought imaginations, but every scrap of information required checking. There was always the long chance that the information might contain a grain of truth. More important was the need for reassuring the public as to the interest and alertness of the security service.

Bad news from overseas had an entirely different and heart-warming affect on one of the citizens of the North Country, Chief Moses of Old Crow in the Yukon Territory. Old Crow is a small, isolated village of log houses on the banks of a river. Members of the Indian band headed by Chief Moses are scattered throughout the surrounding bush country. They and their fellows in the town must work hard and long to eke out a meagre living. Money is hard to come by in that part of the world.

Chief Moses heard of the bombings in London and was deeply affected by the tragic news. As more stories of the bombings reached his village, he became particularly moved by the thoughts of the children who were being killed or maimed or orphaned. With the knowledge of such suffering weighing heavily on him, the old gentleman could not sit idly by, even though the holocausts were being visited on a city and a people thousands of miles away which he had never seen and to whom

Law and Order comes to a 'vast lone land.'

George Arthur French, CNG, first commissioner of the NWMP. His mission: to bring peace to the riotous Northwest. In 1874 he led the Force on its famous march to the foothills of the Rockies

Fort Calgary, now the city site, was built by Inspector F. A. Brisebois and "F" troop of the NWMP in 1875. The photo, April, 1879, is the first ever taken of the Fort

Third from left, James F. Macleod, CNG, second Commissioner

This group of officers displays the original uniform of the Force 1875

Dr. Kitson; Miss Graham, first white woman to enter Fort Walsh 1878

Horse Camp near Fort Walsh where black horses used by Force were bred

These Mounties endured three months of slogging, starvation, and thirst in their epic 1,000-mile trek westward from Fort Dufferin

Two officers of the North West Mounted Police standing by their mounts at Banff in 1888, create an impressive picture of authority

The North West Mounted Police 1888. Standing left to right, Inspectors Routledge, Nathan, Moffat, Norman, Cotton, and MacPherson. Seated, from left to right, Superintendent Jarvis and Inspector Constantine and son

NWMP Detachment near Revelstoke, British Columbia. Seated in the chair is Inspector Samuel Benfield Steele (later Major-General Sir Sam Steele). He was the third man sworn into the NWMP

This photo, dated 1900, is of the now-famous Musical Ride which began with the NWMP

A full dress Mounted Parade on the occasion of the visit of the Duke of Cornwall and York to Calgary, September, 1901

Tent and horse lines, Rockcliffe, 1921, now the site of "N" Division, training centre for eastern Canada, RCMP Air Division, and Laboratory

Harvison attending to his mount, Regina, 1932. "We had just escorted the Lieutenant-Governor to the opening of the Provincial Legislature."

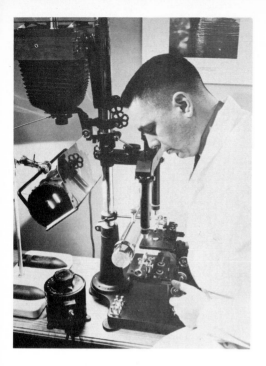

The
Force
continues
to
expand
and
'Maintiens
le
Droit.'

This RCMP Laboratory at Ottawa is one of the four scientific laboratories across Canada

Communications Centre at Headquarters in Ottawa

At Interpol Conference, Madrid, 1962, Assistant Commissioner W. L. Higgit, Deputy Commissioner G. B. McClellan, and delegate from France

LEFT:
At "N" Division, Ottawa, 1962. Haile Selassie, Emperor of Ethiopia, leaves barracks to see special performance of Musical Ride

OPPOSITE LEFT:
Vancouver, B.C., July 1958. H.R.H. Princess Margaret attends theatre. Behind, Colonel the Honourable Frank Mackenzie Ross, Lieutenant-Governor of B.C.

OPPOSITE RIGHT:
May 23, 1961. The late Governor General Georges P. Vanier arrives at "N" Division for annual Mess Dinner commemorating founding of Force in 1873.

Mrs. Jacqueline Kennedy arrives with Mrs. Diefenbaker at "N" Division to see performance of Musical Ride

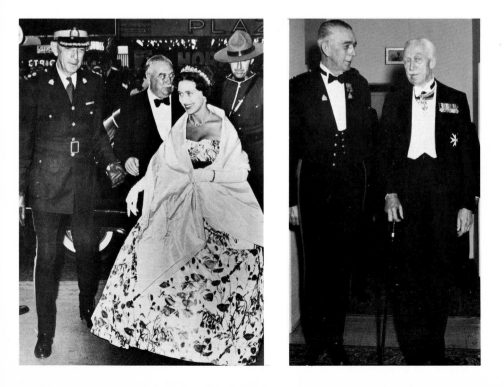

*Formations
in the
Musical Ride*

The Star

The Maze

The Dome

This photo of an RCMP Beachcraft (one of the eighteen aircraft belonging to the Force) illustrates how well-equipped the Force is today

"Commissioner" class patrol boat, custodian of the Atlantic seaboard

Western Arctic Patrol

Early justice in the Northwest. "Trial of a Whiskey Trader, High River"
PHOTO – *Glenbow Foundation. Artist; Neavit*

Igor Gouzenko, former Russian Embassy clerk whose revelations cracked Soviet spy ring in Canada, 1946, conceals his identity during an interview with columnist Drew Pearson at an undisclosed place in Canada
PHOTO – *World Wide* (AP). *Wheeler Newspaper Syndicate*

Lucien Rivard, "cocky and in control." Charge of breaking out of Bordeaux Jail withdrawn to speed up extradition to U.S. for narcotics conspiracy charges
PHOTO – *Toronto Star Syndicate*

Hal Banks, 15-years' President of the SIU, ousted and sentenced to five years in jail for conspiracy to assault a rival union leader
PHOTO – *Toronto Star Syndicate*

Adrien Arcand, long-time leader of the Canadian Fascist Party. He died in Montreal, August 1, 1967, after a prolonged illness
PHOTO – *Toronto Star Syndicate*

Gypsum Queen Inquiry, 1934. Captain Freeman Hatfield, defrauder, caught after long pursuit, sentenced to four years' imprisonment
PHOTO – *Toronto Star Syndicate*

The RCMP *Band*

The Farewell Mess Dinner on the retirement of Commissioner Harvison

he and his people owed nothing. Something, some effort, must be made to help the children.

Chief Moses visited all of his people, which, in that country, where travel is hard, was of itself a goodly effort. In his travelling, he sought subscriptions to a special fund which he had set up, and the good people of Old Crow raised a sum of seven hundred dollars, every dollar of which had been hard-earned and none of which could be easily spared. Seven hundred dollars is a sizable fortune in that area. The money was placed in an envelope and addressed to the King of England, London. A note was enclosed in which it was directed that the money was to be used for the poor children who suffered from the bombings.

Chief Moses was named a member of the Order of the British Empire in the next List of Honours granted by the King. Never has recognition been more deeply deserved or more proudly received. The old gentleman died in 1965, but I had the great pleasure and privilege of meeting him in 1960 when I toured the Yukon to inspect the RCMP detachments, one of which is located at Old Crow.

It was winter, and our ski-equipped police plane landed on the ice of the river close to the rather high embankment on which the village is built. As is always the case in small northern communities, almost the entire population was waiting for the plane to welcome the visitors, but the Chief was not there. He had followed his customary, self-developed, and imposed procedure. On the approach of the plane, he had donned his parka, put on the cap with the word "Chief" in gold letters, pinned on the insignia of his Order, and walked to the foot of the village flagstaff from which the Union Jack fluttered. Visitors were required to climb the embankment and proceed to the flagstaff to present themselves to Chief Moses, O.B.E. In my view, this could not have been improved on by all the learned masters of procedure and protocol in the land.

There had usually been reasonably satisfactory co-operation between police forces in Canada – federal, provincial, and municipal. But the demands and pressures of the war years brought them even closer together. This worked to the advantage of all police in their efforts to combat increasing crime. In the carrying out of new duties imposed by the war effort, the spirit of close liaison and co-operation brought incalculable benefits to the Royal Canadian Mounted Police. Other forces, despite the fact that they, too, were under strength, and that many of their experienced officers and men were serving overseas, extended the utmost assistance in response to every request. The work of our Force would have been much more difficult, if not impossible, but for the willing help received from other law-enforcement bodies.

This spirit of close team-work was continued after World War II and has been enhanced by the work of the Canadian Association of Chiefs of Police, by regional police associations, the Canadian Society for Industrial Security, and, of course, by personal friendships that had developed. Despite stresses and strains brought about by questions of jurisdiction, responsibility, some necessary secrecy, and, occasionally, by political pressures, the police in Canada work in close harmony. When it is considered that the combined strength of all forces policing Canada, an area somewhat larger than the United States, is twenty-six thousand, or approximately the same as the strength of the New York City Police, it will be realized that close co-operation and teamwork is essential.

The war also brought closer ties and co-operation with police and Intelligence services in other countries, partly because of confidence and friendships developed and partly because the changing patterns of crime and counter-espionage necessitated close international relationship. In the police field, the opening of liaison offices in London and Washington, membership in Interpol, and in the International Association of Chiefs of Police assure the continuance of team-work among law-enforcement agencies of many countries.

Throughout the war years, necessity dictated an acceleration in the rate of change and modernization within the Force, improvements that under normal conditions and normal resistance to change would have taken many years were speedily brought about. By 1945, the Force had completed the transition from a frontier police to a modern, law-enforcement, security, and counter-intelligence organization. Some pride may be taken by members of the Force and its civilian employees and Reserves in the fact that during those busy years normal policing duties were carried on without serious let-up while, at the same time, the heavy burden of new duties received close and efficient attention.

At the end of the war, files of the German Intelligence services came into the hands of the Allies. While those files revealed a great deal of information regarding the operation of enemy espionage services, there is not the slightest indication that the Germans, or the Italians, were successful in any of their attempts to plant agents in Canada, or to secure classified information from Canadians. Probably I should emphasize that I am speaking here of our success in countering the espionage agencies of the countries with whom we were at war. Subsequent events were to prove that the Soviet Union had been successful in setting up several widespread nets of spies, both Russian and Canadian.

14

-»»-»»-»»-»»-«-«-«-«-«-

Igor Gouzenko
and
Soviet Espionage

I was just beginning to enjoy the relief and relaxation brought about by the ending of hostilities when, early in September of 1945, orders were received from the Commissioner by which I was transferred to Winnipeg. As was the custom, very little time was allowed for the move. I was given two weeks in which to wind up outstanding matters, hand over my work to my successor, get the household furnishings packed and shipped, and report to the Officer Commanding in Winnipeg.

Doris and I realized that we had been extremely fortunate. Transfers were frequent and, in the case of officers, postings averaged about three years. We had been married eighteen years and had been permitted to spend all of that time in Montreal. We had not suffered the disruption of friendships and the breaking of contacts that result from frequent moves. We had been fortunate in another way. Our son, Weston, had been able to complete public-school classes and reach the final year of high school without interruption. An overall consideration was that Winnipeg is considered one of the more desirable postings and is the site of an excellent university.

My duties in Winnipeg were to be those of Officer in Charge of Detectives, and I looked forward to working in a Contract Division, in which the Force, apart from federal work, acted as provincial police and, in about a dozen towns, as municipal police. The posting promised valuable experience. As it developed, it was to be more than a year before I could settle into the work in Winnipeg.

We had been there only two or three weeks and were just in the process of moving into our new home, when urgent instructions were

147

received that I was to report to the Commissioner in Ottawa as quickly as possible. On boarding the plane for the flight east, I met Inspector Anthony from Vancouver, who, I discovered, had also received a summons to Ottawa. Our instructions had contained no hint as to the reason for the hurried trip, and this gave rise to some concern. The ever-present possibility that we had done or were thought to have done something that was about to bring the wrath of the Commissioner upon us was discussed as a first possibility. That theory was discarded on the grounds that, since we had never worked together, we could not have erred together. The rest of the trip was taken up with guessing the reason for the sudden call. The unusual procedure of summoning officers from widely separated divisions indicated that there had been developments of considerable importance. It seemed a reasonable guess, since Anthony and I had spent most of our service in criminal-investigation work, and in the counter-intelligence efforts of the Force, that the work ahead would be in one of those fields.

We were not left long in doubt. Commissioner Wood received us immediately following our arrival in the headquarters building. For the first time, we heard the name Gouzenko, and the story of his defection from the Russian Embassy, the story of a courageous man who risked his life to do a great service for Canada and the Western World, by supplying, for the first time, an authenticated revelation of the sprawling subversive and espionage networks operated by the Soviet Union.

The so-called Gouzenko Spy Case was destined to receive world-wide publicity. It has been the subject of a voluminous and very informative report by a Royal Commission. Several books have been written around the story, and it has even been turned into a motion picture. Thousands of newspaper articles have appeared, and magazines have serialized the tale. The name "Gouzenko" became almost a household word, but all that was very much in the future when Anthony and I were called in. Gouzenko had told his story. If true, it would be of inestimable value because it would alert the Western World as to the existence and methods of the burgeoning Soviet espionage apparatus. In the early stages, the big question in the minds of those who had been brought into the still top-secret matter was, "Is his story true," and if so, "Can the truth be established beyond a reasonable doubt?"

Having brought us up to date on these developments, Commissioner Wood went on to say that the Government had not reached a decision as to the course of action it would follow, partly because it was waiting for some confirmation of Gouzenko's allegations and partly because Prime Minister Mackenzie King considered it a very "hot potato." Pending a decision, the Commissioner was determined that the Force should be fully prepared to play its part in the event that the Government decided on stern measures.

Experienced investigators had already started on the huge task of minutely checking and seeking proof of every detail contained in Gouzenko's statement and in the documents that he claimed to have removed from the Soviet Embassy. Inspector Anthony and I had been chosen to handle the interrogation of persons named in the documents, if such interrogations were made necessary by future developments. For the present we were to prepare ourselves for these possible duties by studying Gouzenko's statement, examining the documents, checking all relevant intelligence files, and by interviewing Gouzenko himself.

While the story of this espionage case has been told over and over again, there are parts that bear retelling from the point of view of one who was engaged in the investigation and there are a few bits and pieces that have not yet been told.

For some years the Force had been aware, through its counter-intelligence work, that the USSR's Embassy in Ottawa was engaged in espionage and in recruiting espionage agents. On several occasions, warnings and some evidence regarding the penetration of Government departments had been given to the Government. But the Gouzenko documents disclosed an espionage apparatus that went far beyond our knowledge or suspicion, an apparatus that had successfully penetrated many departments, including the Armed Services, the National Research Council, the Department of Munitions and Supply, the Wartime Information Board, the Canadian Information Service, and Parliament itself.

Scientists, university professors, officers of the Armed Services, secretaries, and clerks had been recruited into the espionage nets from the Communist Party of Canada. The network reached into the office of the High Commissioner of the United Kingdom in Canada. Other ramifications extended directly to the United Kingdom, to the United States, and to France.

Through their espionage networks, which had operated under the direct control of Moscow, the Soviets had secured a great deal of information and copies of many documents regarding matters of top-secret nature, including secrets that had been entrusted to Canada by other countries. Gouzenko's documents established, also, that Soviet espionage and the NKVD, or Soviet Secret Police, had been active in Canada since the early twenties – thus exploding the myth that the Communists in Canada were independent of control from Moscow.

Leaders of the Party in Canada, working under the direction of the Soviet Embassy, had selected persons from the Party or its front groups as prospects for espionage work, conditioned them to undertake such treasonable activities, and after receiving Moscow's approval through the Embassy had recruited them into the network. In several instances, notably that of Fred Rose, the Canadian Communist leader and a Member of Parliament, Canadian Reds had served as spy masters, but always under the close control and direction of the Embassy.

In the early stages, a defector is always regarded with caution and scepticism by professionals in the intelligence field. The basic questions require full and convincing answers. Why did the person defect? Is his story true? In the case of Gouzenko, there was also the need to establish the authenticity of the documents he brought with him. In replying to questions as to the reasons for his defection, Gouzenko gave convincing answers.

In conversation, after some preliminary stalling while he tried to take the measure of his interrogators, Gouzenko was direct and abrupt. In addition to having a remarkable memory, he was obviously a highly intelligent and gifted man. This early appraisal was born out by the calm, cool manner in which he withstood the attacks of the many defence counsels during the subsequent trials. Some years later, his novel *Fall of a Titan* became a bestseller and received wide acclaim from the critics. He had ability, too, as an artist. Professionals who have examined his paintings claimed that he might well have made a career in that field.

Gouzenko was not a humble man given to underestimating his own ability. In fact, one got the impression that his considerable talent was somewhat outstripped by his estimation of that talent. Undoubtedly, the reasons for his defection were as given in his statement to the Royal Commission, but I believe that his vanity provided additional motivation. The Soviets had failed to recognize him as a borderline genius, or to promote him to a rank more in keeping with his intellectual powers. Resentment of that slight might well have been blended with his other reasons for defecting.

Members of the Force assigned to him experienced little difficulty in establishing the authenticity and accuracy of the documents that had been part of the secret files of the Soviet Embassy. Handwritten reports, said by Gouzenko to have been received from Canadian agents, were compared with the known writings of the Canadians mentioned and found to be identical. Typewritten documents submitted by agents had been typed on machines in offices of the suspects. Photographic and photostatic copies of secret documents were checked with the departments concerned. We discovered that the originals had been drawn from the files by the suspects just before the receipt of the copies by the Soviet spy masters. The dossier of one Canadian agent mentioned a streetcorner meeting with a Soviet Embassy man during a very heavy downpour. The meeting, according to the dossier, had taken place months before the defection of Gouzenko. Records of the Meteorological

Bureau showed that at the time and date given for the meeting Ottawa had had the heaviest downpour of the month.

The files contained frequent mention of the movements of members of the Soviet Embassy staff and of Canadian agents. Some of these were verified from our own files, which contained reports from members who had had the persons mentioned under surveillance at the very time referred to in the Soviet documents. Other dates and places were confirmed through hotel registers and travel agencies.

Even the folders that held the documents were found to have been purchased by the Soviet Embassy from an Ottawa stationery supply company. Beyond question, the Gouzenko documents were authentic; and beyond question, they established a conspiracy that had been controlled from Moscow through its diplomatic representatives in Canada and with the connivance and willing support of at least some of the leaders of the Communist movement in Canada. Through this conspiracy, the Soviets had succeeded in securing a great deal of secret and important information, including details in the field of atomic research, radar, the American "vt fuse," and samples of Uranium-235, enriched with Uranium-233. In commenting on the material secured by this espionage network, the report of the Royal Comission says:

> *In conclusion, therefore, we can say that much vital technical information, which should still be secret to the authorities of Canada, Great Britain, and the United States, has been made known to the Russians by reason of the espionage activities reported herein. The full extent of the information handed over is impossible to say. As we have already pointed out, these operations have been going on for some time. We should emphasize that the bulk of the technical information sought by espionage leaders related to research developments which would play an important part in the postwar defense of Canada, the United Kingdom, and the United States.*

Inspector Anthony and I spent about three months studying the Gouzenko story and documents, and in familiarizing ourselves with the backgrounds of the various persons involved. As no decision had been reached by the middle of December, we were told to return to our respective divisions and await further instructions.

Almost four months had elapsed since Gouzenko walked away from the Embassy laden with deeply incriminating papers, which the Government now knew to be authentic, but there was still much apprehension and doubt in high places. In Ottawa, the indications were that the Government, or at least Prime Minister Mackenzie King, regarded the entire affair as a politically dangerous and a personally embarrassing annoyance. It has been said of Mackenzie King that he never made a decision on a controversial matter so long as it remained controversial. However, the Gouzenko affair did not allow much room for manoeuvring. It could not be shelved indefinitely, nor did the circumstances permit the often-used device of sampling public opinion before committing the Government to a definite course. The matter was of vital importance to the United Kingdom and to the United States and could not, therefore, be treated as a matter for Canadian consideration alone. Further, a member of Parliament, officers of the Armed Services, and scientific and professional employees of the Government were involved. A too-lengthy delay would bring criticism at home and from abroad, while whatever decision might be made would, beyond question, bring great controversy.

Mackenzie King had reached the twilight of his career. Concern with the affairs of state had given way, in large measure, to consideration of the niche he would occupy, or hoped to occupy, in history. The Gouzenko affair threatened to disturb that niche, and King seemed to regard it as a personal problem and affront. His first reaction on being told of the defection, and of the contents of the documents, had been to urge that Gouzenko be taken back to the Embassy, together with the papers he had removed. Having been brought to reconsider that suggestion, there had remained, in the early weeks, some hope that the situation might prove less serious than it appeared, but investigations confirmed his original fears and brought new evidence of Communist penetration of Government departments. He still hesitated.

In the meantime, it was becoming increasingly difficult to maintain secrecy regarding the investigation. The somewhat massive inquiries being carried out in Canada, the United Kingdom, and the United States started to give rise to rumours. Some of these reached newspaper columnists who started guessing games as to what was going on. Drew Pearson, an American syndicated columnist, announced in his column that the biggest story of intrigue and espionage since the war was about to break, and that it would involve the leakage of information regarding atomic research. Newsmen began to make inquiries at RCMP headquarters and at various Government departments; the "no-comment" answers served only to increase the mounting stream of rumour.

There was also the highly important task of providing complete security for Gouzenko and his wife and child. The usual problems of finding new identities and safe living quarters for defectors were made more difficult in this case by several important factors and complications. The Soviets knew the impact his story would have on the free world and on their own spying networks. It seemed probable that attempts would be made to silence Gouzenko by liquidation or abduction. A safe, secret hiding place had to be found, where he and his family would have complete protection, but at the same time he had to be readily available for interviews with investigators. The facilities to be provided had to allow for the presence of several guards, but under conditions that would not arouse the curiosity of neighbours. Rationing was still in effect, as was National Registration, and while these regulations could be circumvented, there was need for caution in making the arrangements. There was an added and very important complication: Mrs. Gouzenko was pregnant. Medical attention – and later, hospitalization – had to be provided for.

The considerable responsibility of arranging for the security, accommodation, medical services, and all other requirements of the Gouzenko family was assigned to Inspector George B. McClellan who, at that time, was the Criminal Investigation Branch officer for O Division, which covered most of the Province of Ontario. McClellan ultimately succeeded me as Commissioner of the Force.

Although about twenty years have gone by since Gouzenko's break from the Communists, and despite the fact that in recent years he has shown a tendency toward abandoning commonsense rules for his own safety, I believe it would be indiscreet and improper for me to go into details as to the manner in which the family was hidden, or as to the various locations and identities that have been used. Quite a few people have met the Gouzenkos under their assumed names at various times and places. The publication of details could possibly lead to disclosing their present location. That McClellan and the carefully chosen men who worked with him did an excellent job is well established by the fact that the Gouzenkos were afforded new identities and complete safety.

One amusing part of the story of the protection of the Gouzenko family can be told, however, since the identities used for that particular incident are not traceable. Mrs. Gouzenko was about to have a child. For reasons of security, the father was unable to make the necessary arrangements, and it was encumbent upon McClellan to make plans for her hospitalization and medical care. Having consulted with friends in the medical profession, he decided upon a small, well-equipped hospital located in a town in Northern Ontario. Someone would be required to pose as the husband, and for this duty he chose a member of the Force who spoke Russian and could, when occasion demanded, embellish his English with a heavy and authentic Russian accent.

The "couple" were provided with National Registration Certificates, which included details regarding address and employment. Since these details would not have stood up under very close scrutiny, there was some concern lest, at the last moment, some difficulty might develop with the hospital authorities in securing admittance for the expectant mother. Inquiries elicited the information that the "father" would be required to supply details that would enable the nurse at the admitting desk to complete a rather lengthy questionnaire. A copy of this form was secured by discreet means, and it was learned that its chief purpose was the fixing of responsibility for the payment of hospital and medical costs. A plan was worked out which, it was hoped, would enable the "husband" to avoid potentially troublesome questions.

As Mrs. Gouzenko's time approached, she was taken to the hospital where she and her "husband" presented themselves to the admitting desk. The father was properly nervous and concerned, and seemed to become increasingly upset as he tried to understand the question posed by the nurse who, in turn, had trouble with the heavily accented English. He managed to give his name and address but became somewhat irritable when called on to produce the Registration Cards. The next question concerned money, and this annoyed him to the point of hostility.

"You don't trust, ay," he shouted. "You want money. All right, I pay now."

Producing a huge roll of bills, he proceeded to peel off more than enough to meet any possible contingency. Slapping these onto the desk in front of the startled nurse, he ended the conversation with, "No more talk. No more ask questions. Now you put wife in bed for get baby."

The baby was not born for several days, and during that time the worried "father" spent most of his time at the hospital, an unusual but excellent cover for a security guard. The day following the arrival of the child, he made a brief visit to his headquarters in Toronto, where he continued his role of proud father as he solemnly went from office to office handing out cigars.

Anthony and I had a few weeks with our families before being recalled to Ottawa at the beginning of February, 1946. At headquarters we were advised that an Order in Council was about to be passed which would appoint a Royal Commission comprising two Judges of the Supreme Court of Canada, the Honourable Mr. Justice Robert Taschereau and the Honourable Mr. Justice J. H. Kellock. The Order in Council would empower the Royal Commission "to investigate the facts relating to and the circumstances surrounding the communication by public officials and other persons in positions of trust of secret and confidential information to agents of a foreign power."

Action subsequently taken under these Orders in Council brought widespread criticism of the Force at home and abroad on the grounds that its members acted without lawful authority in detaining twelve persons and holding them incommunicado for some days and in searching their homes and offices. In fact, an earlier Order in Council provided full authority for the actions taken by the Force. The powers granted were extraordinary. It was the extent to which these powers abrogated or interfered with the rights and freedom of the individuals concerned that was to bring a storm of criticism against the Government and police; but the critics were not those who had the responsibility for – or were called on to act toward – the protection of the State, or in the interests of friendly powers. The decision to take firm and positive action was reached by the Government only after long, hard consideration and much hesitation. Certainly, the conspiracy could not have been broken up, or the details of secrets that had been secured by the Russians discovered, or the methods employed by the Soviets established without authority such as granted by the Orders in Council.

Many of the most severe critics have been people who see, or pretend to see, the dangers of a "police state" in almost every action of law-enforcement bodies. Surely that danger arises only when the police disregard or refuse to follow the enactments of Government. In the Gouzenko affair, it was not the part of the police to question the action of the Government, even had there been an inclination to do so, which there was not.

During the early morning hours of February 16, members of the Force, acting on orders issued by the appropriate authority within the terms of the Order, detained ten persons in Ottawa, Montreal, and Toronto and carried out searches of a number of dwelling houses and offices. The following day, two more persons were detained – one was an Army officer who was apprehended as he disembarked from an overseas flight at Montreal; the other, a scientist, was located in Western Canada. The persons detained were taken to the RCMP training establishment at Rockcliffe on the outskirts of Ottawa where, during the next few days, they were interrogated by Anthony and me, as provided for by the Order in Council.

The searches produced valuable evidence in support of Gouzenko's story. It was quite apparent that the Russians had not told their Canadian dupes of Gouzenko's defection or warned them of the possible consequences. It was apparent, too, that our investigators had carried out their widespread and difficult inquiries without breaking the wall of secrecy, a very credible performance. Possibly the lengthy delay on the part of the Canadian Government had encouraged the Russians in the belief that no action would be taken and that they could conceal the fact that the Canadian members of the espionage net had been endangered through the disillusionment and desertion of a member of the Embassy staff. Possibly there was a breakdown in the line of communication between the heads of the Communist Party in Canada who might have been told and the members of the net; or, most probably, the Russians simply abandoned the people they had been using. Whatever their reasons may have been, they did not warn their Canadian spies regarding the impending danger, although they did take the precaution of protecting the Russians involved by sending them out of the country.

The arrests, and particularly the fact that the persons arrested were being held incommunicado, unleashed a storm of criticism. As was to be expected, the Communist press and Communist-inspired speakers were loud and vicious and lying in their attacks. Less expected were the cries of indignation and outrage from the legitimate press which, with few exceptions, burst into banner headlines. True, a cloak of secrecy still surrounded Government and police action, and certainly the press and the public had reason to be disturbed at what appeared to be high-handed police activities; but their inability to secure authentic details because of Government-imposed secrecy did not justify the guessing games and "rape-of-justice" sensationalism that crowded the papers.

Unfortunately, some of the writers in their outrage and in their search for new "angles" were not too discriminating in their choice of sources. As a result, many of the propaganda pieces released by the Communist Party, which was busily engaged on their well-worn tactic of building a "strawman" to cloud the issue, gained wide circulation in the non-Communist press. For a time it was made to appear that the Government and the police were on trial, rather than the group of people who had been undermining the safety of their country.

There were the inevitable charges of police brutality and "Gestapo tactics." As is so often the case, no scrap of proof or anything vaguely resembling evidence was offered to substantiate such charges; and it is of interest that no such complaints were advanced during the subsequent trials. Some of the fantastic though widely circulated stories held that the detainees were being kept in small, dark, dungeon-like cells. Other tales held that they were kept under glaring lights so that they could not sleep, and that they were being kept on a diet of bread and water.

In fact, the RCMP establishment at Rockcliffe is a training centre. There are no cells or detention quarters. The rooms provided for the accommodation of the detainees were those normally used by officers and NCO's during training classes. The food served came from the very well-equipped kitchens which are under the supervision of qualified dieticians and was of the same high quality served to the members of the Force.

Probably the best answer to these charges is to be found in the report of the Royal Commission:

> We may mention that none of the witnesses who had been detained under Order in Council P.C. 6444 made or suggested any complaint to us about their interrogation, the methods of their interrogation, the living conditions in their place of detention, or their treatment by their custodians, the Royal Canadian Mounted Police.

Despite this assurance from two judges of the Supreme Court of Canada, and although no complaints of mistreatment were heard or hinted at during the subsequent trials, some of the stories have persisted and are still occasionally raised by the press or in the House of Commons.

Five days after the arrests, the Soviet Government attempted to raise a different sort of smoke screen. In a note delivered to the Canadian Embassy in Moscow, they brushed off any suggestion of espionage, although admitting that: "In the latter periods of the war, certain members of the staff of the Soviet military attaché in Canada received, from Canadian Nationals with whom they were acquainted, certain secret information which did not, however, present great interest for the Soviet organization." The note went on to state that the information was of no value, and in any event, could have been secured from published works, and that it would, therefore, be ridiculous to affirm that delivery of insignificant secret data of this kind could create any threat to the security of Canada. Having downgraded the value of the material secured by their busy espionage net and having evaded reference to that net, the Soviet note switched to the attack – a manoeuvre that has become very familiar – by holding that the entire affair was a plot by the Canadian Government against the Soviet Union.

On the morning of the arrests, Inspector Anthony and I established ourselves in offices at Rockcliffe. It had been decided that Anthony would interview those suspects who were thought to be part of the net centred on Toronto, while I would concern myself with the Montreal group which included: an army officer who had been seconded to the War Information Board; a professor of chemistry, who had carried out research work on explosives for the National Research Council; a geological engineer employed in the Records Division of the Ammunition Production Board; an electrical engineer employed on secret work connected with the developments of a radar; a scientist engaged on research work in the microwave section of the National Research Council; and a professor of mathematics who had been granted an army commission to work on the development of explosives and weapons.

Immediately following their arrival at the training centre, the detainees were brought before Anthony or me so that the reason for their detention and the authority under which that action had been taken might be carefully explained to them. They were told that serious allegations had been made and that evidence had been gathered which tended to implicate them in the espionage activities of the USSR. They were advised briefly regarding details of the information that had reached us. There was no interrogation at these first meetings. The detainees were told too that they would be interviewed during the next few days and that during those interviews it was their right, if they so wished, to refuse to answer questions or provide information. They were asked, in the meantime, to give careful thought to the situation that had been brought about by Communist activities in Canada, particularly their own beliefs, loyalties, or disloyalties.

These preliminary meetings served the very useful purpose of allowing Anthony and me to take stock of the suspects. We had read both the Soviet Intelligence assessment of the characters of these people and the details of their recruitment as given in the files taken from the Soviet Embassy by Gouzenko. It was an intensely interesting experience to talk with the individuals concerned and estimate the accuracy of the appraisals that had been made by the spy masters for the information of their Moscow control centre or "director."

In their "talent-spotting" and recruitment work for this espionage net, the Soviet spy masters had not found it necessary to resort to their frequently used techniques of blackmail and bribery. According to the Soviet records, these people were ideological spies who had been brought into Communist-front groups, most of them through a Red-controlled "scientific association," and from there, after careful indoctrination and training, into the espionage apparatus.

These Soviet documents and the statements subsequently given by the persons involved established that most of the so-called "talent-spotting" had been done by Fred Rose and another leader of the Communists in Canada, Sam Carr. Having selected individuals from the membership of the Communist-front groups as likely material for espionage work, Rose and Carr had been required to submit detailed reports regarding the character, financial standing, salary, family life, habits, weaknesses, and employment. Particular attention was given to the value of the information to which the prospective spy would have access through his employment.

These reports were studied by the spy masters in the Embassy and then sent on, with his comments, to the control centre in Moscow. As often as not, Moscow had asked for more details. Recruitment into the espionage net was a patient, painstaking process. The system was slow and somewhat cumbersome, but it had the advantage of controlling any overly enthusiastic or optimistic action on the part of the local spy master by applying the brakes of distant and dispassionate professionalism. If the man in Moscow gave the go-ahead signal, as he had for each of these detainees, the prospect was then moved from the "front" group into a smaller and secret "study cell." Commenting on these secret study groups, the Royal Commission report said:

> Linked with these studies at all stages, moreover, goes on organized indoctrination calculated to create in the mind of the study group member an essentially uncritical acceptance at its face value of the propaganda of a foreign state. Accordingly, the study groups are encouraged to subscribe to Com-

munist books and periodicals. The Canadian Tribune *and* Clarion *of Toronto,* New Masses (*a periodical published in the United States*), National Affairs *of Toronto, and* Club Life *have been among those mentioned as regular objects of study and discussion in these groups, as well as selected books on Russia. In some cases, the effect of these study courses seems to be a gradual development of divided loyalties or, in extreme cases, of transferred loyalties. Thus it seems to happen that through these study groups some adherents, who begin by feeling that Canadian society is not democratic or not equalitarian enough for their taste, are gradually led to transfer a part or most of their loyalties to another country, without reference to whether that other country is in actual fact more or less democratic or equalitarian than Canada.*

Indeed, a sense of internationalism seems, in many cases, to play a definite role in one stage of the course. In those cases, the Canadian sympathizer is first encouraged to develop a sense of loyalty, not directly to a foreign state but to what he conceives to be an international ideal. This subjective internationalism is then usually linked, almost inextricably, through the indoctrination courses and the intensive exposure of the propaganda of a particular foreign state, with the current conception of the national interests of that foreign state and with the current doctrines and policies of Communist parties throughout the world.

Apart from the undermining of old loyalties and the transferring of loyalties to new ideals, these secret study groups have another basic objective. The need for secrecy is constantly emphasized. An atmosphere of conspiracy is gradually developed. Members are warned of the dangers of frankness or honesty in the expression of their political views outside the cell meetings. In rare instances a member of the cell finds the conspiratorial atmosphere of the meetings alarming or repulsive and drops out, but this indicates an error in the assessment of the individual by the talent-spotter rather than an error in the curriculum of the study group.

For most of the prospective spies, attendance of cell meetings leads to a gradual acceptance of a double life and double standards. The Communists are never in a hurry in developing prospects, and the secret-cell method of indoctrination and brainwashing usually lead to the disintegration of normal moral principals, beliefs, and character. Although I had known of and studied the Soviet methods of recruitment, indoctrination, and training, I was, nevertheless, surprised by the calibre of men who allowed themselves to be duped by these methods and drawn into treason and treachery against their own country.

These were not men embittered by failure or goaded by unusual desire for success; nor were they men who had been badly used by their country. It may be argued that their willingness to work for the Reds stemmed from a desire to help all humanity rather than from self-interest, but until their recruitment and indoctrination they had been quite content to gather the benefits of the system under which they lived, and were content to believe that that system of democracy and freedom held the best hope for mankind. The fact that highly intelligent, learned, and able men, who had been respected and trusted by their colleagues, employers, and Government, had been deceived away from honour and turned into willing tools of Communism is in my view the most disturbing aspect of the Gouzenko case and of the numerous Soviet espionage cases that have been uncovered in recent years.

During the questioning of the Montreal members of the espionage net, I attempted to probe the interesting and disturbing matter of their motivation and reasoning that had led otherwise competent and disciplined minds into participating in a criminal conspiracy that called on them to cheat and lie. Why had these men, trained and skilled in scientific analysis and in the search for truth, abandoned that training when listening to the mouthpieces of Communists?

So far as I was able to learn during lengthy interviews with the detainees, not one of them had fully accepted the Communist ideology. Surprisingly, three of them were extremely critical of Communism, of the lies, shifting opportunistic policies, and blatant propaganda used in the attempts to spread the Communist cause. The teachers in the secret cells to which they had belonged had not done a very thorough job of indoctrination. But they had been successful in undermining their faith in the democratic system. In so doing this they had whittled away moral fibre and loyalties. The spies had not carried out their treachery on behalf of a great ideal or sincere conviction that their work would benefit mankind. They were not working for something that they believed to be good. Less understandably, they were working *against* something – their own country, which the Communists had convinced them was bad.

The detainees all advanced reasons or excuses for their association with the Communists. One, who had been a student in Italy when Mussolini came to power, claimed that in spying for the Russians he had been trying to protect Canada against Fascism. Two of the scientists advanced the belief that there should be a free international exchange of information in the scientific field and that their efforts had been directed toward breaking down all barriers of secrecy. Two others held that Jewish people were not receiving fair treatment in Canada. Another believed – or offered as an excuse – that all politicians and the entire political system in Canada was corrupt, and that in handing over secret documents to the Russians, he had been trying to help bring an end to such corruption.

But these explanations were too simple, too pat. I formed an opinion at that time – one that has since been strengthened by the study of other espionage and by discussions with heads of counter-intelligence services in the United States, the United Kingdom, Australia, and Europe – that the so-called "ideological spy," the national who willingly betrays his own country, is not driven by a complete acceptance of Communist teachings but by an intellectual arrogance, an arrogance that places his judgment ahead of that of all others. Certainly Communist indoctrination plays a large part in this, particularly in that the tearing down of old beliefs tends to confirm the inflated value that the subject places on his own opinions and views. He becomes more and more convinced that all others are bunglers.

The conspiratorial atmosphere at the meetings of the secret cells appeals to him on several grounds. Here is an opportunity to strike out at the bunglers. His arrogance overrides the fact that he must abandon normal codes of loyalty, honour, and decency. Such codes are meant to control lesser intellects. There is a further attraction. Espionage is a risky business. The challenge of pitting his superior intellect against that of counter-intelligence forces offers a thrill, a sort of grown-up game of cops and robbers. I have seen little evidence of ideological spies being activated solely by a desire to help build a better society.

The Soviet spy masters had erred badly in accepting two of the men I questioned. One was the type of individual an interrogator encounters on very rare occasions, a person burdened with a martyr complex, with an urge toward self-destruction in the fight for some lost cause. The other – an even more rare individual – was a man utterly incapable of evasion or lying.

The "martyr" welcomed the opportunity to give a statement and filled a notebook with details of his work for the Soviets. An interesting sidelight is that following his release from Rockcliffe, pending trial, he was approached by the Communists, who enticed him into another martyr's role, that of silence. He was called as witness for the prosecution in several of the trials, and despite his earlier statements to me and his statements under oath to the Royal Commission, he steadfastly refused to answer questions. This earned him a total of nine months' imprisonment on three separate charges of contempt of Court before his own trial, which brought another six years.

The other man, incapable of evasion, gave direct and complete answers to all questions and rounded out those answers by writing a lengthy review of his recruitment, training, motivation, and acts of treason.

The Soviet professionals had erred badly in another way. A cardinal rule of espionage is that each link of the chain must be kept, as far as possible, in ignorance of the others. Usually knowledge is circulated according to this rule on a strictly observed "need-to-know" basis, but the spy masters had been exceedingly lax in this regard. The man with a martyr complex had been used as a go-between in the direction and control of three other spies. The "truth-teller" had been made aware of the activities of other members of the net by his contact man, Fred Rose, and on at least one occasion by one of the professionals from the Soviet Embassy.

During the time that the interviews were being held at Rockcliffe Training Centre, the Royal Commission was conducting its inquiries and hearing witnesses in a room on one of the upper floors of the Justice Building. A room on the floor below was used for the filing and storage of exhibits that had been seized during the numerous searches carried out in furtherance of the inquiry. Quite often Anthony and I found it necessary to visit this exhibit room in order to examine seized documents to keep abreast of developments.

On one occasion I spent an entire afternoon going over recently seized papers. Having completed my work, I started for the elevator, still somewhat preoccupied with the new evidence provided by the documents I had examined. As the elevator door slid open, I saw that the two occupants were members of the Royal Commission, both Justices of the Supreme Court of Canada. As I entered the elevator to my utter amazement these normally austere and dignified gentlemen raised their hats, bowed deeply, and greeted me as "Your Excellency." In the meantime, the elevator had descended to the ground floor. Again, as the door opened, the Honourable Mr. Justice Taschereau and the Honourable Mr. Justice Kellock uncovered, bowed deeply, repeated "Your Excellency," and solemnly walked away. I was too astounded to ask questions.

The following day I went to a luncheon which was attended by the Commission Counsel and secretaries, the Commissioner, and other officers. As I stepped across the threshold, everyone in the room bowed low while the mess secretary announced the arrival of "His Excellency." By that time I had learned the story back of this unusual behaviour and had rather expected the greeting. I had armed myself with a very long cigarette-holder and a few words of Russian to play the role that had been accorded me.

What had happened was that the previous day one of the members of the Montreal espionage net had been summoned before the Royal Commission. He was one of the weaker links and an extremely nervous, agitated man. His appearance before the Commission, his conscience, and the preliminary questions of Counsel upset him to a point where he could not think clearly, or answer intelligently. In an effort to put him at ease, the examining Counsel picked up a book containing photographs of many of the persons involved in the inquiry. Opening the book at the first page, which held the picture of a tall, thin, rather cadaverous-looking man, the Counsel asked, "Do you know who that is?"

There was a sigh or relief from the witness. Here was a question that he could answer clearly, without fear. "Yes. I know him. That is Inspector Harvison of the Mounted Police." The picture was actually that of Mr. Zarubin, the Soviet Ambassador to Canada. Hence my subsequent and very temporary elevation to the exalted rank of "Excellency."

The interrogation and documentary evidence taken during the searches strengthened the case against Fred Rose, the Member of Parliament, who had still not been detained. Now his arrest was justified. A warrant was sworn out and he was arrested in his apartment in Ottawa and taken directly to Montreal where he was placed in the custody of the Quebec Provincial Police overnight and taken before the Criminal Court the next morning. Immediately thereafter the Communist Party set up a defence fund. In the literature and releases issued in an effort to secure contributions, the party screamed about the "gestapo" methods of the police. By ambiguous wording, they implied that a Member of Parliament had been arrested and held incommunicado at Rockcliffe for an extended period. This they knew to be a flat lie, but it did not prevent them from basing their appeal for money on the Rose case, nor has it hindered critics in recent years.

Fred Rose was the first of the spies to appear before the courts, and his was the first case in which Gouzenko appeared as a witness. By that time the Gouzenko affair had received headline attention internationally, and the case brought reporters to Montreal from many countries. The Force was concerned for the safety of Gouzenko, not only during the court proceedings but in the years ahead, and there was particular concern over the possibility that the press would secure and publish photographs or drawings of Gouzenko.

It was decided that a press conference should be called and that we should appeal to the press to avoid carrying pictures or descriptions of the defector. Some sixty reporters and photographers attended the meeting which was held in the police offices. At first they tended to ridicule the suggestion that the publication of photographs would increase the dangers to Gouzenko. Surely, they said, the Communists knew what he looked like and already had a number of pictures of him. We readily agreed but went on to point out the difficulties of establishing new identities for him and his family, and we pointed out the ways in which those difficulties would be increased if everyone in the country knew what he looked like. The point was accepted immediately. Without further argument, the newsmen reached unanimous agreement to forego pictures or sketches, although these would have added greatly to their stories and brought fair sums of money to the photographers. The agreement reached at that meeting has never been broken. Without the co-operation of the press, it would have been extremely difficult, if not impossible, to find safe cover for a man who had earned protection and freedom in Canada. Probably the Force was over-cautious. Probably nothing would have happened to him had the security measures been less rigid, but his execution would have served grim notice on other potential defectors. The risk could not be taken.

There was concern within the Force and among the prosecution lawyers as to how Gouzenko would conduct himself in the witness box and how he would withstand cross-examination. Leading counsel had been employed to defend Rose, and it was clear that the preliminary hearing would be a tough testing ground. A great deal of evidence had been gathered, in addition to that provided by Gouzenko, but if the defence could succeed in upsetting or confusing our star witness, the outcome would be in some doubt. Our worries faded soon after Gouzenko began to give evidence. His amazingly accurate memory, his assurance and control, and the fact that he enjoyed every moment in the spotlight made him one of the best witnesses I have ever heard in court. Defence counsel tried every trick in the bag in their efforts to trip him. They soon learned to respect his ability and obvious truthfulness. They found, also, that he was quite capable of foreseeing their gambits and turning them against the defence.

During the Rose trial, before the Court of King's Bench some weeks later, the defence tried a new approach in their efforts to upset Gouzenko. One of the most able cross-examiners among the defence lawyers in Montreal had been added to the team representing the accused Member of Parliament. He started his cross-examination in low key by asking a seemingly unimportant question. Had the witness, during his boyhood in Russia, heard of the Royal Canadian Mounted Police. Gouzenko replied that he had. Watching Gouzenko, I knew that he had already guessed the direction that this line of questioning would take. The lawyer went on to explore the extent of the witness' knowledge regarding the Force before coming to Canada, and in the process he started using such terms as "world-famous police organization," "model Force," "body of men known for their integrity."

The witness answered the questions without hesitation. He admitted that since boyhood he had had a great interest in the Royal Canadian Mounted Police. In answer to further questions, he said that he had maintained that interest after coming to Canada and had purchased several books dealing with the work of the Force. Then came the question toward which the lawyer had been building – and for which Gouzenko had been waiting.

"Why didn't you go directly to the Royal Canadian Mounted Police after leaving the Embassy on the night of your defection?"

The answer was the one the defence counsel had hoped for. "I thought there might be spies in the Mounted Police."

The Counsel then staged a very credible act for the benefit of the jury in an effort to discredit the witness. Pointing an accusing finger, he shouted, "Do you expect us to believe that? You have told us that you knew the high reputation of the Mounted Police. You claim that you were in great fear for your safety and for that of your family. Yet when you needed help, you went to a newspaper and then to several other offices before you were taken to the police. And you expect us to believe that you avoided the police because you thought there might be a spy in their ranks."

Turning to the jury, he enlarged on his theme. How could this story be believed? And if the witness could not be believed in this part of his story, the entire explanation must be viewed with suspicion. The man was not a reliable witness. His story that he had avoided the police because there might be a spy in their midst was ridiculous.

At this point the lawyer paused for breath. In the witness box, Gouzenko had been waiting for the right moment. He nodded toward the accused and said in a loud, clear voice, "Why not? There was one in Parliament."

There were no further questions from the defence.

The trial lasted several weeks during which the Crown built a massive case against Rose. At one point the prosecution ran into a small snag when four witnesses – all of whom had been connected with the espionage net and all of whom had been charged – flatly refused to answer questions. The evidence hoped for would have provided corroboration for the evidence of the other witnesses, but it was not vital to the case. Toward the end, proceedings dragged somewhat as counsel for the prosecution piled fact upon fact in an effort to remove any last lingering doubts from the minds of the jurors as to the guilt of the accused.

The jury was out for only a few minutes before returning a verdict of guilty. After the jury had been dismissed, the senior prosecution counsel and I made a point of chatting with the man who had served as foreman. We were interested in knowing what part of the evidence had impressed the jurymen; at what stage had they reached a decision as to the guilt of the accused? We learned that they had been vastly interested in – but not completely convinced by – the weight of direct and documentary evidence produced before them. In the words of the foreman, "It was not until those four Commies refused to answer questions that we made up our minds and agreed. We knew then that Rose was guilty, and we would have said so, had you stopped the trial right then. We didn't need the rest of the witnesses."

Rose was sentenced to six years' imprisonment and at the end of that time departed for his native Poland. Eight others were convicted and sentenced to terms ranging from two and one-half to six years. One man was fined. But much more important than the punishment of the offenders was the fact that Soviet espionage methods had been exposed. That exposure was made possible by the decision of the Government, reached only after long delay, deep consideration, and reluctance to take stern measures to uproot treason. Those who were thoroughly familiar with the affair knew that the Government had only one alternative to the Gouzenko exposure – that of leaving the door wide open for treachery unlimited.

It is now over twenty years since the Gouzenko case, and the years have brought many changes. Stalin has gone, along with most of his apparatus for repressions within Russia. Khruschev brought an easing in the strains of the Cold War, and this "peaceful coexistence" has continued under the present Russian leaders. In Canada, the top men in the Communist Party have grown old and tired, frustrated by the sudden shifts in Soviet policies and leadership. Most of their fire has been dampened by the general prosperity and improvements in our social system. The Canadian Communist Party itself seems less militant and has suffered a membership decline. There is a growing tendency to regard Communist leaders in Canada as rather pitiful antiques, and the party as a group of almost harmless crackpots. In the meantime, too, Russia has become one of the largest customers for Canadian exports.

But Soviet attempts to subvert Canadian nationals still goes on as before. The Gouzenko case served only to expose some of the Communist methods and to warn Moscow that their methods needed overhauling. Such names as Fuchs, Vassall, Hiss, Rosenberg, Petrov, Houghton, Gee, and Lonsdale remind us that Soviet agents are still searching for – and finding – people willing to commit treason. Almost all Western countries can produce a list of Soviet bloc embassy officials who have been expelled because of alleged espionage activities. In the United Kingdom, the Government has even found it advisable to issue a warning against Soviet espionage in the form of a book *Their Trade Is Treachery* which has been given to all civil servants.

There has been a change in Soviet espionage targets over the years. Today the Russian controls want a knowledge in depth of all the affairs of the democracies – trade, economy, politics, planning, objectives. There is a constant drive to find weak spots through which to secure details that will enable them to out-manoeuvre the West in international affairs. At the time of the Gouzenko case, seventeen persons – or about one-third of the Soviet Embassy staff in Ottawa – was employed to operate the various espionage nets. The situation has changed only in that the Ottawa staff is larger than ever. As well, we now have embassies and trade missions representing several Communist bloc countries which are generally far larger than those of similar non-Communist nations. This compels the opinion that either the Communists are exceedingly inefficient in carrying out their legitimate business or that many of their employees are engaged in duties in no way connected with the normal work of embassies and trade missions.

While doing business with the Communists – and prospering thereby – and working for peaceful coexistence, we should bear in mind that the trade stems from their needs and not from a desire to help a capitalist state. It would be wise to use some part of the profits of the trade to strengthen security, or at least to make sure that in reaching for their money we do not leave ourselves wide open to attack.

15

-»»-»»-»»-»»-«««-«««-«««-«««-

With the Manitoba
Division

After I completed my task with the Gouzenko affair, I returned to Winnipeg early in December of 1946. Although on paper I had been a member of the Winnipeg Division for fourteen months, I had spent most of that time in Ottawa and Montreal and was still a stranger to my new duties. The transfer had served only to move my wife Doris and my son Weston to Winnipeg, where they had to face almost all the chores of setting up a home alone. We all hoped that I would be allowed to settle down for awhile so that we might get acquainted with and enjoy our new surroundings. I was anxious, as well, to take up my new duties and gain experience in the work of the Force in a Contract Division, but family life and personal wishes are seldom given preference over discipline, training, and the exigencies of the Service. Just a few days before Christmas, my Officer Commanding received a brief letter from the Commissioner instructing that I was to return to Ottawa on January 3, 1947, in order to attend the Canadian Police College for three months.

The Canadian Police College is an advanced training course conducted by the Force for officers and Senior NCO's. Attendance is open to the Armed Services, to Canadian Police Forces, and to police forces in other countries. It is usual for half of the thirty-two members of each class to come from other services. Police officers from many countries have attended too, and at times the College becomes a miniature United Nations. Four years ago when, as Commissioner, I visited Pakistan, I was given a luncheon in Lahore by sixteen graduates of the Canadian Police College and was delighted to learn that the course was held in high esteem there. Each of the graduates had done well in the police service of that country.

The lecturers were top-level men drawn from Government departments, universities, industry, religious bodies, welfare agencies, the Armed Services, and from a number of police organizations. All were expert in their fields, and most lecturers presented their subjects in an interesting and informative manner that almost always led to discussions during the evening bull sessions. As with any training course, those after-hours sessions add greatly to the value of the class, particularly because they enabled us to hear the views and experiences of policemen from other forces and other countries.

I recall one lecturer in particular who held the undivided attention of the class throughout an entire afternoon. This chap was explaining the law of probability and in order to make his points used a deck of cards as a teaching aid. With extreme care, he solemnly worked out the probability of success in drawing on two pair or to an inside straight or to innumerable other combinations in the game of poker. We had some difficulty in relating his subject matter to police work but, nevertheless, it was added to our after-hour subjects; and we spent long sessions in studying and attempting to apply his techniques.

After three months, I returned to Winnipeg, satisfied that the time had been well-spent and that I was in somewhat better health due to physical training and drill that formed a regular part of the training class. I had also earned some small rewards through very persistent efforts to grasp the law of probability.

We spent five pleasant and very profitable years in Winnipeg. The Division is responsible for federal and provincial law enforcement for the Province of Manitoba, and for the enforcement of by-laws in twelve municipalities. Because the area is more easily administered from Winnipeg, a part of Ontario, from the head of the Great Lakes west, is attached to the Winnipeg command. At that time, the work was handled through three Sub-Division offices and some sixty-five Detachments, the strength of the various posts ranging from about a hundred men in Winnipeg down to some one-man Detachments.

While there was a fairly steady and heavy volume of federal work, the cases were less complicated and exacting than the narcotic drug, illicit alcohol, counterfeiting, and espionage conspiracies experienced in the Eastern cities. But the enforcement of the Criminal Code, provincial statutes, and municipal by-laws brought constant pressures to bear on the resources of the police with investigations ranging from minor traffic violations and locating lost hunters to thefts, hold-ups, rapes, and murder.

The various levels of Government are not at all times in complete and whole-hearted agreement on matters of law enforcement, and I had wondered about the degree to which varying viewpoints might interfere with the carrying out of impartial police work. It had seemed possible, too, that since local governments are closer to the scene, there would be a greater likelihood of attempts to bring political pressures to bear on the police. The terms of the contracts under which the Force carried out provincial and municipal policing provide some safeguards, such as the placing of matters of discipline, promotion, and transfer in the hands of the police authority. But such safeguards cannot provide complete assurance against attempts to influence proper law enforcement, or against the difficulties and unpleasantnesses that might be brought about by such attempts.

In practice, in Manitoba, and later in other contract provinces, I found that such safeguards are rarely needed. Problems and differences do arise on matters of manpower, equipment, and accommodation, but almost invariably such differences are worked out satisfactorily and on the basis of maintaining adequate police resources as economically as possible. Insofar as investigations and prosecutions are concerned, it has been my experience that the police are given strong support by members of provincial and municipal governments. Instances of attempts at political interference do occur, but they are rare indeed.

The contract system of policing by a federal force has been questioned on the grounds that the extension of the system will lead to the setting up of a "police state" – that old, overworked alarm of critics. Any real or fancied fears on these grounds overlook one very important point. Under the contract system, the Force serves Liberal, Conservative, and Social Credit Governments in the various provinces. Until the defeat of the New Democratic Party in Saskatchewan, the Force had served that Government for many years too. The system is, therefore, a guarantee against the development of a police state, or a police force that is the tool of any political party. Political impartiality on the part of the police is a built-in and very important requirement.

After about two years as Chief of Detectives, I was transferred to the position of Officer Commanding, Sub-Division; and several months later, to the desk of Officer in Charge, Criminal Investigation Branch. The changes were advantageous in that I was brought in touch with all the work of the Division and all types of police work, from the one-man Detachment maintaining law and order in a small or isolated community to the large municipal policing Detachments.

For the first time, I experienced the problems of highway-traffic control and came to realize the heavy demands made on police resources by the necessary and continuous efforts to get drivers to stop killing or maiming themselves and others. I came to understand the feeling of bitterness and frustration that build up in members employed on traffic patrol through their close contact with the scenes of tragedy and senseless slaughter on the highways. Finely drawn arguments by defence counsel and light sentences by courts cannot be taken in stride by men frequently called on to remove dead, crippled, and screaming bodies from wreckages brought on by drunken, idiotic, and reckless drivers.

A major problem facing police on the prairies in those years was that of safe-breaking and theft during the fall and winter months when the wheat harvest was being marketed. Keen competition between grain-elevator companies and the demand of farmers for ready-cash payment necessitated the distribution of hundreds of thousands of dollars to elevator operators and payors, usually the general stores in small communities across the prairies. Some of the storekeepers had safes, but many of these were of the tin-can variety that could, as the saying was among policemen, "be opened with a toothpick." While such safes afforded a slight impediment rather than a secure protection, they were, nevertheless, preferable to the shoe boxes and empty tins used by some of the payors for the storage of large sums of money. The carelessness with which the flood of cash was handled served as an invitation to all the criminals in the area, and the invitation was accepted with enthusiasm every harvest season.

Increased police patrols in the vicinity of grain elevators and payors' stores were effective up to a point, but such patrols were spread very thinly among the thousands of grain elevators in the vast wheat country. The safe-breaking fraternity added manpower difficulties by developing a few tricks of its own. Sometimes one or two well-known criminals would be sent into a town to act as decoys in an attempt to draw the police out of position so that robberies could be carried out elsewhere, or fake informers would be used to try to clear the patrols out of the area marked for the next break-in. On several occasions, fires were started as a means of keeping the police and citizenry busy while a robbery was taking place.

On the police side, there were constant efforts to discover methods to curb the annual rash of safe-cracking. Efforts were made to convince payors to keep a list of the numbers of a least some of the bills in their safes or tin cans or shoe boxes, but these efforts met with very limited success. The payors were fully insured against loss and were inclined to be careless. As a result, very little of the stolen money could be identified, and criminals found in possession of large sums of cash could get away with the old tale that they had won it gambling.

An ambitious project was started at headquarters in Ottawa where, working with experts of the National Research Council, members of the police laboratory staff carried out a number of experiments with a by-product of the atomic-energy plant at Chalk River. The by-product, a harmless liquid, was radioactive to a degree that would register on a geiger counter. Experiments established that bills impregnated with the substance could be quickly located over a fairly wide area by use of the geiger apparatus. The laboratory staff added a small quantity of a colour-fast dye. We now had a liquid that would discolour currency a faint red and also make the currency radioactive.

The next problem was to find some means of putting the liquid to use. A cash box was developed in the lid of which a phial of the liquid and a spring-activated plunger were concealed. When opened by anyone not familiar with the mechanism, the phial would be broken and the liquid would sprinkle on the money in the lower part of the box. The idea was intriguing, but there were flaws that caused some of us to doubt its practicability. In the first place, it was reasonable to wonder if the thieves would visit any of the safes in which we had installed the some-what complicated apparatus, since the cost would allow only extremely – almost infinitesimally – limited distribution. If the old law of probability gave us a break, there remained the possibility that the thieves would be suspicious of the dampened money. Then there was another drawback. The radioactive material would provide identification of stolen money, but that money, in turn, according to the experts, might contaminate all other money with which it came in contact, so that identification could not be positive. Further, in the event of thefts occuring at more than one of the "plants," the matter of identification would be very complicated indeed.

Despite these handicaps, it seemed worthwhile to experiment. In-stallations were made in the safes of twenty reliable payors in each of the three prairie provinces. In hopeful anticipation that the thieves would break into some of our trick cash boxes, arrangements were made with the banks whereby all branches across the prairies were asked to be on the lookout for currency with a slight pinkish tint. If such discoloured bills came to their attention, they were asked to immediately notify the nearest police office.

Unfortunately the thieves did not co-operate by attacking any of the prepared premises, but the experiment did produce some results that were more embarrassing than helpful. In circularizing the banks, we had not reckoned with the fact that many farmers, particularly oldsters of foreign extraction, have doubts about savings accounts. They preferred to place their money in hiding places around their farms, such as receptacles buried in the ground, or in manure heaps, or hidden in the walls of sheds and stables. Quite often the hiding places were damp and the money was subjected to moisture. Within hours of the receipt of the circulars, the tellers gave ample proof of their eagerness to co-operate with the police. Calls reporting pinkish bills flooded our Detachments, although our trick cash boxes were still intact. We learned the hard way that currency that remains damp over a long period takes on a pinkish tinge.

A regular part of the safe-breaking season was the receipt of complaints from grain-elevator operators and insurance companies demanding more police protection. Certainly the situation was far from satisfactory, but since the losses were the result of gross carelessness in the handling of large sums of money, the fault was not entirely – or even chiefly – that of the police. The concern of the elevator companies was not too deep since they were insured. The insurance companies objected strenuously to the widespread annual losses, but they, in turn, could ease their hurt by increasing premiums. The annual complaints to the police had become almost ritualistic.

Inspector Lloyd Bingham (now Assistant Commissioner and Director of Criminal Investigation at headquarters) visited Winnipeg during the Summer of 1947 in his capacity as co-ordinator of anti-safe-blowing efforts in the three prairie provinces. During our discussion of activities planned for the fall, we touched on the matter of basic responsibility and the degree to which carelessness on the part of the companies contributed to the outbreaks. Having explored that angle, we decided that the situation should be placed squarely before the companies concerned. The elevator companies and the interested insurance organizations were invited to attend a joint meeting for the purpose of planning protective measures for the coming fall. The meeting was well attended, and in response to our invitation for frank comment regarding policing methods, we received severe criticism from spokesmen for both groups.

The attitude of the companies opened the door for equal frankness from the police, and we took full advantage of the opportunity. Case after case was cited, wherein sums of money running into the thousands had been handled in a manner that outraged the most elementary security precautions. Some of the merchant-payors had adopted the habit of hanging "this is not locked" signs on their safes in order to avoid the damage to their stock that might result if intruders blew the safe open. In other cases, thousands of dollars had been kept behind rows of canned goods on the shelves of payors' stores, and the money was revealed to everyone present each time a payment for wheat was made. In one robbery, the thieves had made an easy haul by removing a cardboard shoebox containing twenty thousand dollars, which the payor, a general merchant, had kept conveniently handy on a shelf under the cash register.

Even a rank amateur could make a fair haul under the existing, lackadaisical ways of handling money. We referred to a case that had occurred the previous fall in a small town close to Winnipeg. The door of a "tin-can" type safe had been pried open with a crowbar and the sum of $642.29 stolen. It was found that the crowbar was the property of a neighbour who had used it to prop his garage door closed. That the thief knew where to get the bar was an indication of local amateur talent, and the thief was rounded up without difficulty. He was a hired hand from an adjacent farm. The day before the robbery he had watched the storekeeper pay out some money and return the cash box to the safe. That night he gained entry through an unlocked window and tackled the safe with a screwdriver – a slightly optimistic effort even for that type of safe. Having succeeded in bending a part of the door outward with the screwdriver, he was unable to get enough leverage to gain access. He then went for the crowbar that he had seen against the door of the nearby garage. Having completed the theft, he did something that I wish, without hope, more criminals would do. In this pocket diary under the date of the theft, he made an entry "To loot – $642.29."

The company executives seemed to be impressed by our recitation of incidents which established that payors, comfortable in the knowledge that losses of grain money would be covered by insurance, showed very little concern in the safeguarding of money distributed to them. Having made that point, we went on to provide details of the thousands of miles of road and of the many grain elevators and payors that required police protection. We made it clear that during the coming fall the police would do the best they could with the manpower available, but as our resources had not been increased the best would be about the same as in previous years. Unless they took steps within their organizations to stop the widespread negligence that amounted to an open invitation to every thief in the countryside, they could anticipate many thefts.

The meeting produced surprising results and accomplished more than could have been done by any number of police patrols. One company installed good tubular safes mounted in concrete in each of their nine hundred elevators, and others fell in line by installing equally satisfactory equipment. Many payors were eliminated, and a system was worked out whereby the amount of cash in the hands of the payors at any one time was greatly reduced. Insurance premiums were adjusted to compensate for the cost of the improved security measures. As a result, the grain elevators and payors ceased to provide an annual happy-hunting ground for criminals. Safe-breaking was reduced to a minimum.

The experience and resources of the police are frequently tested in many ways other than those connected with the prevention or investigation of crime and arrest of criminals. The public rightly expects that in the event of an emergency adequate action will be taken, and in most emergent situations the police must play a major role. Quite often it falls on the police to mobilize the resources of an area to work together in the meeting of some sudden tragedy or catastrophy demanding immediate action.

An event of tragedy and mass death occurred shortly after nine-thirty on the night of September 1, 1947, at Dugald, Manitoba, a little village about fifteen miles east of Winnipeg. The eastbound Canadian National Railway's transcontinental had drawn into the station a few minutes earlier and was delayed there awaiting the arrival of a special loaded with holidayers headed for their homes in the Winnipeg area. According to the arrangements, the special would switch onto a siding, leaving the main line clear for the transcontinental.

In the flickering light of the gas lamps in the old-fashioned wooden coaches of the holiday special, passengers were starting to prepare for their arrival in Winnipeg. They could not see the headlight of the waiting transcontinental, nor could they know that the clicking wheels of their train had gone on past the switch and were rushing toward the worst collision in Western Canada's railroading history. The tremendous force of the collision telescoped the two locomotives, derailed some of the cars of the holiday special, and overturned others. Fire roared through the tinder-dry wooden coaches as passengers tried to find a way of escape through windows that would not open and doors that jammed. Twenty-nine people died, and scores were injured in the crash or in the holocaust that followed. The coaches burned until only gaunt steel skeletons remained.

At the moment of impact, the Dugald operator was on the phone talking with the chief dispatcher in Winnipeg. The dispatcher heard the tremendous crash and immediately spread the alarm. In the meantime, a resourceful young woman in the telephone office at Dugald lost no time in calling the nearest RCMP detachment at Transcona, about seventeen miles away, and then in calling her assistants back to handle the many messages that she knew would flood the switchboard.

Members of the Transcona Detachment were among the first to reach the scene. A call for help was radioed to Division Headquarters in Winnipeg, and all available men were rushed out. Calls went out for assistance, and soon ambulances, doctors, fire-fighters, trucks, and even tractors were at the scene of the wreck. Everything possible was being done to contain the flames and aid the injured and the dying. All the while, news of the tragedy had spread throughout the area.

In Winnipeg, radio stations interrupted regular programs to carry special news items. Within an hour of the crash, all roads leading to Dugald were crowded with cars and taxis trying to reach the scene of the accident. Some of the vehicles carried anxious relatives and friends of persons known or thought to have been on the wrecked train. Some of the passengers were reporters, but for the most part they were the usual run of sightseers who inevitably rush to the scene of an accident seeking morbid thrills without regard for the fact that their presence may interfere with essential rescue work. Fortunately at Dugald the rush of traffic had been anticipated, and police patrols at traffic-control points were set up. Throughout the initial confusion, a way was kept clear for ambulances and cars bearing rescue workers, and for the return journey of the ambulances carrying injured persons to hospitals.

At the wreckage, fire-fighters, railway workers, and police were fighting a losing battle with the flames. The only water available was that contained in a nearby ditch, and this was soon emptied. A tank car of water was moved in by rail, but the torn tracks made it impossible to bring it within range and again the crowding sightseers who walked along the tracks in the hundreds added to the difficulties and, in so doing, endangered their own lives. A storage warehouse near the tracks had caught fire and the gasoline and oil drums within threatened to blow up at any moment. Closer to the station a grain elevator started to burn, and the spectacle of flames shooting high in the air brought more people to join the crowds pressing in on the rescue workers. Railway men and policemen, who were sorely needed to help in the work of fire-fighting and aiding the injured, had to be taken from those essential tasks to force the crowds back to a position of safety and hold them there. Other men had to be detailed to clear onlookers and vehicles from a nearby roadway where it was expected there would be explosions and the collapse of buildings. When the exploisons came, gasoline barrels and flaming debris were tossed high in the air, but fortunately they landed in areas that had been cleared. Again, when the grain elevator collapsed with a roar and spewed its red hot contents across the right of way, no one was injured.

In Winnipeg, police, railway, hospital, and newspaper switchboards were crowded with calls from anxious relatives of persons thought to have been on the train. In the early stages, the only information available to callers was that a serious accident had occurred. As the confusion cleared, information regarding known passengers and their whereabouts was passed on, but there was one anxiety-laden gap in the information, a gap that remained for some days. Most of the bodies could not be identified; they had been burned beyond recognition.

The coroner set up a temporary morgue in Transcona, and the remains were taken there as soon as they could be removed from the debris of the burned coaches. For several days the wreckage was searched and sifted for traces of articles that would establish identification. In almost all cases these efforts proved futile. Police offices had many visitors seeking information regarding loved ones, and teams of policemen scoured the countryside from which the train had drawn its passengers in an effort to definitely establish the number and names of persons who had boarded the train. In a few instances the information secured for anxious relatives was good. Several families had changed their minds and decided to remain at their cottages for a few days. One family missed the train. In one case, fate in the form of a faulty outboard motor had stranded a family in the middle of a lake until after train time. They had paddled back to their cottage and remained for the night. Many of the cottages were isolated, and some of the persons who had changed their plans or missed the train did not learn of the accident until visited by the police.

A great deal of hurried but painstaking inquiry resulted in the completion of an accurate list of the passengers on the ill-fated train. Only then was it possible to establish beyond question the names of the persons who had died in the crash. In all but one or two instances it was impossible to establish identification of the charred victims. The victims had been of many faiths, and this raised complicated and deep problems as to the form religious services should take. After several meetings with the pastors of the various religious denominations and with relatives of the deceased, agreement was reached for a joint service and mass burial.

Members of the Force were detailed to mount a searching investigation to determine the cause of the accident. This necessitated research into the rules and regulations governing the operation of railroads as those rules applied to the stretch of rail, signals, and timetables governing the Dugald track and switches. Another team, working with experts in that field, made a detailed study of the instruments in the engine cabs, brakes and brake marks, conditions of lights and switches, and the speed at which the special was travelling as indicated by the force of the impact. Still another team prepared drawings and took hundreds of photographs so that a comprehensive brief could be prepared for the information of a public hearing that had been ordered by the Board of Transport Commissioners. The results brought a commendation from the attorney-general, the coroner, the members of the commission, council for all parties concerned, and from the Railroad Brotherhood. Tragedies that involve mass deaths are fortunately very rare, but when they do occur the police in the affected area must be equipped and prepared to move at once, to mobilize rescue forces and aid in that work, set up methods of communication, control traffic, protect the public from the possible serious results of curiosity that brings crowds surging around an accident scene, and to start an investigation at the earliest possible moment in order that all of the facts may be placed before the courts of inquiry that inevitably follow such tragedies.

It is to the credit of police forces that their varied work in such emergencies is usually carried out so smoothly and efficiently that the public tends to forget this aspect of police work. There are many occurrences – traffic accidents, persons lost in the bush, missing children, fires, floods – in which it is the part of the police to serve the public in a manner no less important but not as well known or publicized as their work in the criminal field. Such work does not fit into work-assessment forms, nor can the volume be anticipated with any degree of accuracy in drawing up estimates for future manpower and equipment requirements. This is one of the factors that contributes to a situation wherein most police forces are continually understaffed.

During 1949, the fact that I had seniority in the rank of Inspector brought my name toward the top of the list. Along with several other officers, I was called to Regina to write promotional examinations. These examinations last a week and cover lengthy papers on such matters as criminal law, evidence, investigative techniques, handling of riots, crowds, emergencies, police administration, management, communications, equipment, finance, filing methods, crime prevention, and the very wide subject of "general knowledge." Officers are required to write these examinations at each rank, from Sub-Inspector to Assistant Commissioner. Participants must average seventy per cent if they are to become eligible for promotion to the next rank. Should an officer fail, he is given another opportunity a year later. Those selected to participate are advised several months in advance so that they have ample opportunity for study and preparation.

I have never been fully convinced as to the reliability of these examinations since there is a wide difference in the ability of people to get their thoughts and experiences on paper, and I have seen several able, experienced officers flunk the examinations. But I am fully convinced of the value of the pressures that compel a great deal of study and preparation in the weeks leading up to them. In my own case, my experience up to that time had been almost entirely in the CIB field. Such limited knowledge as I possessed regarding the administrative, financial, personnel, supply problems, and functions of the Force had been gained almost entirely during study in preparation for promotional examinations or for the exams that form a part of the fairly frequent "in-service" training classes. I was always vastly relieved, and a little surprised, when I managed to squeeze out pass marks on subjects other than those connected with CIB work. My luck held in the examinations. Promotion to the rank of Superintendent followed in the fall of that year. In February of the next year, I was transferred to Vancouver to command E Division, which at that time was only concerned with federal duties in British Columbia.

16

>>>->>>->>>->>><<<-<<<-<<<-<<<

Service
in
British Columbia

Doris and I were thrilled with our transfer to the West Coast. We had heard a great deal of the beauties of British Columbia and of the mild climate along the coastal strip. After the fairly rigorous climate of Manitoba, a sojourn in "Canada's evergreen playground" held a great deal of attraction for us. Our pleasure was not complete, however, in that we had reached the point experienced by most parents who are subject to "transfers." Our son Weston had found employment with the Canadian Broadcasting Corporation and had met "the girl," Edna Middleton, whom he was later to marry. We might have persuaded him to seek new work in Vancouver, but having met Edna we realized that no amount of persuasion would or should convince him to leave Winnipeg at that time. We had to agree, though with normal parental reluctance, that his decision to remain behind was the right one.

We left Winnipeg in sub-zero weather during a blinding snowstorm. Two days later, on February 22, we arrived in Vancouver in bright, warm sunshine. Thousands of crocuses were blooming, lawns were green, and spring was in the air. We lost no time in shedding our heavy overcoats, scarves, and overshoes to go for a walk in the bright sunshine. True, we discovered that this was the first sunshine after many days of rain, but this fact in no way detracted from our surprise and pleasure with the climate and scenery of our new environment.

This was my first Command of a Division, and I was eager to take over my new duties. Headquarters were located in a lovely old building surrounded by beautiful gardens next to a golf course in one of the residential areas of Vancouver. Most of the work was centred in Vancouver which had the largest concentration of drug addicts of any Canadian city. There was some customs and excise work, and a fair volume of the investigations were required in assistance to other federal Government departments, but on the whole the pressures on the Division did not seem very heavy.

My Criminal Investigation Bureau Officer, Inspector George Archer (who on retirement became Chief Constable of the City of Vancouver) and his assistant, Inspector Gerry Bella, were thoroughly experienced and competent officers. Similarly, the Administrative and Quartermaster Branches were in the charge of very capable men. In the field, there were only twelve Detachments, and the members in charge handled their work in a manner that left few problems for Headquarters. All in all, the job of officer commanding did not appear to be very onerous. In fact, the only problem to reach my desk during the first day or two was that of dealing with the pheasants which were eating the tulip bulbs in our gardens. I had become fairly used to heavy pressures, and while the change was welcome and the future promised several years of relaxed living and many enjoyable trips around the province on Detachment inspections, the picture seemed much too good to be true.

My misgivings were justified at the end of the first week when I received a letter from Commissioner Wood, advising me that negotiations were underway with the Government of British Columbia whereby it was expected that the Royal Canadian Mounted Police would absorb the provincial force and a number of municipal forces. The letter went on to direct that I interview the Attorney-General, the Commissioner of the Provincial Police, and other authorities to secure a wide variety of information that would be required in drawing up the contract. Simultaneous news releases by the Minister of Justice at Ottawa and the Provincial Attorney-General appeared in the press the following day. The tulip bulbs had to be abandoned to the pheasants. There was work to be done.

Rapidly increasing population, new and expanding industries, the opening of railways and roads to serve developing areas all brought additional demands on the law-enforcement services. The British Columbia Provincial Police Force was an excellent service with a long, proud record, but it had not been given sufficient financial backing to keep it abreast of the tremendous changes that were taking place all over the province. The Force was undermanned, its transportation and communication facilities were sorely in need of an overhaul, training facilities were inadequate to meet changing conditions, and the accommodation at the headquarters building in Victoria, and at most of more than a hundred Detachments throughout the province, were below acceptable standard. Despite the handicaps imposed by lack of adequate support, the Provincial Police were doing a good job; but in large measure this was due to the high calibre of its members and their experience, ability, and loyalty.

The Attorney-General realized that changes were overdue. During conversations with him, I learned that he was firm in the opinion that the necessary changes could best be brought about through an amalgamation of the federal and provincial enforcement bodies which would result in standardized training, a uniform code of discipline, reduction in the duplication of police posts, and possibly in a reduction in the overall strength required to carry out policing duties on behalf of the three levels of government concerned.

Two other factors interested him, and while he limited mention of these to the requirements of our negotiations, it was clear that they played a large part in his eagerness to discuss a contract. First was the fact that he had been under considerable direct fire from critics unhappy with existing law-enforcement methods and procedures. He anticipated that, by having the police work done under contract, a large part of any future criticism would be directed toward the new Force and the federal Government. The second, and more important point, was the matter of cost. Under the terms of the provincial policing contracts, the federal Government accepts responsibility for a major part, some sixty per cent of all policing expenditures. The Attorney-General, the Honourable Gordon Wismer, emphasized the need for increased efficiency and did not dwell on the matter of costs, but it was clear that in a contract he saw a very desirable method of improving policing facilities and resources while at the same time saving the province a great deal of money. As a skilled and experienced bargainer, he expressed some doubts and made a show of reluctance, but he could not quite hide his eagerness to secure agreements for the province and the thirty-odd municipalities with which the provincial government had policing arrangements.

At the same time, the federal Government, judging from instructions and information reaching me from the Commissioner, seemed even more anxious to conclude a contract. For some years the federal Government's attitude had favoured policing of the provinces by the Royal Canadian Mounted Police on the grounds that such an arrangement made for better policing in that a central Force could maintain adequate recruiting, personnel, and training branches; it brought closer co-operation between different levels of law enforcement and provided a uniform system of administration, discipline, communications, and inspection. On the matter of costs, it was felt that a clause of the contracts – whereby the central Government could withdraw men from the provinces in the case of a national emergency occurring at any point in Canada – saved the cost of maintaining a reserve of manpower as had been the practice prior to the era of the contracts. There was also a saving to the taxpayer through the reduction of duplicated police services. As a final consideration, the federal Government realized that it must accept some part of the cost and responsibility for law enforcement under changing conditions wherein criminals were becoming increasingly well-organized and mobile. Crime could no longer be considered a local problem or responsibility.

Another consideration that loomed large in the minds of both federal and provincial authorities was a problem peculiar to British Columbia. This was the Sons of Freedom Doukhobors, the strange fanatical group which, in the name of religion, and under the leadership of self-seeking and often corrupt leaders, defied the laws of Canada for over fifty years. Some three thousand members of this group were concentrated in the mountainous areas in the southeastern part of the province. The Doukhobors posed a real police problem.

Cunning and unscrupulous leaders had played on the superstitions and religious beliefs of the largely illiterate Sons of Freedom to fill them with hate and distrust for Canada and its Government and laws. While using religion and superstition as clubs with which to beat their followers into a form of mass paranoia, their leaders, always aware of the importance of public relations, also used religion to fool the press, the authorities, and the public by releasing a constant stream of pious-sounding tracts and statements. The Governments, federal and provincial, extremely sensitive of the political danger of interfering with activities carried out in the name of religion, had for years avoided establishing a definite policy; at best, the Governments followed a policy of vacillation. As a result, the Sons of Freedom villages developed into hot-beds of terror from which arsonists and bombers crept out to burn and destroy.

By 1950, when the negotiations for a policing contract were underway, hundreds of depredations by the Sons of Freedom had caused loss and damage running into millions of dollars, and it was becoming increasingly clear that the rapidly deteriorating situation demanded positive governmental action. Even while the negotiations were proceeding, a new wave of violence broke out which necessitated the transfer of a troop of RCMP men from the prairie provinces to reinforce the provincial police in the Doukhobor areas.

This outbreak delayed the signing of the contract while the federal Government reviewed the position in which it might be placed *vis-à-vis* the Doukhobors. For years the Province of British Columbia had argued that since the Government at Ottawa had seen fit to allow the Doukhobors to enter Canada, it should accept basic – or at least some – responsibility for the troubles brought about by that decision. Ottawa had evaded this responsibility by holding fast to the letter of the British North America Act, which places primary law enforcement in the hands of the provincial authorities. Now Ottawa foresaw the possibility that by contracting to have the Royal Canadian Mounted Police, a federal body, take over law enforcement within the province, the federal Government of Canada might be held to have accepted a large part of the responsibility.

In fact, there was no real cause for concern on this score, since the terms of the contracts make it clear that policing would be carried out under the control of the provincial Attorney-General, but Ottawa was well aware of the political dangers inherent in the Doukhobor problem and was anxious to avoid even the semblance of accepting the responsibility. Negotiations bogged down while a series of letters and telegrams were exchanged. Several times during these weeks of delay, when it seemed that the Governments were close to agreement, further outbreaks of bombings and burnings by the Sons of Freedom occasioned more delay and more consideration of the terms of the contract.

Eventually, Ottawa sent me the precise wording of desired amendments and additions. I was instructed to attempt to have the provincial authorities agree to the proposals. The suggested amendments had been drawn up in order to define precisely the responsibility of the two Governments as regards the Sons of Freedom Doukhobors. There was an additional section that would require the Attorney-General to consult with the federal Government on matters pertaining to law enforcement in the Doukhobor area. Ottawa considered this section a desirable safeguard against the possibility that the provincial authorities might take advantage of the financially generous terms of the contract by calling for unnecessarily large numbers of reinforcements. Apart from the financial considerations, Ottawa wanted to avoid large-scale or precipitate action on the part of the Force that might be regarded by the public as an indication of direct involvement of the federal Government in the Doukhobor problem.

Attorney-General Wismer, a shrewd, capable man of long experience as a lawyer and cabinet minister, was more amused than disturbed by the precautionary efforts. Having studied the proposed changes for a few moments, he chuckled and said, "For years we have been trying to get the federal Government to discuss Doukhobor affairs, but they have shied away from all approaches. Now, suddenly, they insist on a contract to bring about discussions. I am afraid that someone will have second thoughts and realize that by insisting on this they are actually putting themselves in the position of guiding policy as regards Doukhobors. They may also realize that this new section is not worth the paper it is written on since I cannot, by contract, abrogate the authority given an Attorney-General by the British North America Act; but while it is not binding, the proposed section will give me a good lever. I can't believe that they will go through with it. Let's hurry up with the contract before Ottawa changes its mind!"

The Attorney-General's views and his willingness to sign the proposed agreement were passed on to Ottawa. A few days later I received the contract in the form desired by the federal authorities. On August 9, 1950, the documents were signed by the Attorney-General on behalf of the province, and by me on behalf of the federal Government during a brief ceremony held at the Vancouver Headquarters of the RCMP. With this contract, E Division had become the largest Division in the Force.

At about the same time, a continent away, another policing contract was signed. The former colony of Newfoundland had entered Confederation, and the RCMP was thereby called on to expand and take over federal and provincial policing in Canada's new and tenth province.

The larger Divisions of the Force are commanded by very senior officers. As I was still a very junior Superintendent, the expansion of E Division meant the loss of my command. Assistant-Commissioner Allan T. Belcher was transferred from Alberta to take over the newly expanded Division. I became Second-in-Command and assumed the duties of Officer in Charge of the Criminal Investigation Bureau.

In advance of the signing of the contract, a team of our personnel officers had visited British Columbia to interview all members of the British Columbia Police Force and assess their suitability. On the recommendations of that team, almost all of the NCO's and men, and a majority of the officers, were absorbed into the RCMP, the exceptions being for the most part members who, for reasons of health or age, could not be taken over. The judgment of the personnel branch proved sound indeed. The Force gained a great deal through the acquisition of some five hundred experienced policemen, men of high calibre who were dedicated to a career in law enforcement.

The effective date of the contract was August 15, which allowed only six days after signing for the Force to become responsible for policing throughout the province, with the exception of municipal work being done within the larger cities. This was the signal for tremendous activity which might best be described as orderly chaos. Divisional headquarters, together with records, supplies, equipment, and some staff, had to be moved from Vancouver to Victoria, where we were to occupy the rather ramshackle offices of the provincial police located in one end of an old drill hall. Telegrams were sent off to Ottawa requesting the immediate shipment of large quantities of uniforms, stationery, books of Rules and Regulations (the Bible of the Force), and a number of items of equipment which we knew had been in short supply at provincial detachments. Fortunately these requirements had been anticipated and requisitioned in advance. The supplies were packed and ready for shipment.

Personnel problems had to be studied and arrangements set up whereby the two Forces would be integrated in a manner most likely to produce, quickly, the desired results. We were fortunate in that the long delay in negotiations had enabled us to gather a great deal of information regarding the work in the different areas of the province. This information, coupled with the reports that had resulted from the interviews of the personnel officers, simplified the task of staff selection and postings. In the event, the "take-over" proceeded more smoothly than we had expected.

There were minor difficulties and frictions, as the newly acquired members adjusted to different methods and disciplines. Problems arose, too, from the fact that the members of the RCMP were not thoroughly familiar with conditions throughout British Columbia, or with the systems and practices of provincial authorities; but in a short time the two Forces became welded into one team, united by a strong desire to get on with the job. The "job" called for the carrying out of the widest possible variety of police work and the giving of assistance to government departments and the public over an area of 366,255 square miles, embracing some of the most beautiful and also some of the most rugged terrain in the world.

While the beauty was appreciated, its features did little to help in the carrying out of our work. A number of Detachments were located in isolated villages along the coast which, with its deep inlets and fjords, winds ten thousand miles from the Washington border to Alaska, by air, a distance of about a thousand miles. These Detachments, as well as those on the Queen Charlotte Islands, were accessible only by boat or plane. Inland, there were Detachments adjacent to the Yukon border. Some were ideally located in the fruit-growing areas; others policed towns and areas that had sprung up in new frontiers which were being opened in the rich, beautiful bustling province.

These new frontiers called for police work somewhat less formal and frilly than that desired by citizens in more settled communities. Reports received from Detachments in the cattle country along the old Caribou Trail were reminicent of the early West, with their frequent mention of horse thieves, cattle rustlers, and over-exuberant Saturday night celebrations. From the Kootenay Mountain region came a steady flow of reports of Doukhobor arson, bombings, and nude parades. At the other end of the scale were the problems of highway-traffic control, of narcotic-drug trafficking, of investigations into murders, bank robberies, burglaries, fraud, and conspiracy – the whole gamut of crime. But of all the problems posed by the wide variety of duties, the most troublesome were those raised by the Sons of Freedom Doukhobors.

Since almost the turn of the century, a large part of the Doukhobor population has defied the laws of Canada and defeated all efforts of Governments, friends, and well-wishers to help or even to understand them. By 1950, when the policing contract with British Columbia was signed, some three thousand of the more radical Doukhobors had joined together to form a sect called Sons of Freedom. Most of the members of this group were concentrated in villages in the Kootenay area, but there were a few scattered throughout other parts of British Columbia and in the prairie provinces. This strange cult, with its admixture of lunacy and religion, of superstitious, frightened illiterate followers, and scheming profligate leaders, of peace sought through murder, arson, and bombing, raised problems that were surely among the most difficult and frustrating encountered by police anywhere.

Here was organized crime operating under the banner of religion which the Sons had learned to flaunt whenever they wished to attract sympathy, to confuse non-Doukhobors, or to embarrass the authorities. Outbreaks of violence were always preceded and accompanied by vigorous wavings of banners and appeals for protection against alleged religious persecution. These repeated cries of religious persecution have fooled most non-Doukhobors and compelled Governments to follow policies of vacillation and forbearance.

One of the minor weapons used by the Sons of Freedom in their campaigns to force the Government to give in to their wishes is the nude parade during which dozens – and sometimes hundreds – of men, women, and even children strip and march. In almost all instances, such parades follow the alleged receipt of a very timely "divine" message by the leader or one of his aides. There may be some grounds for scepticism in the fact that such messages are rarely received in inclement weather and never during the winter months. They do come through with amazing regularity during spring blossom time, and again during the months of heavy tourist traffic when they bring the Sons a great deal of publicity. Aside from the more serious aspects of the problem, the sudden appearance of several hundred naked people on the highway during the tourist season can cause monumental traffic jams, while the tourists crowd in with their cameras.

To those not familiar with the history of the Sons of Freedom and the ways in which their leaders have played on ignorance and fear to pervert religion into fanaticism and hatred of all authority, it may seem an exaggeration to say that their villages became centres of organized crime and the breeding places of terror. But what milder words could be used to describe a group that has carried out almost twelve hundred depredations, caused well over twenty million dollars worth of property damage, and brought about twenty deaths, some of them by murder?

From the time the first Doukhobors arrived in Canada in 1899 until W. A. C. Bennett formed his first Government in British Columbia, the Sons of Freedom have been a cause of concern to provincial and federal law-enforcement bodies. Premier Bennett and several members of his Cabinet had a great deal of knowledge regarding the Doukhobors and the young, brilliant, and energetic Attorney-General, Robert Bonner, was never content to merely follow old, worn out policies. He demanded – and received – the fullest possible support from the police and backed his demands with a readiness to support their requirements for added strength and additional equipment. But he was quick to recognize that permanent solutions were not to be found in strict law enforcement alone.

Working with E. Davey Fulton, then Minister of Justice in the federal Cabinet, Bonner devised a plan to put an end to the migration scheme through which successive leaders had mulcted the rank-and-file Doukhobors of hundreds of thousands of dollars of their hard-earned money. Leaders had just started another campaign to collect funds for their migration scheme. This time the Doukhobors were supposed to be leaving for Russia. The federal and provincial Governments issued a joint statement. If the Doukhobors wanted to leave Canada, the statement said, the Governments would do everything possible to assist in their departure and, furthermore, the provincial Government would foot the bill for transportation, and the Government of Canada would put up an equal amount to give the migrants a fresh start in Russia.

It wasn't much of a gamble since odds were long that the Russians would be unwilling to accept the troublesome Freedomites. The gamble paid off handsomely. The USSR wanted no part in relieving Canada of this particular section of its proletariat; the racket was stopped and the rank-and-file Doukhobors were saved money and provided with a strong weapon to use against any future leaders who attempted to rob them through the migration scheme.

This was a victory, and an important one, but Bonner knew that so long as the Sons of Freedom remained frightened, superstitious and illiterate followers of unscrupulous leaders, other means would be found to rob and deceive them. A way must be found to break through the wall of ignorance and fear and hatred that their leaders had been careful to keep in good repair. And the best hope, the only hope, for a permanent breach was through education.

Having set up comfortable dormitories, recreation, and schooling facilities at New Denver, a town some distance from the Sons of Freedom communities, the provincial Government served notice on the Freedomite communities that the children must attend school and fixed a date on which those not attending a local school would be received into New Denver. Parents were warned that children of school age who were still truant after the fixed date would be picked up by the police and taken to New Denver. A judge thoroughly familiar with and sympathetic to the Doukhobors was appointed to hear appeals and disputes, and a standing committee representing the Government, the Department of Education, the Attorney-General, welfare groups, and the police was set up to closely follow developments.

The plan brought a flood of protests and criticism and, in the Freedomite communities, nude parades and burnings. Their leaders were quick in crying "persecution" and in bringing out the old and well-worked objection that education offended their religion and was "an instrument of the devil." Non-Doukhobors and some sections of the news media, unmindful of the history of the Sons, added their protests against a plan that would "tear children from their parents" and "bring police terror to the settlements." These critics were, seemingly, quite content to permit unscrupulous leaders and fear-ridden parents to condemn the children to lives of poverty and illiteracy.

Bonner and his confreres in government did not give an inch before the threats of the Freedomites, or the storm raised by the critics. The children were going to have the advantage that elementary education would give them in deciding their futures. Police reports from the Doukhobor areas brought some encouraging information. Quite a few parents, when away from the leaders, were expressing pleasure with the plan and hope that the Government would carry it through.

As had been anticipated, few children turned up at the New Denver school on the appointed day. Back in the Freedomite villages, look-outs were being posted and signal systems arranged to warn of the approach of the police. Hiding spots were planned for the children in the bush, in haystacks, and in sheds and out-buildings. But in a few of the houses, mothers were ironing and packing freshly washed clothes, hopeful that their children would be taken to school.

It was an unpleasant and embarrassing task for the police. Additional men had been sent into the area to allow for simultaneous searches in all of the villages affected. The searches were carried out methodically and quietly, as far as the police were concerned, but the villagers, goaded on by the more fanatical among them, staged noisy demonstrations with much screaming and wailing and cries of "Cossack" each time a child was located and taken to the waiting bus, but there were no attacks on the police. And again there were hopeful signs. Some of the parents – and among them some of the noisiest in their cries of "Cossacks" – took advantage of the first opportunity to whisper directions to a policeman regarding the hiding place of their children. Despite the outcries, in a surprising number of instances little bundles of clothing and lunches had been packed in readiness for the leave-taking of the children.

It took the children a few days to become accustomed to the new quarters and routines, but once that phase was over, they settled in willingly and happily. They proved to be very apt, bright students, and most of them showed a great curiosity and interest in learning. They were keen on sports, and before long could hold their own with the juvenile athletes of the town with whom, after a little hesitation on both sides, they became good friends and playmates.

Visiting days proved somewhat disturbing. The parents and friends of the children were quite free to get a pass at the open gate and visit with the children in the dormitories and recreation rooms, but a quiet, well-ordered visit did not suit the purposes of the leaders who had the parents remain outside and talk to the children through the open-mesh wire fence. If reporters were present, the leaders would stir up a great screaming and wailing, while the children, true to their early training, and taking their cue from the parents, would join in the general hubbub. Very soon after the departure of the parents, the children would throw off the upset caused by the parents' visit, and become happy eager youngsters again.

Similar scenes occurred after each holiday season, when buses returned to the villages to take the children back to school. But once aboard the buses, the children became normal, noisy youngsters, anxious to get back to the new way of life. Criticism from sympathetic non-Doukhobors gradually diminished as the critics took a closer look at the situation and its effect on the lives of the youngsters.

Other changes and improvements have been brought about by the long-overdue effort to cope with the Freedomite problem. Gone were the days when the authorities backed away in the face of depredations and rewarded terror with concessions; and gone were the days when a convicted terrorist would be released from prison after serving only a very small part of his sentence. A special prison, designed to serve the needs of the Doukhobors, had been built to house the arsonists, the bombers, and the fanatics who had committed crimes; and the system of paroles had been brought more in line with that maintaining in other parole institutions. Adequate strength, and a few new techniques, enabled the police to increase the number of convictions. The provincial Government had taken hold of the vexed question of the Crown lands that had once belonged to the Doukhobors. An eminently fair plan had been announced, whereby the Doukhobors could purchase the land at far below its value and on easy, long-term payments.

Trouble still erupts from time to time in Freedomite areas. Habits, fears, and superstitions learned through several generations cannot be erased or changed overnight, but they are changing over the years. Each of the well-considered and positive actions taken will play a part in bringing about change in adapting the Doukhobors, especially the Freedomite sect, to Canadian life.

17

-»»-»»-»»-»»«««-«««-«««-«««

Director of Operations
and
Criminal Investigation

In 1952, I was called to Regina to write examinations that would, if passed, qualify me for a promotion. The week-long examinations seemed tougher than usual, and it was with great relief and some surprise that a few weeks later I received the Commissioner's letter advising that I had achieved passing marks. The following year I was promoted to the rank of Assistant Commissioner and transferred to the Headquarters in Ottawa, to take over the duties that come under the Director of Operations and Criminal Investigation. That resounding and cumbersome title, usually abbreviated to DOCI, is given to the officer directly responsible to the Commissioner for all of the police and investigative activities of the Force, with the exception of work in the field of security and intelligence. Work in that field comes under a separate Directorate.

While working in a field Division, there is a tendency to regard the problems of one's area as the most pressing and important facing the Force and to limit the horizons to the boundaries of the Division. From the vantage point of the DOCI's desk, the outlook is changed and, necessarily, enlarged. Reports flow in from every part of Canada and from police forces around the world. There is a steady stream of correspondence with Government departments, federal and provincial, regarding assistance given by or being sought from the Force; and with departments, agencies, and committees studying various aspects of and attempting to learn causes and find cures for some of our social ills. And when Parliament is in session, there are many questions from the floor of the House. Answering these questions is sometimes troublesome and always time-consuming, but apart from any other consideration, they serve the important function of constantly reminding the public and the police that ultimate authority rests with Parliament.

One could not have served for years without being aware of the great changes that were taking place without, in a small way, playing a part in bringing about improvements. But the extent to which the Force had altered and moved forward to meet new challenges could not be fully appreciated without the full view afforded from headquarters. It was extremely interesting to make comparisons between the Force as I first saw it in 1919 and the modern organization that had been built on that old and solid foundation.

The Force had expanded to cover all of Canada to undertake a multitude of new duties, and to meet new responsibilities. It had increased in strength from about three hundred and fifty members at the beginning of 1919 to more than seven thousand. The volume of work had grown from a few thousand inquiries to just over a million a year. This surprising figure has given rise to some confusion and misunderstanding. On one occasion, when Security and Intelligence activities were under fire in the House, T. C. Douglas, Leader of the New Democratic Party, quoted the figure from the Commissioner's Annual Report and jumped to the conclusion that it established that the RCMP had security files on more than ten per cent of the population. This gave rise to some eyebrow lifting and criticism in the press before someone took the trouble to examine the Commissioner's Report. The "more than a million inquiries" figure has nothing to do with security and intelligence work. (For obvious reasons the figures for that Directorate are not published.) Nor does the figure mean that the Force has arrested or charged more than a million people in a year, an interpretation that has caused more eyebrow lifting. Such an interpretation overlooks the fact that a very large percentage of police work is in no way connected with criminality, but rather is directed toward assisting in such matters as naturalizations, first aid at accident scenes, locating missing or lost persons, inspection of small craft under the Canada Shipping Act, visits to isolated villages in the far north, escorting of mentally deranged persons, and a host of other public-service duties.

For statistical purposes, records are kept that show, among other things, the number of official inquiries or contacts with the public by members of the Force. It is the total of those contacts that make up the figure in the Annual Report. A unit in that total may cover an involved investigation of criminal activities or the widespread search for persons lost in the bush, or it may be simply a statistical result of a member calling on a person given as a reference in an application for naturalization. The figure is used mainly as an indication of the volume of the multitudinous duties of the Force. In recent years, the total has increased to one and a half million.

It would be surprising if, in carrying out such a heavy volume of widely varied duties, the police could avoid an occasional error, or seeming error, of action or judgment. And it would be amazing, bearing in mind that many of the inquiries do concern wrongdoing, and that allegations against the police are useful to the defence, if there were no complaints of heavy-handed action by investigators. Certainly members do commit errors of judgment and, unfortunately, it is not possible, despite intense training, to have all members at all times walk the sometimes difficult line between complete impartiality and an overly zealous pursuit of their duties. Complaints are received and, invariably, receive thorough investigation. During my first year as DOCI, fifty-nine complaints were lodged with the Force. Inquiries established that nineteen of these were unfounded; in thirty-three cases, members had been guilty of errors of judgment, and in seven instances the error or action had been of a serious nature. Errors or overly zealous actions on the part of law-enforcement officers cannot be overlooked or excused, and I make no attempt to justify them. However, I am inclined to doubt that there are many public-service organizations that have perfected personnel selection, training, supervision, and management to a point where they receive fewer than fifty-nine complaints from a million contacts.

Sometimes the investigation of a complaint produces interesting and even amusing facts. On one occasion, I received a well-written, completely detailed and quite disturbing letter from a citizen of a small town in Northern British Columbia. The complainant alleged that he had witnessed an affair on the main street during which two of our constables had administered severe beatings to two brothers who were visiting the town. After the beatings, the brothers had been dragged to the lock-up and placed in cells.

Preliminary inquiries tended to confirm the details given by the citizen. The men had been arrested on the date given, and they had been much the worse for wear when lodged in the cells, so much so that a doctor was called in to attend to a black eye and to apply tape to a few cuts and scratches. Instructions were sent out ordering an officer from another area to make a very full inquiry. His report put a different light on the affair. The brothers were located at a small lumber camp, deep in the bush north of town. In their signed statements, they disclosed that, periodically, the isolation of the bush camp became too much for them and they developed great urges to go to town, "to blow off steam, and raise a little hell." They admitted that while in their cups they were quarrelsome. Almost invariably their long, repressed desire to "raise a bit of hell" ended in a brawl of noble proportions.

On the date in question, having consumed enough firewater to attain the desired state of belligerency, they set about trying to pick fights with other occupants of the bar. Usually in that part of the country it is not a difficult matter to find men who are willing to oblige anyone who really desires a test of strength and fisticuffs, but that afternoon the other bar-flies were intent on minding their own affairs. Disgusted with the peaceful atmosphere of the bar, the two would-be gladiators went into the middle of the street from whence in loud and searing language they proceeded to challenge all comers. Their exuberant disturbance brought two Constables on the scene. They were promptly included in the challenge to fight. They declined the invitation but advised the pair that they were under arrest. When they attempted to remove the pair to the jailhouse, the fight was on.

The brothers were husky young men, but so were the Constables, both of whom were only recently out of our training depot. From the account given by the brothers, and by witnesses who flocked out of surrounding buildings, the fracas was a beauty, grand enough to satisfy even the most ardent hell-raisers. Eventually the brothers were carted off to the jail where, after medical attention for both victors and vanquished, they were allowed to sleep off their already dampened warrior spirits. The next morning they pleaded guilty to having disturbed the peace and were assessed small fines.

There were no hard feelings and certainly no complaints from the brothers regarding the actions of the police – just the opposite. They were strong in their praise of the fighting ability of the Constables. In his statement, one of them said, "They licked us fair and square and gave us a darned good walloping, but we got in a few good licks. Complaints? We got no complaints. We asked for it and we sure got it. Why those Mounties are good pals of ours now!"

The other added, "Another three months or so and we'll get the urge again – but we won't go back to that town. We don't want to fight with our pals – and anyway it's no fun when you know, ahead of time, that you're going to be beat."

Back in 1919, the Force's "fleet" of automobiles consisted of three somewhat ancient models. By the time I took over the DOCI's desk in 1953, the fleet had grown to eighteen hundred, well-equipped cars, and to this transportation there had been added forty-two patrol vessels and eighteen planes. In the north country, traction-driven snowmobiles and bombadiers had supplemented the dog-team.

Selection of personnel was no longer based on the comparatively simple method of a physical examination, a few not too difficult tests, and an assessment of character and suitability by a Recruiting Sergeant. The old methods had worked surprisingly well to meet the requirements of the times, but times and the Force had changed greatly, and the changes had necessitated new systems in the selection of recruits. In the old days, the low pay and pension, poor service conditions, and the rough-and-ready, frontier-type police work had called for men with a high spirit of adventure but no great concern over financial gain or prospects for the future. A spirit of adventure was still required in recruits for the rapidly developing organization, but the Force now required a higher standard of education in recruits anxious to make a career in police work. The old method had served well, but it had also resulted in an extremely high turn-over in personnel. Ways had to be found to select career men capable of meeting the increasingly complex and heavy responsibilities.

To meet these requirements, Commissioner Stuart Taylor Wood, under some urging from his alert, forward-looking Deputy, F. J. Mead, had in 1943 requested assistance from the Canadian army and from universities in the setting up of a personnel branch within the Force. The army seconded an officer, well-experienced in their personnel work, Major Roderick Haig-Brown, now a Magistrate at Campbell River, British Columbia, and a highly regarded author. From the universities, the Force received very willing and knowledgeable professional assistance from numerous teachers.

Haig-Brown was given *carte blanche* in the matter of studying the requirements of the Force and travelled thousands of miles visiting Divisions, Sub-Divisions, and Detachments, including a number of posts in the far north. (As a side line while at Coppermine, he taught the Eskimos the art of fly-fishing, since they were not having much luck with their own methods.) His analytical, objective report on personnel requirements – some of which were peculiar to a Force, the duties of which ranged from bush-type police work to the battling of the most sophisticated types of crime – established beyond question the value of having an "outsider" examine the organization and arrive at fresh views. These would be un-inhibited by long association with and training in traditional policies and practices, and unaffected by concern over the reaction of senior officers to criticism of the old, established order. Certainly Haig-Brown pulled no punches, but his report was not resented by the Commissioner, just the reverse. It brought speedy, action in the intended direction, and as an additional bonus established a precedent whereby the views of specialist "outsiders" have been sought in many areas of the work of the Force.

Following his survey Haig-Brown developed a plan to greatly improve selection at the recruit level and to apply modern techniques in the vastly important matter of man-management and the building and retaining of a high standard of morale.

Some of the ideas advanced were radical when viewed from the traditional practices of the Force. Probably the Commissioner had doubts regarding the proposed shattering of traditions and wanted to double-check, or he may have wanted the views of serving members regarding implementation of the plan, but whatever his reason, he called six officers, including me, to Ottawa to study the matter. On our arrival, we were given a brief outline of Haig-Brown's report and resultant proposals, and told that for the next few days we would be subjected to talks from the proponents of change. We got together that evening to discuss this new and surprising approach. It is rare that change is readily accepted by persons trained in an organization that is doing fairly well by following old and tried procedure. We were not too taken with the idea of replacing personal assessments of the character of applicants, or the existing methods of handling problems of morale, by a system involving ideas drawn from psychiatrists and psychologists or intelligence tests and lengthy interviews by specially trained and classified, non-combatant "personnel officers." It was tentatively decided that we would approach the coming exposure to the "head-shrinkers" with a great deal of scepticism.

I was not reassured by my first contact with the professionals. Having been detailed to carry out other duties, I missed the first talks and entered the classroom in the middle of a lecture by one of the professors. As I approached my seat, I could scarcely believe my ears! Shades of the frontier days – the psychiatrist was actually holding forth on "bed-wetting and thumb-sucking," most unlikely subjects for concern in the matter of recruitment and morale-building in the Mounted Police. I could almost hear the rustle of old-timers turning over in their graves.

As I listened, I was somewhat reassured. The professor was not suggesting that these weaknesses were prevalent in or a matter of concern to the Force. He was simply explaining some of the methods used in the profession in drawing inferences from behaviour patterns. These men knew their business thoroughly and, in addition, were convincing salesmen. In two or three days, they had overcome our scepticism – not usually a simple task with policemen – and had turned us into reasonably enthusiastic supporters of the new approach. A few days were spent in arriving at decisions as to the most advisable course to follow in implementing the plan. A report of our discussions, findings, and recommendations was handed to Commissioner S. T. Wood, and it received almost immediate approval.

I have gone to some length in reviewing the background of the Personnel Branch, but I believe this is justified by the important part that Branch has played in the development of the Force. The tests and interviews designed for use at applicant level have screened into the organization men capable of keeping pace with other important changes and developments. A few, but very few, misfits have slipped through the screening, but I know of no organization that has perfected a system of selection that will entirely eliminate error.

Apart from doing valuable work at recruitment level, the Personnel Branch and its Divisional officers have done a tremendous amount toward improving the lot of serving members. Annual and special interviews with and reports on each man assist greatly in career-planning. Careful studies of working and living conditions, followed by persistent and insistent reports to Headquarters, have helped greatly in improving pay, housing, equipment, and life in general for all members. And the right of any member to request and receive an interview with a Personnel Officer, who is allowed somewhat more leeway than other officers in the matter of enforcing strict discipline, assures the member of a sympathetic and helpful hearing. Many careers have been saved and the services of valuable men retained for the Force through such interviews.

In my view, the change from the old methods of recruitment and man-management to a modern approach to this problem was one of the most important developments in the transition of the Force. Without it, progress in other directions would not have been so easily made. I have just one doubt about the Personnel Branch, and it still plagues me. What if there had been a Personnel Branch back in Regina in 1919?

By 1953, the scientific laboratories had been set up at Ottawa and Regina and were functioning with a reasonable degree of efficiency. More and better apparatuses were required, but the securing of needed instruments had to await the availability of funds. In the meantime, excellent staff overcame the gaps in equipment as far as was possible by improvisation and hard work. The key rule in the work of the laboratories was "impartiality." Strict adherence to that rule has earned the confidence of the Courts in evidence given by our experts. It was not unusual for their evidence to favour the accused and bring about an acquittal.

Since 1953, the equipment of the laboratories has been brought more in line with requirements, and additional laboratories have been opened in British Columbia and the Maritimes. A great deal of the credit for these developments must be given to the good judgment and persistence of Superintendent James A. Churchman. As a Corporal in Montreal in 1920, he started studying ballistics and photography and he advocated the setting up of a scientific laboratory. It had required persistence and, at times, tenacious obstinacy to push his ideas through, but the present laboratories and his well-deserved international reputation as a ballistics expert established that he had those attributes.

Churchman was the officer in charge of the laboratories while I was DOCI, and he was still asking for better equipment, more staff, and improved accommodation. Sometimes it was necessary to turn down his requests, but the matter did not end there. A few weeks later, the same requests, couched in different language, and using new arguments, would reach my desk, and this would be repeated over and over again until he found a loophole, or wore down resistance. His requests frequently brought memories of the 1920's, in Montreal, when he was just starting his efforts to bring scientific aid to the Force. For months he tried to convince Ottawa that we should have our own photographic room rather than remain dependent on the sometimes reluctant co-operation of the provincial police or the municipal forces. Eventually, and probably in exasperation, Headquarters supplied an old, huge "con-certina" type camera, but flatly refused to spend money on reflectors, or any other of the requested items. Churchman made arrangements with the cook whereby he was supplied with a number of empty tomato cans from which he fashioned several reflectors. Stands were improvised from lengths of old pipe found in the garage, and he scrounged electrical wiring by locating and cutting dead lines in the old building. An inch was cut off the front legs of a discarded office chair in order that the occupant would be compelled to sit upright while being photographed. A tomato can served to make a frame for numbers to hang around the prisoner's neck. The numbers were cut from calendars. We were in business with our own photographic room and, to our surprise, Churchman's make-shift set-up produced passable photographs. I believe the drive toward scientific aids for the Force had its beginning in that "Rube Goldberg" – equipped photographic room.

Prior to the early thirties, Mounted Police officers, from headquarters down to the smallest detachment, were almost invariably located in unsatisfactory, run-down premises. On arrival in a strange town, it was scarcely necessary to ask directions. One need only head for the oldest building in sight to find the police office and cells crowded into dilapidated quarters. Economy and strict discipline overrode such tender considera-tions as morale and public relations, which remained high in spite of, rather than because of, the continuation of policies that had fallen behind the times.

Under the Commissionership of S. T. Wood, and with the reluctant blessings from the Treasury people, a limited but forward-looking build-ing program was started. Wood's successor, as Commissioner was Leon-ard H. Nicholson, who was quick to realize the importance of the plan, and after some pulling at federal and provincial purse-strings, he was able to greatly enlarge the building program. By 1953, it had advanced to a point where Headquarters, most Divisions and Sub-Divisions, and many detachments were housed in suitable premises. The program was continued by Nicholson's successor, until today the deplorably housed, poorly equipped Force office or deachment has become almost a thing of the past. The passing was unlamentable.

Great strides had also been made in the matter of training. At basic levels, physical training, drill, riding, and the use of small arms still played an important but no longer major part in preparing men for a career in law enforcement. Lecturers, many of them brought from other Departments, business, and universities, covered a wide variety of subjects that provided the trainees with the background of knowledge now essential in the police field. Members employed in special areas of police work were brought together, periodically, for training by experts in their particular fields. Other specialists received training and studied training methods overseas, and senior officers regularly attended the National Defence College and the Imperial Defence College. The Canadian Police College, started by the Force in the early forties had, by 1953, established a reputation that brought trainees from many countries.

Advantage had been taken of opportunities to send members to universities to study law, commerce, political history, and scientific subjects that would help in the work of the laboratories. This program had developed by 1953 to a point where the Force was receiving about twenty graduates a year. The candidates for these university courses are carefully chosen members with a minimum of four years' service. In recent years, several hullabaloos have been raised in and out of the House of Commons on the grounds that our men were engaged in undercover work to spy on other students. Since applications for enrollment are made by the Force, and cheques covering tuition and other costs are paid by official cheques, and since our members turn up at Convocation and other university ceremonies with full uniform under their gowns, it seems apparent that charges of "spying" are utter nonsense, or that the Force is incredibly naïve in attempting such an "undercover" operation.

The rapid expansion in volume of work forced changes in the handling and filing of correspondence. The Central Registry, the repository for all information and intelligence gathered by the Force, had undergone great changes, and by 1953 had become a well-equipped, smoothly operating department. Similar modernization had brought the Fingerprint Section, which services all police forces in Canada, and occasionally those in other countries, to a high degree of perfection. The trend toward utilization of up-to-date methods has continued and in recent years the steadily increasing work-load has brought about the use of computers.

After some hesitation and some difficulty in the matter of securing necessary funds, a reasonably satisfactory radio-communications network had been installed. Since 1953, the Force has kept abreast of developments in the field of police communications. Today the widespread use of radio and telex ensures speedy communication between more than seven hundred offices and the cars, planes, boats, and national and international law-enforcement agencies, including Interpol. The need for speedy means of communications can hardly be over emphasized when persons in, say, Montreal may plan a crime, carry it out in Toronto, and be in Vancouver or Mexico or London the same night.

The Force had moved a long way to meet new challenges. These changes, some brought on by outside pressures, some by a desire to do a better job, were not peculiar to the RCMP. Most other law-enforcement agencies had moved forward with the times and were in a better position to serve their communities through improved police forces, the getting together of police administrators in such bodies as the Canadian Association of Chiefs of Police, the International Association of Chiefs of Police, based in the United States, and Interpol, based in Europe.

But social attitudes and practices had not remained static while police forces attempted to catch up and keep abreast of modern times. Nor had crime continued to follow old patterns. There had been many changes in our society, mostly for the good, but some had brought about conditions that tended to offset and defeat the best efforts of the police to fulfil their function of maintaining law and order – and this despite the fact that the police were better trained, better equipped, and better organized than ever before.

Crime – serious crime – was on the increase, and the percentage of juveniles involved in crime had increased to disturbing figures and was still increasing. Various theories have been advanced to explain the cause back of increasing criminality. Blame has been placed on a feeling of insecurity in an unsettled world, on the aftermath of two wars, on a breakdown of the home, on a weakening of religious influence, on Communist propaganda, on resentment of authority, on the fact that the police were enforcing an increasing number of restrictive rather than criminal laws, on allegations that the police were too active, that the police were not doing enough, on soft treatment of criminals by the courts and that the courts were not sufficiently harsh, and on a host of other real or supposed causes. Despite a great deal of study and effort, in spite of theorizing answers, solutions had not been found or at least had not produced substantial results.

There was and is today a continuing and increasing attitude that law enforcement concerns only the police and the criminals and that in that context it is desirable that the odds be weighed heavily in favour of the offenders. More and more the police seemed to be regarded as a group somehow separate from the public and bent on imposing discipline and restrictions of their own making. Somewhere along the line the old belief that the keeping of peace in the community was a matter for concern for the entire community had been lost or sidetracked.

Apart from the problems posed by the apathetic attitudes of large sections of the public and by its general unwillingness to consider law and order as of any direct concern to the individual – unless, of course, he was victimized – there were indications of another and even more serious trend in public attitudes, particularly among young people. There was an increasing incidence of cases in which the police were assaulted by bystanders while attempting to make an arrest, and of reports of groups of juveniles attacking policemen for no apparent reason. Sometimes these attacks would be witnessed by scores of people, juvenile and adult, but rarely did a bystander go to the aid of the uniformed citizens who were being beaten. Seemingly the old spirit of fair play had suffered a setback, or it was no longer accepted as applicable to policemen.

Great efforts were expended within police forces and in seeking advice from outside consultants. A great deal of time and money was spent, and is still being spent in an effort to define causes and improve public relations. The problem is not peculiar to Canada. Law-enforcement agencies in other countries have tried to develop measures that would correct or at least ease this particular problem, but despite all of their efforts the trend of hostility toward the police continued. By 1963, the last year during which I was in close touch with the situation, there were 1,037 assaults on policemen, an increase of 9.3 per cent over the previous year. In England and Wales, where the Bobby had hitherto held the respect of the community as a quiet, understanding minion of the courts, the figures for assaults rose by 10.8 per cent to a startling 6,964. In the United States, there were 9,621 recorded assaults on policemen.

The courts in Canada were not uniform in their views regarding the beating of policemen or of the need to extend such protection through adequate sentencing. Sentences varied from terms of imprisonment to fines of five or ten dollars, and in at least one case to admonishing the police for having laid charges. The judge held that the police should expect and accept hostility and resistance. The prosecutor, in the latter case, did not point out that the judge might incur hostility from persons sentenced by him but that he would not expect to accept beatings as a normal part of his work. As regards fines of five or ten dollars, in such cases – and at the risk of having levelled at me that increasingly popular charge of "seeking revenge" – I would like to suggest that such fines are, in fact, a reasonably priced licence to assault and batter policemen.

The question of public confidence and support is the most important single question facing law-enforcement bodies today. Police officers may be better trained, equipment may be improved, they may become completely competent in the mechanics of their work, but they will continue to lose ground in their battle against the criminal elements in our society until such time as they have gained the full support of the Governments, the courts, and most important of all – the public.

It has been said frequently that in order to secure the confidence of the public the police must first earn and deserve it. No one can quarrel with that proposition. The police cannot be surprised should public support waver in the face of wrong-doing on the part of any member; nor can the police be surprised should there be a drop in public confidence whenever a policeman abuses his authority or neglects to pay proper attention to the fine balances and counterbalances that have been designed to protect and preserve the rights of the individual. But I cannot believe that the police are solely or even chiefly responsible for the antagonism that has built up during recent years. The police are doing a better job today than at any time in the past, yet they are meeting constantly increasing opposition in their efforts to enforce laws enacted by our government to maintain free, safe, peaceful communities.

The pattern of crime had changed in response to changes in society. In addition to normal crimes – crimes that are as old as sin – and in addition to the steadily mounting involvement of juveniles, professional law breakers have improved their organizations and techniques. Fast means of transportation and communication, coupled with better planning, enabled national and international criminal organizations to carry out crimes that cost communities millions of dollars. Many of these offenses by criminal organizations were crimes of violence – the protection racket, hold-ups, bank robberies, drug trafficking, and murder. Some were smoother, more sophisticated, and very complicated methods of plundering the public – bankruptcy, stock frauds, fake loan companies, and other "white-collar" crimes. All of these wrinkles present the police with special and difficult problems. The perpetrators are experienced criminals who in their planning take into account the risks and means of reducing those risks to a minimum. Often they are assisted in their planning by a lawyer, wise in the ways of building a defence in advance of a crime, as a precautionary measure against the possibility that things may not go precisely according to the plans. Usually those about to participate are warned against talking if they are questioned by the police after the crime, but at times the traditional rule of silence is reversed and criminals are rehearsed in a statement that they are to give if arrested. This is a far-sighted manoeuvre in that if things go wrong and the criminals are arrested, defence counsel is in a position to call policemen to the witness box to repeat the statement made by the accused. Thus the accused gets his version of the events before the judge or jury without being subjected to cross-examination.

The difficulties the police face securing evidence in connection with organized crime do not end with the bringing of the culprits before the courts. The big-time criminal can afford the best available lawyers and can pay witnesses to give false testimony. He or his lawyer knows how to take advantage of every protection that has been built into our laws. It is the experienced criminal, the member of the mobs, who benefits most from those safeguards.

The gangsters are also the chief beneficiaries of our gaming laws, laws that are the outcome of years of efforts by legislators to find a politically safe middle-ground between those who favour more liberal and practical legislation and the anti-gambling groups. The resultant hodge-podge falls far short of fulfilling the avowed purpose of protecting the public. Indeed, in some ways the gaming laws border on hypocrisy. How can the police or the public reconcile or regard as a serious attempt to protect the public a set of laws that permits a man to lose a month or a year's pay at the racetrack but make it an offence for him to spend his last dollar on a lottery ticket or his last dime on a punchboard? How can we accept the reasoning that it is legal and proper to buy a *pari-mutuel* ticket at the track, but illegal and wicked to take a flyer for two dollars at the handy corner bookie?

There is ample evidence that the general public – at least that part of the public that is not opposed to gambling – does not accept the reasoning back of the legislation. And there is ample evidence that many if not most Canadians are not averse to taking the odd gaming risk. It follows that the gambling laws are not taken very seriously and that for this reason the police receive very little support in their efforts to enforce laws which are, even by many policemen, regarded as somewhat ridiculous.

This situation is made-to-order for the gangsters whose organizations depend on gambling for the largest part of their income. Through bookie shops, numbers rackets, and gaming houses, they reap a harvest which provides the funds with which to finance other criminal activities. They experience little difficulty in securing batteries of telephones with which to service local customers, and direct lines to centres in the United States for the receiving of track-side information and "lay-off" betting. In the climate created by such laws, it is not surprising that the gangsters are sometimes able to buy protection.

While I was DOCI, the Senate set up a committee to inquire into gambling. Commissioner Leonard H. Nicholson was invited to appear before the Committee, and I worked closely with him in preparing his statement to the senators. He drew attention to the weaknesses, contradictions, and impracticability of the existing laws and the ways in which these ineffective laws enable criminals to milk the public of millions of dollars. The fact that great numbers of Canadians placed bets or bought lottery tickets or played number rackets through gangster-operated organizations was held to be an acceptable indication that a large part of the public likes to gamble and will gamble – legally or otherwise. On the basis that millions of dollars were being channelled into organized crime under the existing but unworkable laws, Nicholson suggested that a new and frank approach should be tried to assure the public a fair run for its money by keeping the hands of the syndicates out of the pot. The plan advanced was straightforward. Gambling that could be operated under strict control should be legalized with the Government exercising discretion as to the amount or volume of the gambling that would be permitted. Games of chance that could not be kept out of the hands of gangsters and could not be operated under close supervision would be made illegal. The cost of supervision, accounting, and taxes would, under the plan, be taken from the money wagered and would be far less costly than the "take" of the gangsters.

Commissioner Nicholson's idea was not novel or radical. Race tracks have operated under this system for many years in Canada. Races, gambling casinos, and betting pools have been legalized and conducted under Government supervision in many countries. But novel or not, the suggestion brought the wrath of the righteous down on Nicholson's head. Anti-gambling groups published scathing objections. A few newspapers expressed surprise, editorially, that a Commissioner of Police would come out in favor of widespread gambling. Actually he had done no such thing. He had suggested that there be a frank recognition of the fact that gambling was already widespread and would continue as long as a considerable number of people wanted to participate. It is extremely doubtful that implementation of the plan would have increased gambling, but it would have forced the gangsters out, given the public a good measure of protection, and provided some revenue.

Arguments against the plan were that it would be immoral for the Government to legalize gambling and wicked to accept as taxes any part of the proceeds. This may be so, and I am not arguing the morals of the matter, but rightly or wrongly the Government, through race tracks, is already guilty on both counts. It was also said that the opening of off-track betting offices, branches of the track *pari-mutuels*, would encourage betting, an argument that cannot be taken too seriously by anyone familiar with the present situation whereby bookie joints provide more widespread service than would be the case with Government-supervised betting offices. Nor would legalized off-track betting provide favourite hang-outs for juveniles, as do the shady businesses that now handle betting.

There were also loud protests at the thought of legalizing lotteries and gaming houses. Again the protests overlooked the existing betting houses and lotteries, all of which are operated by mobsters, and most of which are crooked. It seems to me to be pulling a long bow to take the stand that it is more righteous to close our eyes to illegal operations than it would be to bring gambling out into the open where it could be seen and supervised and controlled, or to hold that it would be immoral for the Government to take some of the profits out of the gambling and thereby deal a heavy blow to organized crime. Many old, conservative countries have legalized lotteries and gaming houses and sports pools, as well as racing, without any noticeable effect on their morals or well-being, at least not as much effect as organized crime exerts whenever it is allowed to flourish.

The Senate Committee submitted a lengthy and fairly discerning report, but the hodge-podge of unworkable law remains, and organized crime continues to milk the public for funds which are used to finance other criminal enterprises and spread corruption even further.

From the DOCI's desk, it was easy to see the extent to which organization, speedy communication, and rapid transportation had influenced the methods employed in carrying out many types of crime. Counterfeiting, fraudulent cheques, bankruptcy frauds, stock rackets, the traffic in narcotic drugs – all had become complex, well-planned, and carefully executed criminal activities. Most of the wrong-doers were local talent, but the influence and guidance of the United States syndicates was increasingly apparent. Police forces drew closer together in their efforts to cope with the situation and their efforts met with a fair degree of success, but the initiative rests with the criminals, and crime continues on an upward trend.

My two years at the DOCI's desk were fascinating, sometimes frustrating, and immensely valuable. They gave me an opportunity to see all of the work of the Force, the developments that had taken place, and they made me realize all the challenges that law-enforcement agencies have to face when pitted against law-breakers.

18

➤➤➤-➤➤➤-➤➤➤-➤➤➤-◄◄◄-◄◄◄-◄◄◄-◄◄◄

Espionage
and
Treason

Does Canada have any secrets that are really worth stealing? Is it necessary to maintain a counter-intelligence service? I have been asked these questions many times by Government officials employed in departments in which security is not too important, by the press, business men, and the general public. Opposition members have raised the issue in the House of Commons on several occasions. It is a fair question for several reasons, chief among them being the fear that most counter-intelligence work implies secret prying into the affairs of others and therefore an invasion of the privacy and freedom of individuals. The operations of an effective security service cost a great deal of the tax-payers' money.

A ready if not completely convincing answer is provided by the espionage activities of the USSR and other Iron Curtain countries. Their persistent efforts to penetrate Canadian security, to recruit Canadians into their networks through the use of liberal payments or blackmail or pressures on relatives in the homelands establish beyond any reasonable doubt that they place a high premium on information that they may filch from Canada. There is absolutely no doubt regarding their eagerness and continuing activities in the espionage field. Nor can it be doubted that they have established and now maintain a sizeable apparatus for the carrying out of espionage and subversion in Canada.

Espionage did not end with the revelations of the Gouzenko case – it simply became more expert as the USSR and its satellites benefited from the mistakes and experiences of that case and other cases throughout the democracies. In recent years Canada has witnessed several prosecutions for charges arising from espionage and quite a number of attachés and employees of Iron Curtain embassies have been declared *persona non grata* and asked to leave the country because of their involvement in efforts to steal classified information from Canada. Not all the cases in which espionage leads to the explusion of diplomats are published. At times the Government takes the stand that such publicity might offend the ussr and probably result in the expulsion of a Canadian from Russia on a tit-for-tat basis.

The latter consideration has merit in that it is troublesome and costly to send replacements. As to offending the Soviets by letting the Canadian public know of well-established espionage cases, I doubt that there is much cause for concern here. It has been frequently demonstrated that the Russians are not particularly thin-skinned on that score. Even Kruschev admitted espionage operations during his appearance before the United Nations. Russian controls are fully aware of the accuracy of charges made against their agents – no country could hope to operate a world-wide network without an occasional slip-up – but outraged protests and "strawman" methods of defending by attack have proven invaluable in spreading confusion among their opponents and providing arguments for their supporters. A large part of the success of Soviet operations in the field of espionage stems from the hard-minded, practical manner in which the Kremlin approaches the problem of espionage. Our sometimes too tender regard for their sensibilities in this field seems more likely to cause ridicule than engender appreciation among the tough-minded men who direct their operations.

It has been argued that the Soviets refuse to accept as accurate the vast amount of information open to them in Canada and that they are convinced that they must double-check everything through espionage. This sort of argument goes on to hold that after all the Russians are just doing what all other countries are doing. These arguments do not stand up very well in the face of facts. It is true that, at times, the Kremlin does go to great lengths to secure information that it could get very readily from published, unclassified documents or through the press. But these could be "double-checking" operations; it is definitely known that at times such simple assignments are used in their early efforts to draw someone into their web, and at others times these form part of the training of contacts and agents. However, it is also clearly established that many of their "targets" lie well within the security screen that protects classified or secret information.

As to the argument that the Soviets are only doing what is done by all other countries, this is simply not true as regards Canada. Canada does not have an intelligence organization which operates in other countries. Certainly foreign information is received by Canadian embassies abroad, but this information is secured from "open" sources, not through the activities of secret espionage apparati. The gathering of such "open" information is part of the normal function of an embassy. Through the Royal Canadian Mounted Police, Canada does operate a counter-intelligence organization, the purpose of which is purely defensive. The Force does not send espionage agents abroad, but it does attempt – and with considerable success – to protect the security of the country by meeting the challenges posed by secret agents of foreign powers. One could wish that the Government and the politicians would be a little more forthright in asserting Canada's sovereign right to protest against and take action toward preventing the setting up of potentially dangerous underground organizations within our own boundaries.

It is important to remember that Canada does have secrets of her own, as well as top-secret information directly entrusted to her by friendly nations, or received through membership in NATO and other international bodies. It is doubtful if the most ardent advocate of the "we-have-no-secrets" school of thought would argue that the Cabinet should sit in public while discussing affairs of vital interest to the business and future of our country; or that ministers, departmental heads, the armed services, and all committees should make their planning matters of open record. Certainly there are matters the premature disclosure of which would do great harm to our legitimate interests. This is particularly true at a time when the Soviets are as much interested in securing information that will enable them to outmanoeuvre us at the "peaceful co-existence" conference tables as they are in gaining information of military value.

When secrets are entrusted to Canada by other powers, the very acceptance of such confidences carries with it responsibility for measures that will assure their safekeeping. Some of these confidences, such as those received through membership in NATO, are given only after the recipient country has undertaken certain steps to maintain security. Although there may be a choice as to the degree of security imposed to protect our own secrets, there is no leeway in the matter of safeguarding the trust of other nations.

When confidential and important information is in the possession of several collaborating nations, the offensive intelligence services of opposing powers, if they are efficient, will probe to find the spots where security can be most easily breached. The Soviet intelligence services are efficient, skilled, and persistent; it is probably the most formidable espionage organization in history, and it has the advantage of aid from local subversive groups. Still the skilled professionals of the Russian intelligence service do not have a great deal of confidence in local Communist parties. To a limited extent they use them in the recruitment of contacts and agents, but even in that important endeavour they proceed with great caution. Local Communist parties are used – "used" is the proper term – chiefly for spreading propaganda and raising issues that will weaken or bring criticism to the Government in power unless of course that Government is Communist. Local parties are also used to create friction between friendly powers. The efforts of local Communist parties are always toward creating conditions of chaos during which it is their hope, the disciplined "activists" of the party will be able to seize power. The extent of their activities depends on conditions within each country, but the objective never varies. This point is easily verified by a brief study of Communist activities in the trouble spots in the world today.

If we accept the foregoing views, which can be supported by a mass of evidence, then the answers to the two questions raised in the beginning of this chapter seem clear beyond reasonable doubt. Canada *does* have secrets worth protecting; and it *is necessary* that we maintain an efficient counter-intelligence and security service. But this gives rise to another question. Is the counter-intelligence service provided by the RCMP competent and efficient? Does the force handle well the problems that are the concern of a national security and intelligence service?

The Force frequently comes under fire because of its security functions. According to some critics, members employed on the work lack the background, training, and knowledge that would enable them to appreciate the sensitivity of their task. Because of these shortcomings, it is alleged, the Force inclines toward a jackbooted approach to delicate matters that, at times, borders on infringement of fundamental rights and freedoms. Unfortunately it is rare indeed that such critics take the trouble to get the facts straight. It is unfortunate also that, because of the necessary rule of silence, the police are rarely in a position to answer the critics, even when the most widely inaccurate allegations are being levelled at them.

The recent Gerda Munsinger and Victor Spencer cases serve as good examples of the wide gap that often exists between criticism and fact. In the early stages of both cases, it was alleged that the Force had been bumbling and inept in its inquiries and in the essential task of keeping the Government informed. But the rule of silence was removed only when Royal Commissions were set up to arrive at the truths of the matters, and then the Force had an opportunity to publicly present the facts regarding the role it had played. The reports of the Commissions clearly established that the security and intelligence service had functioned throughout in an alert, efficient, and entirely proper manner. The persons involved in the inquiries, particularly in the Munsinger affair, held widely divergent views regarding the setting up and conduct of the Commission, but the Force appreciated these rare opportunities to present an accurate picture of its work.

In 1955, I was transferred from the DOCI's desk to become the Director of Security and Intelligence, a post that carries responsibility for the supervision of the work of the Directorate across Canada. I had been closely associated with counter-intelligence work since 1936 in the divisions in which I had served, and I welcomed the opportunity to play a part in the supervision and planning of this very important work of the Force. I was pleased also to have the chance to acquire top-level knowledge regarding the extent and methods of subversion and espionage in Canada by studying the files of the Directorate. I also had a chance to meet frequently with the heads of other national security services in other democratic countries.

The counter-intelligence responsibilities of the RCMP had their beginning almost fifty years ago when the Government learned of the presence in Western Canada of paid agents sent by Moscow to form a revolutionary party. The Force was called to make arrangements whereby the Government would be kept advised of developments. A handful of men was assigned to the task. The fact that a Sergeant, working undercover of course, attended the first organizational meeting of the Canadian Communist Party, and that other members of the small Special Branch – as it was then known – became minor executives of the party, indicates that these fledgling counter-intelligence men made up for lack of experience and training by hard work and enthusiasm.

Between the wars, the Canadian Communist Party grew and became increasingly active. This necessitated an expansion of the Special Branch and the establishment of arrangements whereby members would receive training in the United Kingdom and the United States and, later – as senior members became sufficiently experienced in "trade-craft" – in Canada itself. The approach of World War II and the urgent need for close observation of the Nazi, Fascist, and Canadian Fascist parties gave impetus to the growth of the counter-intelligence service and brought a wealth of experience. That the lessons of the prewar years were well learned is indicated by the fact that the arrangements made by our enemies were completely disrupted on the outbreak of war. There was not one case of enemy sabotage, and as far as is known, or could be discovered from the files seized in Germany after the war, no enemy agents were able to operate in Canada.

The war years also brought about very close co-operation with the intelligence services of other countries, and this has continued since the war. The benefits to be derived from close liaison at the investigational level and by frequent meetings between the heads of the services in different countries are obvious. What better way is there to keep abreast of new developments in the spying activities of those trying to penetrate our security methods? Yet this co-operation with friendly powers has brought some severe criticism on occasions when it has been disclosed that information – developed in Canada regarding subversive, security or espionage matters in other countries, particularly the United States – has been given to the counter-intelligence service of the country concerned. It is interesting to speculate on the possible reaction of these critics if it became known that the security service of a friendly nation had failed to pass on information of vital interest to Canada. Co-operation must be a two-way street.

Shortly after the war, because security (as distinct from counter-espionage) had been made a responsibility of the Force, the name of the Directorate was changed from Special Branch – a title copied from the United Kingdom – to Security and Intelligence. Briefly, the work of this force within the Force is divided into three main categories: counter-espionage, security, counter-subversion. The Directorate in Ottawa and the branches in divisions across the country are staffed by members carefully chosen after some years of observation by the Personnel Branch. They receive extremely careful training by fully qualified and experienced instructors. Members still go to other countries for training, but in assessing the capability and quality of the Security and Intelligence Directorate, it is significant that members of other services frequently come to Canada for training by the Force. Many of the Officers and NCO's have spent most of their service in this work. In addition to "regular" members of the Force, the Directorate has on its staff a number of highly qualified civilian members and civil servants who give assistance in the analysis of reports, in researching developments in the Communist world, and in preparing reports to the Government.

I have said that the spies of Iron Curtain countries are well-trained, highly skilled, and totally professional, but they are by no means supermen who never make mistakes. True, in their service mistakes are costly, but the very pressures under which they work and the high cost of error sometimes bring about a conflict between persistence and caution, and this leads them into actions that border on the ridiculous.

I recall an incident that occurred at a garden party given at the Experimental Farm in Ottawa in honour of a delegation of agriculturalists visiting from Russia. I had only recently been appointed Director of Security and Intelligence, a fact that was undoubtedly known to Soviet Intelligence, since the appointment had been mentioned in the press. As my wife and I approached the receiving line, I noticed that a Soviet embassy employee, known to us as a member of their intelligence service, was standing directly behind the Soviet ambassador, who headed the line of agricultural experts. The intelligence agent was flanked by two men, one of whom had a moving-picture camera and the other a still camera. While we were being presented to the ambassador, the attaché signalled the photographers who at once moved into position to take photographs – of me – a rather silly procedure since the press had carried several pictures at the time of my appointment. After chatting for a few minutes with the ambassador, my wife and I moved away a short distance and turned to watch the proceedings. As we turned, the attaché was in animated conversation with the Ambassador, and it was quite obvious that I was the subject of the conversation. After a few moments, the Ambassador nodded, seemingly in agreement with whatever proposal had been advanced. From that point on, we were "shadowed" openly and obviously by the attaché who remained about thirty feet behind us. We had a bit of sport by doubling in our tracks and walking in circles, but he persisted in his utterly ridiculous "close surveillance." After about one hour we walked across the grounds to our car. Our watchdog kept his thirty-foot distance. As we entered the car, he took out a notebook to jot down the licence number. This man was one of their fully trained professionals. It is impossible to reconcile his behaviour with our knowledge of their training and ability, and it is difficult to arrive at even a reasonable guess as to what it was hoped the performance would accomplish. Certainly persistence, for some unknown reason, had overridden caution. The fact that it had also overridden courtesy – the garden party had been held to honour the Russian visitors – did not, apparently, enter into their considerations.

But Russian security people can be and usually are extremely cautious. Their meetings with agents and contacts are often so surrounded with precautionary measures, checks, and double-checks, that a writer of spy thrillers would hesitate to include them in a script as being too improbable.

In one of their operations in Ottawa, they arranged a "dead-letter drop" by loosening a stone in one of the walls along a driveway. As a signal to the agent that a message had been placed behind the stone, a cross would be chalked on the side of a building near the bus stop used daily by the agent. The messages left in the "drop" were one way only – control to agent – and contained cryptic and coded directions for a meeting, messages which, if discovered, would be probably taken as clues in some juvenile game of "treasure hunting." In other operations, various surreptitious methods are used in arranging "meets." Messages are left at "live-letter drops," if the address of a go-between is known, or between pages of a given book on the shelves of a bookstore or library. Sometimes the agents used the classified columns of the daily newspaper or a seemingly innocent telegram from a fictitious address to set up a meeting. In dealing with new contacts or agents, the messages would be so coded as to give the date, time, and place of the meeting. Fully trained and trusted agents are usually aware of the time of day or night and the place fixed for the next meeting through instructions received during their last encounter and so they need only to be told the date. In some operations, a trained agent is told the day of the week on which all of his meetings with his master will take place and will be told the manner in which he will receive a message that a meet is "on." Thus, if the weekday fixed for him was a Saturday, and during the preceding week someone stood next to him in a bus-line reading a certain out-of-town paper, or if he received a phone call asking for "Mabel", he would know that the following Saturday was "active." The frequency of meetings depends on the type of work being done by the agent, but the spy-masters are rarely hurried to a point where eagerness to secure the product of the agent will override extreme caution. Weeks and sometimes months may go by before they arrange an encounter, and even then the meeting may not take place because of the deliberate failure of the control man to show up, or because for some reason that develops at the last minute the meeting is considered unsafe. When an arranged "meet" falls through, the agent may have been given instructions to be at the same place at the same time the following week or the following month, or he may have to wait for another signal from his master. Again the traffic is one-way only. "Don't call us, we'll call you."

When a meeting does take place, it is usually surrounded by precautionary measures, so extreme as to seem silly in the open, free, and easy social atmosphere of Canada. That such involved, round-about methods are employed in the espionage networks is complimentary in that it indicates a high regard for the efficiency of the counter-espionage service.

For several hours before a meeting, the area is kept under observation by the spy-master. The slightest indication that they are themselves under surveillance is enough to cause an agent to cancel the arrangements to meet his Canadian contact. As the appointed hour draws close, the number of observers is increased until as many as six or eight men or women may be loitering at strategic points on the street or watching from parked cars or from windows in nearby buildings. Usually the control agent, who is to make the "meet," is preceded and followed by other agents whose job it is to be on the look-out for police "tails."

There may be no actual contact at the meeting place between the control man and the agent being contacted, as the arrangement may be that, having spotted his "control," the agent follows him at a discreet distance. After many twistings and turnings and doublings back, they may get together on a park bench, or get into a car that immediately moves off, or there may be no actual getting together of the two men. If the purpose is to give instructions to the agent, the master may casually stroll through a park, sit for a few minutes on a bench to read his newspaper, and then leave the paper in which the instructions have been folded on the bench, to be picked up by the watching agent; the control man may have thrown away a bit of branch that he had been carrying, a branch that had been hollowed to contain a metal cylinder. If the agent is delivering material, the positions are reversed, and he does the leading and discarding of articles that contain his "product," always under the watchful eyes of the control man and several observers. In many cases, the agent has been provided with photographic equipment for document-copying, and his "delivery" is a roll of film in a trick container, which in turn may be concealed in a "throw-away" article, such as a cigarette package, a hollow stick, or a chocolate-bar wrapping. The "product" may also be passed on by using such old tricks as the switching of similar briefcases on a park bench, in a bus, or on a train. The variety of contrivances used is endless and calls for a great deal of alertness, imagination, and knowledge on the part of the members of the counter-espionage service. The constantly shifting precautionary measures offer a quite understandable explanation of the inability of the police to consistently produce the hard, clear, readily understood sort of evidence that would be expected in, say, a case of fraud, a fact that makes counter-intelligence men prone to grey hair and ulcers.

When such operations as I have described are under the direction of an embassy or consulate or other official office of a foreign country, they are known in intelligence circles as "legal" – a literally inaccurate term used to differentiate between them and "illegals," or between them and espionage networks that are controlled by master spies working independently of the official foreign offices in Canada. "Illegals" use many of the same methods as their brother spies from the embassies but are even more devious and cautious in their work. However, one noticeable difference in their operation is that very often the "illegals" will spend a great deal of time and effort and money in developing an agent and then fail to make use of his services. Such "sleepers" may be well paid for carrying out meaningless little tasks, or they may hear from their masters – often through a member of the crew of an Iron Curtain ship, or a member of a delegation visiting from the Soviet – only at long intervals, sometimes as long as a year apart. As it is reasonable to assume that there is a purpose back of their recruitment, it seems equally reasonable to conclude that this deep underground network of "sleepers" is being built for use if the time ever comes when it will be impossible to operate "legal" nets.

In their recruitment procedures, the espionage nets are much less cautious than in their handling of contacts and agents. There have been many instances in which their approaches are crude and blunt. Persons holding positions that give them access to classified material have received invitations to a cocktail party or to other innocuous social functions at an Iron Curtain embassy. Attachés or members of the embassy staff attempt to become very friendly, in most cases through an ability to discuss the hobbies and likes and dislikes of the prospect, a fact which indicates that inquiries are made in advance of such "chance" conversations. At the slightest opening, the friendship is put on a personal basis, with visits to the home of the prospect, during which direct and sometimes openly prying questions are asked regarding the prospect's salary, financial standing, mortgage, drinking, and entertainment habits. An offer of substantial rewards for "a little co-operation" is often made during the second or third meeting. The Soviet agents must be aware that information regarding such crude efforts at recruitment will reach the counter-intelligence service, but this does not appear to be of any great concern to them. If they are confronted with details of their own activities, they simply denounce the informant as an alcoholic, or as part of a Fascist plot to discredit the USSR.

Another favourite ground for attempts to recruit spies is among New Canadians from Soviet bloc countries. Russians have received many rebuffs for their efforts in this field, but still they persist. A desire on the part of New Canadians to get relatives out from behind the Iron Curtain, or anxiety over the welfare of relatives, or a visit to their old homes and parents and friends – these often lead to approaches from the Soviet bloc intelligence services, approaches that are not always free of threat of reprisals against relatives.

Blackmail has always formed an important part of the recruitment of Soviet agents, and in recent years it has been promoted to a position of prime importance by the espionage bosses. When their efforts at "talent-spotting" turns up a prospect, they go to great lengths to discover weaknesses in his character. Is he a spendthrift, an alcoholic? Is he overly fond of women? Is he a homosexual? If his weakness is over-spending, or too great a love for the bottle, they attempt to use this knowledge to man-oeuvre him into a position where he is in sore need of help, and they become the good samaritans – always for a price. If his character weaknesses are in other directions, they provide the means by which he may satisfy his desires, and they have hidden cameras to take photographs for purposes of blackmail. An agent so recruited is less expensive and more easily held in check than a person brought into the networks on ideological grounds or for pay only. It is my personal belief that, unknown to the principals, the Profumo case in England and the Munsinger affair in Canada were the beginnings of operations of this sort.

In their preparation of identities to be used by agents in the international field, they go to great lengths to provide a background story that will stand up under close scrutiny. Names of deceased persons of the desired age are secured from the offices of registrars or from tombstones. Sometimes they are able to have alterations made in records or to have records destroyed. A false identification is then built up from the birth certificate and other records that will stand examination by the counter-intelligence services. It is interesting and disappointing to note that birth, death, naturalization, and passport records in Canada are such as to make Canada a favourite "homeland" in providing false papers for international spies.

The Lonsdale case in the United Kingdom provides an excellent – and unusual – example of this tendency to use false Canadian identification. A Londsdale was born in a town in Northern Ontario at the time and place shown in the identification papers of the spy master arrested in England. At the request of the United Kingdom authorities, the Force carried out extensive investigations and located the father. According to his story – and he was very frank and straight-forward in telling it – his wife had deserted him some thirty years back and had returned to her native country, Finland, with their eight-year-old son. The dates and other rather vague information fitted the story told by the man under arrest in England. Unfortunately the father could not recall any birthmarks or scars or peculiarities that would either provide positive identification or refute the claims of the arrested spy master to Canadian citizenship. Obviously the description of an eight-year-old was of little help in checking the story of a thirty-eight-year-old man.

In police and intelligence work, patience and persistence are prime requisites. Fortunately the Force member who was handling the inquiry had learned that lesson well. He returned again and again to the father to ask more questions in the hope that he could jog something helpful out of his memory of the boy. His patience paid off. One night he was chatting of times gone by and got the father reminiscing about his early married life. The old gentleman recalled that his wife had cost him a lot of money. Having cited several examples of her extravagances, he mentioned an incident which to him seemed to have been a needless expenditure of hard-earned money.

"Why," he recalled, "she insisted on having the baby circumcised – and that cost me twenty-five dollars."

The investigator realized that he might have come on to something useful.

"Circumcised? Are you sure?" he asked.

"Course I'm sure. Should be. I told you the Doc charged twenty-five bucks, and it only took him a few minutes. Did the job right on the kitchen table, and the kid raised a hell of a row."

An unusual cable was sent to the United Kingdom intelligence service. "Our boy was circumcised. How about yours."

Their first reply indicated that, complete as their search of the suspect had been, it had not provided the personal information that might make our discovery important. A few days later, however, we were advised in very formal language that, as it seemed probable that the suspect would remain in custody for some time, the authorities had decided that he should be given a thorough medical examination. The examining doctors had satisfied themselves that the man who called himself Lonsdale was in good health and had not been circumcised. This means of refuting assumed identification must be rare, even in the sometimes extraordinary annals of counter-intelligence work. It developed later that the details of the Lonsdale boy had been discovered by Soviet agents in Finland

and the information used in providing one of their agents with identification as a Canadian.

If it seems incredible that espionage networks are active in Canada, and that they follow the tactics I have described, I can only assure the reader, with regret, that Iron Curtain countries have been active in this field for many years, and that despite an apparent improvement in the relations between Canada and the Soviet, there has been no indication of a falling-off in their espionage activities. Nor has there been any falling-off in the work of the Force. The Canadian public may rest assured that their counter-espionage service knows its job.

In my view, mention of Soviet espionage at this time is not the stirring of old and troublesome matters that might be better left alone. First, it is not an old discarded problem, but a continuing one. Second, the espionage service of the Iron Curtain countries – loud protests to the contrary – know the truth of the matter and are not so thin-skinned as to be greatly upset or dissuaded from their endeavours by any true statement that may be made. And if their countries are upset by the giving of facts regarding their espionage activities, they have an answer that would be most welcome in Canada. They can stop spying. The first sign of their withdrawal from that field would be a reduction in their embassy staffs which are overstaffed compared with those of other countries.

Security work – the checking of persons being considered for employment in or promotion to sensitive departments of Government – is handled by a separate branch of the Directorate and is a time-consuming, difficult task. There is a fairly general misunderstanding as to the methods and responsibilities of this branch and, as a result, it attracts an unfair amount of adverse criticism.

It is obvious that the RCMP does not operate a security branch for its own purpose or benefit, and it should be equally obvious that the Force does not make or operate underground rules of its own design. The work is carried out under instructions and terms of reference that give in precise detail the duties of the Force in measures designed to ensure reasonable security within the country. Under these measures, which compare very favourably with those developed in other countries to cover the important and delicate problem or internal security, the RCMP is appointed as the agency that will service other departments in the carrying out of security inquiries. It is no part of their function to decide what applicants or employee being considered for promotion should be the subject of inquiries. That responsibility rests with the security officer of each department, and he in turn is guided by rules drawn up by a central committee. Having received a request for information regarding an individual, the police proceed to carry out the work assigned to them under the overall plan by making inquiries. The report that is subsequently sent to the departmental-security officer details the information secured during the police investigation, but it does not – and this point bears repeating, since it has given rise to a great deal of misunderstanding – it does not give an opinion as to the suitability or otherwise of the candidate. From time to time departmental heads and the central committee have attempted to have police reports advance some comment on this point, but the police have steadfastly resisted such pressures on the grounds that the Force serves as a fact-finding agency and that responsibility for action properly rests with the departmental-security officer who must, and should, make the decision regarding suitability. If in doubt as to a proper course of action, he may request guidance from the central committee – not the Force.

Information regarding the volume of requests for such inquiries is never published, but it can be said that requests run into many thousands each year. As they do not, in any way, imply wrong-doing, but result from an application for employment or an opportunity for advancement, the inquiries are not of a particularly secret nature nor is there any good reason why they should be. Nevertheless, the fact that such inquiries are being carried out is frequently viewed with some alarm. There would be much more real cause for alarm if sensitive departments were employing men without bothering to check backgrounds. Complaints and criticisms frequently end by expressing grave doubts as to the ability of the police to make judgments concerning an applicant's suitability. I could argue that point in favor of the police, but this is not necessary since, as has been said, the police do not make the decision in these cases.

Cases have been publicized in which an unsuccessful applicant was known to have a close relative who was an active member of a subversive group. In such cases the cry "guilt by association" has been raised, usually with the alleged fault attributed to the Force. The applicant's close relationship with a person known to be subversive may have been referred to in the police report, but again the decision as to what bearing the fact would have on the suitability of the applicant is not made by the police. And it is always possible that the applicant lost out to another more suitable person simply because he was better qualified. In any event, the "guilt by association" complaint cannot be seriously regarded as well-founded. The question involved is not one of guilt but of the suitability of a person to be given access to matters of a secret and confidential nature. It seems to follow – indeed, it must follow – that if there is any doubt, the question must be resolved in the interest of the state.

Mistakes, inexcusable but unavoidable in the face of thousands of inquiries, do occur on the part of the security service, but fortunately these are rare and every effort is made to eliminate the possibility of error. In a recent case, the police report referred to a man of known subversive leanings as an uncle of an applicant, a brother of the applicant's father. The family name was an uncommon one, and the inquiries took place in a small industrial town. The investigator was told by the employment office of the company where the father and the subversive chap worked that the men were brothers. A town official volunteered the same information, as did several local storekeepers. The investigator accepted the information as accurate and reported the alleged facts. When the case came to light, it brought a great deal of deserved criticism to the Force. Subsequent inquiries at the Bureau of Vital Statistics revealed that the two men were not related. Of course, the investigator erred in a too ready acceptance of the information received from several sources. As has been said, mistakes in the security field are inexcusable, but they are made a little more understandable when all the facts are known.

It is part of the duty of the Directorate of Security and Intelligence to keep a watchful eye on subversive groups in order that the Government may be kept fully advised. It is not always easy to distinguish between a subversive group – the purpose of which is to undermine the morale of citizens, promote social confusion, dislocate the economy of the country, and abrogate the rule of law, the ultimate of which is seizing power during conditions of chaos – and a radical movement that takes full advantage of the rights of free speech and association, of belief and thought, to bring about, in a democratic and legal manner, the changes in the social pattern that they consider desirable. When it is established that revolution, the violent overthrow of the government, is the aim, the activities of the group are of continuing interest to police and intelligence services. If the aim is to speed up evolutionary changes within the framework of democracy, then the movement may be worrisome to the Government and politicians, but it is no longer the concern of the police. It is not an easy task to discover whether a group is working toward revolution or trying, within the laws of the land, to accelerate evolution, particularly as those whose ultimate aim is to create chaos are, at least in the early stages, loud in their denials of revolutionary intent and in their protests against any form of inquiry.

In its counter-subversive work, the Force, if it is to fulfil its function of keeping the Government informed, must at times tread on thin ice. Not only because revolutionary groups by their very nature are secretive, wily, and much given to shouts of "police state" at the first indication that they were under observation. If it can be established beyond a reasonable doubt that their aims are subversive, the police can justify their inquiries. But inquiries must be made in order to gather the facts, and it is at that point that the police are in a difficult position. If it develops that the group is not, in fact, subversive, investigation by the police may be defended only on the grounds of necessity connected with the safety of the state.

Inevitably a great deal of criticism has been levelled at the Force because of its work in the counter-subversive field. The counter-subversive branch must, at times, come perilously close to inquiring into activities that are, in fact, simply the exercising of the basic rights of freedom of speech and assembly and of opposition to the Government. It is doubtful, however, if even the most severe critics can suggest a satisfactory alternative. The welfare of the country demands that the Government must be aware, well in advance, of plotting and planning against the safety of the state. That essential awareness can only be achieved through the work of a counter-subversive service, and that service must in turn make inquiries. It is not entirely facetious to say that the police cannot do their job with ouija boards or crystal balls.

Since World War II, the chief target of the counter-intelligence service has been the Communist Party of Canada and its front groups. That party has suffered a loss of membership, partly because some of the members became disillusioned by the many shifts in policy by Moscow, and partly because Communism does not grow well alongside prosperity. The Canadian leaders are getting on in years and are unable to find causes that will attract any sizable number of young people. The Communists are a legal political party, and it has been argued that the police have no right to attempt to keep abreast of developments within that movement.

The party has been comparatively quiet, but it is far from dead. Given the slightest opportunity it could and would cease being just a propaganda mouthpiece for Moscow and again become an active and vastly troublesome revolutionary party. It should not be too quickly forgotten that the only member they ever succeeded in putting into the House of Commons was convicted and jailed for espionage; nor should one forget that in 1939 and 1940 they tried their best to disrupt Canada's war effort or that Communists served willingly, as recruiting offices for spies. The Communist Party may have run its course in Canada, but it would be foolhardy to suggest that we should be so optimistic as to take it for granted that Canadian Communists do not constitute a very real potential danger.

Quite frequently it is alleged that the Force maintains secret files on organizations and individuals, and that these files may even contain information concerning members of Parliament, cabinet ministers, and other prominent persons. Judging from the amount and tone of publicity given to such allegations, it would appear that there is a considerable amount of public concern regarding the surveillance of politicians. In most instances, the Force's critics hint darkly at dangers inherent in the keeping of secret dossiers, and these innuendos have given rise to fairly widespread charges that the keeping of such records by the police is a reprehensible practice. The RCMP does keep secret files, and since records are not maintained on a basis of class or casts, it follows that they may contain references to persons of some prominence or importance. It is true, also, that there are dangers inherent in the keeping of secret records, since the information they contain could be misused, but to my knowledge there has never been an incident in which misuse of information by the Force has been established, or even seriously charged.

If the keeping of secret files is reprehensible or dangerous, what are the alternatives? Should the police discard all the information that reaches them which cannot be used at once for purposes of prosecution; or should all police files be opened to examination by interested or merely curious passers-by? Clearly those suggestions are impracticable and nonsensical, but I can think of no other alternative to secret dossiers other than keeping files open only to authorized persons. Recent events, inquiries, and commissions have established the need for secrecy and the maintenance of secret records. There is a fair body of opinion that holds that, as regards some of the recent scandals, it might have been better, in the overall interests of the country, had the information been allowed to remain in the secret files.

A final point about the security and intelligence work of the Force. It operates for the benefit of and under the direction of the Government. It was not brought into being by a desire on the part of the police to pry into the affairs of the citizens but by the need to maintain the security of the state. Traditionally, and unavoidably, an intelligence service takes the brunt of any criticism or attack. Governments and ministers do not often rush to admit direct knowledge of the work of the counter-intelligence service, or to take their share of criticism. From the political point of view, that attitude is understandable to some extent, but it does little toward building public confidence in its security and intelligence service. And it does nothing toward creating public awareness of the need for that service.

19

➤➤➤➤➤➤➤➤➤➤◄◄◄◄◄◄◄◄◄◄

Return
to
British Columbia

The work of any of the Direcorates at Headquarters is interesting, often challenging, and sometimes of national and international importance, but one is always "under the gun," subject to immediate pressures and controls from many points, the Commissioner, the minister in charge, the Cabinet, Parliament, and many committees. By comparison, the Officer Commanding of a Division, while engaged on interesting and important duties and still subject to many controls, is free of the immediacy of many of the pressures and problems that develop in the capital city.

After three years at Headquarters, in 1956, I began to look with some envy but not much hope at some of the divisional postings. Circumstances seemed to indicate that I might expect to finish my remaining six years of service in Ottawa, and while that prospect was gratifying in some ways, it was not sufficiently so to offset my desire to return to field work.

It was with a great deal of delight and some surprise, therefore, that I received the information from Commissioner L. H. Nicholson that I was being posted again to British Columbia, where I would take over command of E Division, the largest in the Force, from Assistant-Commissioner Charles Rivett-Carnac who was being transferred to Ottawa as Deputy Commissioner.

Doris and I had fallen in love with British Columbia during our previous posting there, as anyone must who has had the opportunity to visit that beautiful province. We lost no time in preparing for the move and were "champing at the bit" by the time the date for our departure rolled around.

Rivett-Carnac had run a good Division, and it was a pleasure to step into a command and find everything ship-shape and running smoothly. Morale was high, and any differences between the members of the two forces that may have existed in 1950, when the RCMP absorbed the old provincial police, had long since disappeared. The thirteen-hundred members of the Division worked in close harmony in carrying out their heavy and multifarious duties. Had I been given the opportunity to handpick the officers and NCO's, I could not have selected a better group than those who were running the affairs of E Division. Many of them were old friends – among them the erstwhile Corporal "Pete" Bordeleau, with whom I had worked in Montreal during the war years. Pete had then attained the rank of Superintendent, and is now Deputy Commissioner of the Force.

The Honourable Robert Bonner was still the Attorney-General and the Minister to whom the Force was directly responsible for the carrying out of the provincial duties that formed the bulk of the Division's work. Bonner demanded and received a high level of efficiency from the police, he was always forthright in giving the backing and support required to maintain high standards as, indeed, were all members of the Government and departmental heads.

In the adjoining province of Alberta, Assistant-Commissioner G. B. McClellan (the present Commissioner) was Officer Commanding K Division. We were old friends, and this assured close and easy co-operation. In fact, there were numerous occasions when co-operation extended into collaboration as McClellan and I joined forces in an attempt to outmanoeuvre headquarters over a ruling or when it came to trying to get our ideas across. Nicholson and other officers at head-quarters were quick to realize that we were "ganging-up" and backing each other's moves. The Commissioner, probably recalling that he had done a fair bit of "ganging-up" against Ottawa during his service in the Divisions, became wary, but he did not attempt to discourage our "plot-ting against the whites." Across the border we enjoyed the best possible liaison and co-operation with the Oregon, Washington, and California State Police, and the Federal Bureau of Investigation. From the official, working point of view, conditions were about as close to ideal as could be hoped for.

Our good fortune extended to Doris' and my social life. The o.c.'s house, one of the best owned by the Force, was in the Uplands, a choice residential area, and again, if we had a choice, we could not have picked more friendly, sociable neighbours. For some reason a myth has spread across Canada regarding the city of Victoria. People being trans-ferred there are often told, as we were, that the city was dull and mid-

Victorian in its outlook, and that the citizens are aloof and cold to persons not native to the city or its immediate environs. Whoever started that canard must have had his cities mixed or been locked up in his hotel room during his stay in Victoria. We discovered very quickly that it takes an iron constitution to hold up under the enjoyable strain of social life. It took us just a month or two to learn that our constitutions were not quite up to Victoria's standards, and we were forced to slow down a bit. If this social life is mid-Victorian, then the men and women of that era were grand, friendly, and rugged.

The Province of British Columbia was bustling with development. Power sites, new rail lines and highways, lumbering operations, an aluminum plant, and explorations for mines and oil were being pushed forward. The population was increasing at a rapid rate, and cities and towns were bursting with housing projects. This expansion, and the pressing forward of the frontiers of development, had necessitated the opening of several new detachments and the strengthening of others, but except for an increase in volume, the work of the Division had not greatly changed. Traffic control was still a major problem. The accident and death rate were among the highest in the country and were on the upward trend. With the vehicular population increasing by almost ten per cent annually, it was clear that definite and fairly drastic action was called for. With the co-operation of newspapers, radio, and television stations, a safety campaign was started throughout the province. Pleas for safe and sane driving, which formed part of the campaign, were followed by warnings that on and after the date fixed for increased highway patrols the police would crack down on any and all offenders.

The police offensive started on a holiday weekend and included the use of radar and "ghost cars." Every available member, including the clerical staff, was turned out to man additional patrol cars. Our increased activity brought a large crop of prosecutions, a general – and temporary – reduction in speeding, and a great deal of adverse public reaction, particularly aimed at the use of radar and ghost cars. These were not considered "cricket." But we were not playing cricket; we were using every means at our disposal to cut down the accident toll on the highways. Our campaign continued, as did the opposing outbreak of criticism. When it comes to criticism, as with most other activities to which they put their minds, the citizens of British Columbia are not backward or half-hearted. The criticism had almost reached the scalding point when three fortuitous happenings – fortuitous for the police but not for the individuals concerned – turned the tide.

The first of these occurred when one of the "ghost" cars chased, overhauled, and stopped a car that had been rolling along at better than ninety miles an hour. The driver was the able, energetic Minister of Highways, the Honourable Phillip Gaglardi, whose driving habits had earned him the sobriquet "Flying Phil." He was promptly charged. A few weeks later a patrol car stopped a driver who, while driving at a more conservative speed than "Flying Phil," had been exceeding the speed limit. The driver was our Minister, the Honourable Robert Bonner. A short while later the Leader of the Opposition was called to Court for speeding. These three prosecutions received wide publicity. That these citizens of such prominence in the life of the province had not escaped the impartial vigilance of the police seemed to impress the public with the fact that traffic laws were to be taken seriously – and that the police meant business. The campaign for safety on the highways started to receive encouraging support.

The Attorney-General and the Leader of the Opposition raised no objection to the action of the police in laying charges against them, but Gaglardi expressed some very caustic comments regarding the use of ghost cars. I suspect that his real objection arose from the fact that the ghost cars were fast enough to catch him. But "Flying Phil" was caught speeding again a few months later and, once again, he was charged. On that occasion there were no caustic remarks, but he did call me to register a minor complaint on the grounds that he is an exceptional driver and can safely handle a car at ninety miles an hour. Our conversation was quite friendly, and after some discussion of safe speeds, I suggested that when he was next in Kamloops, his home riding, he should go to the air strip where, forgetting his abilities at speeds of ninety, he should drive his car at an even sixty and then stand on the brakes as he would be forced to do if a child had suddenly appeared in front of him. He promised that he would make the experiment and call me to tell me of his reactions. I never heard from him. Apart from his heavy tasks as a Minister of the Crown, Phillip Gaglardi is a minister of the Gospel who fills his tabernacle at Kamloops to overflowing. As regards his driving skills, I am inclined to believe that his good fortune in avoiding an accident thus far is due much more to "somebody up there liking him" than to his driving ability.

The RCMP offices in Victoria were in a building that had been a hotel prior to our takeover. I was frequently reminded of an incident that occurred during the very early stages of our occupancy, when things were still a little chaotic. The member detailed for the evening to the information desk in the front lobby had left his post for a few minutes to give a hand in the moving of furniture and files in the next room. During his absence, a gentleman who had hoisted a few too many drinks staggered into the lobby and up to the vacant reception counter. Having waited in vain for attention, his patience ran out and he headed for the stairs leading to the next floor on which was located the office of the Officer Commanding. The O.C. was still working at his desk, but his secretary had gone for the day. The drunk waited in the hallway, but still no one showed up to look after him. His temper was mounting by the minute. Through the open doors of the secretary's office and the inner sanctum, he could see the Officer Commanding, who was wearing civilian clothes and was too engrossed in his work to notice the visitor. Having suffered what he considered gross neglect, the inebriate stumbled through the open doors and began pounding the desk of a somewhat startled officer with: "This place is a dump. Stayed here before, but service wasn't lousy like it is now. What's idea keeping customers waiting. I came in here for a room and by God, I'm going to get one!" Drawing himself up to his full and wavering height, the confused visitor demanded, "Now get off your fanny and give me some attention."

Buzzers sounded in several parts of the building, and the required attention was quickly forthcoming. The man was in no condition to wander the streets so he was provided with sleeping quarters for the night. While the accommodation was not up to hotel standards, it had the advantage of being free.

I had never served on what might be termed a "frontier-type" detachment, and there were a number of these in the expanding northern areas of British Columbia. The reports that reached me were vastly interesting, and I decided that I should attempt to get more first-hand information than that provided by fairly standard and routine examination of records and interviews. Accordingly, on my next inspection trip to the northern areas, I made a point of travelling in patrol cars and accompanying members in the carrying out of their duties. I was familiar with the responsibilities of the Force, but I was, nevertheless, surprised at the wide variety of work carried out on these patrols. The differences between police work in rural areas and that which I had experienced in the larger centres astonished me.

I recall one patrol during which the constable served two summons; answered a radio call to the scene of a motor accident; gave first aid to two persons who had suffered injuries; radioed for help in getting them to a doctor; arranged for a truck to tow the damaged car to a garage; made several inquiries in an attempt to locate a California car, the owners of which were urgently required to call their home; took statements from two witnesses concerning a recent cattle theft; responded to a radio call by visiting a beer parlour to settle a small fracas; stopped to chat for a few minutes with the proprietors of several gas stations and general stores and to give them *Crime in Your Community*, a booklet which forms part of the crime-prevention program of the Force; pushed an abandoned car well clear of the travelled portion of the road and requested, by radio, that the detachment make inquiries regarding ownership; and, on the way back to the detachment, stopped in for a short visit with a troop of Boy Scouts. That seemed to me to be a fair amount of work for a patrol that lasted less than eight hours. I was aware, of course, that the presence of "brass" might call for particularly impressive efforts, but an examination of the constable's diary established that this patrol had not been outstanding or even different from routine patrols except in detail. The itinerary for my inspection trip was arranged so that I could spend a Saturday night in one of the larger communities in the interior of British Columbia which, according to reports that had reached me, deserved a reputation for the enthusiasm and exuberance of its Saturday-night celebrations. The routine, formal part of the inspection was concluded in the afternoon, following which I had a brief meeting with the NCO and members. I told them that I would be back at seven o'clock and would remain until the small hours of the morning, during which time my purpose would be to watch a detachment in action and not to check on or criticize their work. They were asked to forget that I was there, an admittedly difficult task with the Officer Commanding "breathing down their necks," as the senior NCO pointed out.

Things were fairly quiet when I arrived at the detachment that evening. The cells held a man who had been caught in possession of a stolen car. In the "ladies" section, a woman who had been found wandering about the streets in an advanced state of intoxication came out of her stupor occasionally to comment, loudly, on her views regarding the ancestry of the matron and the constable who had brought her in, but the evening was young and the NCO told me that I could abandon all hope that the quiet would continue. The experience of many Saturday nights had taught him that even a modicum of optimism would be uncalled for.

About eight o'clock, an irate citizen telephoned to complain of juvenile rowdyism in the lumberyard next to his house. A constable left for the scene at once, and a few minutes later radioed in that the juveniles were troublesome and that he would appreciate a little help. Two more men were dispatched to the scene. They had scarcely left the detachment office when a telephone call reported that a fight was in progress on a street corner near the centre of town. Two constables took off to quell the disturbance. About fifteen minutes later, there was a commotion at the entrance of the detachment, as the policemen struggled to get the late combatants through the door. The men had forgotten their grievance against one another and joined forces to resist arrest. Eventually they were deposited in the cells after being searched and relieved of their shoes, belts, and suspenders, an operation that required some persuasion because of the violent resistance of the prisoners. The removal of belts, shoes, suspenders, and neckties is a precautionary measure that serves two purposes. First, it reduces the possibility of suicide. Prisoners have been known to use shoelaces and other articles of wearing apparel to hang themselves. Second, a bare-footed man whose pants lack support is not in a good condition to assault the guards or attempt an escape.

In the meantime, three juveniles had been brought in from the disturbance at the lumberyard. They were still trying to act cocky and defiant, but the trip in the police car had given them time to think of parental reactions. They were all known to the sergeant who listened carefully to the report of the constables. The disturbance had been noisy, and gang bravado had lead to threats against the police, but the threats had petered out and no damage had been done to the police or the lumberyard. The Sergeant read them a stern lecture, seemed to debate the advisability of locking them up, and then sent two Constables to drive the boys to their homes and advise their parents that any future trouble would lead to the laying of charges.

The men who had brought in the fighting drunks had apparently had a rough time – their uniforms and shoes were covered with dust. Whisks and polishing cloths were on hooks in readiness, and the constables, apparently following their normal routine, brushed their clothes and polished their shoes to be tidy in time for the next call. They did not have long to wait. Reports of overly noisy celebrations, disturbances, and fights were being received with increasing frequency. Sometimes the members detailed to answer a call were able to settle the trouble without arrests; often the appearance of a police car at the scene was enough to bring quiet; but at times the circumstances called for arrests. Most of the persons taken into custody submitted quietly, but there were several instances in which our men met stiff resistance and had to wrestle on the ground with the prisoners to bring them in.

In the detachment, the noise level was mounting steadily. The cells were getting crowded, and while most of the occupants were in a subdued state of mind or sleeping off their binge, others created a considerable din by shouting to one another or at the guards. One or two made sporadic attempts at singing. Each time a new prisoner was brought in, he was greeted with cat-calls, and if he showed any signs of belligerence toward the police, he was egged on to put up a fight. After each arrest, the policemen brushed and cleaned and waited quietly for the next foray. I found no cause for criticism of their actions, even when the going was at its roughest; I just admired their patient – and sometimes necessarily rough – attention to the job at hand.

About midnight a call came in regarding a serious car crash a few miles out of town. A car was dispatched to the scene at once. A few minutes later the constable radioed a grim report. Two cars had collided head on. Three people – two men and a woman – were dead and three others had been badly injured. The cars were a tangled wreckage, and the policemen were having difficulties removing the injured and dead. The area reeked of gasoline fumes. The Sergeant acted quickly. Additional men were rushed to assist; doctors and ambulances were arranged for; a garage was asked to send a tow truck with the necessary equipment to cut open the wrecked cars; and the fire department was asked to hurry to the scene. Later, when identifications had been established, there came the heavy task of advising relatives.

The grim work at the wreckage was still in progress when a citizen reported a breaking and entering at a grocery store. The two guards were sent from the cells to attend to the matter. For a while, the Sergeant and I were alone in the detachment, and I had to take over the duties of telephone and radio operator. During that period, a few calls were received reporting fights, but all the Sergeant and I could do was hope that the best man would win.

Twenty-seven persons had been locked up when I left the detachment at about two o'clock in the morning. Most of these were drunks, but the number included two men caught in breaking and entering, two prostitutes, and a man detained at the request of another detachment. Again, examination of the detachment diaries revealed differences in detail but not in volume for previous Saturday nights.

Several of the drunks brought in that Saturday evening were Indians, and this gave rise to a discussion of recent provincial legislation that had opened beerhalls to Indians, and of planned changes in the liquor laws that would remove the prohibition against Indians buying hard liquor. The subject was of direct interest, since easier access to alcohol would mean more drinking by Indians and, therefore, more trouble for the police in the towns and on the reserves where trouble occasionally led to serious and violent crimes. Nevertheless, most policemen were in favour of removing the old restrictions. The general feeling was that, given a few years to accustom themselves to the new freedom and to the new drinking habits, the incidence of trouble would decrease.

The subject of Indians and liquor is a matter that is frequently discussed by law-enforcement men whose duties bring them into direct contact with the problem. The consensus is that there is no basis of fact in the old belief that because of some difference in the chemistry of their bodies Indians react to alcohol more quickly and violently than do people of other races. The white man has for many generations had easy access to liquor and has had the opportunity to develop sensible drinking habits and is still far from master of its use. Until recently, Indians in Canada were forbidden the use of alcohol in any form – liquor, beer, or wine. It is not surprising, nor should it be taken as an indication of some hereditary weakness, that when Indians do manage to get a supply of liquor, which they were compelled to drink in secrecy, some are inclined to overdo things by getting as drunk as fast as they can. It is quite true to say that Indians may be quarrelsome and troublesome when drunk; and that while under the influence of liquor they have committed many crimes, some serious, some atrocious – I had a considerable amount of experience in this regard, and a few spots of serious trouble during my days patrolling Indian reserves in Eastern Canada. I have read many reports of serious crimes, but I have never seen or read of an Indian committing a crime that has not first been committed by other men – white, black, brown, or yellow.

In a lighter vein, the usually depressing business of dealing with drunks does provide the odd bit of humour. This was the case some years ago when the members of a very remote detachment arrested a huge, powerful, fighting man of Swedish ancestry. He fought every inch of the way to the detachment office and into the cell, a small cubicle that had been erected in the rear of the building. It costs a great deal of money and time to transport a steel cell to an isolated post, and this was when economy took precedence over most other considerations. Besides, there was not a very great demand for jail accommodation in that sparsely populated area. Accordingly, the detachment members had been instructed to build a cell. As a concession, they were provided with a can of "battleship" grey paint with which to hide the fact that the cell was of wooden construction. Having fought the prisoner into the cell, and locked the door, the members stood back to take a breather but the Swede was made of sterner stuff. He turned his attention to the cell and, finding that the lattice-work bars gave way under his shaking and charging, he set to work with a will. Suddenly the whole thing collapsed about his ears. The sudden and unexpected victory pacified him. The Swede sat down on top of the wreckage and, sadly shaking his head, muttered over and over again, "This is a hell of a yail."

In the busy Vancouver area, narcotic drugs were one of the major concerns of the Force. There was the sad procession of addicts in and out of jails for having possessed narcotic drugs and for offenses resulting from their efforts to get money with which to buy drugs. Occasionally the work of the police would result in the arrest of a trafficker, but such successes only caused a short disruption in the traffic and an increase in the price of drugs to the addicts. The profit for the trafficker is high, and there are always racketeers anxious to break into the vicious trade.

We began to hear a great deal about the "British System" under which, it was alleged, the addicts were supplied with enough drugs free or at a small cost to maintain their addiction and keep them happy. A committee was formed in Vancouver and in other Canadian cities to bring pressure on the Government to adopt this method. Actually, the system that had been put into effect in England was not as simple – or as successful – as the publicity indicated. Under the "British System," an addict could, after registering as an addict, secure drugs very cheaply, but the law did not give doctors the authority to prescribe narcotic drugs to maintain addiction. As in Canada, drugs could be administered or prescribed in an effort to cure the patient but not to perpetuate the habit. In practice the main difference between the more liberal English view and the restrictive Canadian one was the point at which the treatment became the maintenance of addiction, and certainly British doctors were given a great deal of freedom in their interpretation.

On the surface, the giving of free or cheap drugs to addicts seems a simple and attractive answer to the narcotic-drug problem. Traffickers would be put out of business; addicts would be able to find and hold steady employment; addicts would no longer be forced to resort to criminal activities in order to satisfy their craving. Simple and attractive, indeed – until one stops to seriously consider the whole matter and to question the details. Who makes the decisions as to the quantity of narcotics to be given an addict? The doctor or the addict? If the former, and if he was trying to hold or reduce the degree of addiction, the addict would be grateful for whatever quantities he received but he would go to the underworld to make up for any shortage. Most medical authorities with experience in this field hold that addiction is progressive and that an addict, left to his own resources, will require more and more drugs. Therefore, if decisions as to quantity were left to the addict, his addiction would develop, and the Government and the medical profession would be in the position of assisting in that development.

Another question requiring careful consideration is the matter of the actual administration of the drugs. Would this be done in the doctor's office, or would the patient be given a week or a month or several months' supply? It is difficult to understand how an addict could hold employment if he were required to go to the doctor's office for his injections, which might be anywhere from one to eight a day, depending on the length of time during which he had been addicted. If the patient were given a stock of drugs, there would be a decided possibility that some part of that stock would reach the illegal market to supply non-registered addicts or those who were being treated by less-generous doctors. This was the experience in the United States where the "free drugs for addicts" method was tried until it failed in the late twenties.

The argument most commonly advanced by those who favour the almost unrestricted giving of drugs to addicts is that traffickers would be put out of business. This is a somewhat doubtful proposition, unless all addicts are given all the drugs they desire, a step that would open the way for abuses. It would be unduly optimistic to believe that all addicts would register, or that those who did admit addiction would be entirely truthful regarding their requirements. Thus there is a decided possibility that users of narcotics who did not want their addiction made a matter of record would receive supplies from a new type of trafficker, the registered user. Those who point to the elimination of traffickers as one of the desirable benefits of the "British System" overlook the main objective of their efforts to cope with the problem of drug addiction which should be the reduction of the number of addicts, not the elimination of the traffickers, as desirable as that would be.

My view is that of many others who have been close to the problem for years – that the "free drugs for addicts" approach offers more risk than hope. The removal of the stigma of drug addiction and the provision of easy sources of supply would open the doors very wide for those who have resisted temptation through fear of acquiring what the addicts call "a monkey on my back." Under the present system in Canada, the "monkey" is expensive and soul-destroying. It would be less expensive but no less destructive if the "monkey" were a gift from the Government.

Conditions in England were much more favourable than those in Canada for the experiment with free drugs. Narcotics addiction was never as widespread as in North America, nor did the English have a three-thousand-mile border separating them from the country with the greatest number of addicts. Despite these advantages, it became apparent fairly early in the experiment that there were serious flaws in the system. Recent announcements from the police and other authorities have expressed grave concern over the spread of addiction to the use of morphine and heroin, a clear indication that the flaws have become serious and that the method is not producing the anticipated results.

The best solution to the problem of illegal trafficking in drugs lies in the treatment of addicts. There has been some advancement in the methods of treatment, but the outlook in that direction is not very bright. Cures are being effected, but the number is disappointingly low. I am not aware of any study which establishes the percentage of persons cured who had become addicted while looking for "kicks" and those who developed the habit because of the need for a crutch to face the facts of life. It seems most probable that the former are much more likely to receive lasting benefits from the treatment than the latter. Doctors tell us that it is a fairly simple matter to gradually reduce a patient's dosage until he has been completely withdrawn from the use of narcotics, and that he may then be built up physically until he is in good health. But the desire for a crutch – the inadequacy that first made him an addict – will in most cases lead to a return to the habit very soon after his release from the treatment centre.

For too many years the illegal traffic in narcotics was considered entirely a matter for the police. It is good to see legislators, doctors, psychologists, psychiatrists, and social workers showing an interest in the problem of addiction. Treatment centers are being built, and a great deal of experimentation is being carried out. Let us hope that a cure or a better method of handling the problem is on its way. Until better methods are found, the police will have to continue their efforts to curb the traffic.

In the early Spring of 1959, I was called to attend a conference in Ottawa. During the week at Headquarters, Commissioner Nicholson invited me to have dinner with him and his charming wife Mary on the last day of the meeting. Dinner with the Nicholsons was always an event to look forward to not only because of the pleasant surroundings and conversation but also because Mary was a cook *par excellence.* I anticipated an enjoyable evening but had no indication that there would be anything unusual or that I would leave in a state of euphoria.

Dinner lived up to my expectations, and I was leaning back to enjoy the excellent brandy when Nicholson, always direct in conversation, said something that ended my relaxation for days to come. Very casually he advised me that I was to be transferred to Ottawa, as Deputy Commissioner, to be prepared to succeed him as Commissioner when he retired in a year or two. The transfer was to take place in a few months and, following my arrival in Ottawa, he planned to make a number of lengthy inspection trips to accustom me to the duties of the Commissioner.

Surprise would be too mild a term to describe my reaction. There were several officers senior to me, and although most of these would have gone to pension by the time of Nicholson's retirement, succession to the Commissioner's desk had not always been decided by seniority. Obviously I had considered the possibility that some day I might get to the very top, but that possibility had always been laden with "if's" and "but's". I had high hopes of reaching the rank of Deputy Commissioner. Beyond that any hope depended on too many factors. I am not sure that I thanked Nicholson for his confidence in me, but I do recall that his surprising news caused me to make heavy inroads into his brandy. I could not get back to Victoria quickly enough to give Doris the tremendous news. She was as surprised as I was, and for several weeks we enjoyed high expectations. But developments at the other end of Canada – in Newfoundland – were to directly affect our future.

One evening in March, we were listening to the radio when we received shocking and disturbing news. Commissioner Nicholson had submitted his resignation because the Government had refused to send sorely needed re-enforcements to support the members of the Division in Newfoundland who were handling a serious situation there. The woodworkers were on strike, and the strike had developed into a vicious struggle between the opposing forces. Bloody riots had occurred, during which a member of the local constabulary had been killed and a number of persons, civilians and police, were injured. Further violent outbreaks seemed probable. The Officer Commanding the Division, Assistant Commissioner A. Parsons, had been through many emergencies, and he was not the man to press the panic button without good reason. It was his considered opinion that, should the predicted riots occur, the normal strength at his command might not be able to maintain control of the situation. His views were also those of the Attorney-General of the Province. Commissioner Nicholson was asked to send fifty men as re-enforcements.

Under the terms of the policing contracts entered into with the provinces, the provincial authorities may, in the event of an emergency, call for assistance from the federal Government, and such additional manpower as may be required will be sent to the troubled area – provided, of course, that they can be spared from other duties. There were no other emergencies in Canada at that time, and it was Nicholson's decided opinion that fifty men could be spared for temporary duty in Newfoundland without seriously affecting the work of other Divisions. He so advised the Minister of Justice, the Honourable E. Davey Fulton.

The men were being assembled, and arrangements had already been made for their transportation by air to Newfoundland and their accommodation there, when the Minister suddenly decided against sending aid to the over-taxed Division. His reasoning, as given later in the House of Commons, was an exercise in semantics, based on a finely drawn interpretation of the policing contract. Nicholson could not accept what appeared to him an outright breach of a contract to which he had been a signatory, nor was he willing to accept, without strong protest, a situation that could endanger the lives of civilians – that would abandon the police of the area to their own limited resources. His resignation was promptly submitted and accepted.

Deputy Commissioner Charles Rivett-Carnac, who had been on retirement leave, was recalled by the Minister and offered the appointment as Commissioner. Although he had been in indifferent health for some time, he agreed to take on the heavy task.

Rivett-Carnac's appointment as Commissioner left the post of senior Deputy Commissioner vacant. The second post of Deputy Commissioner was also vacant, as the former incumbent had retired some months earlier. In April, I was transferred to Ottawa to assume the duties of Deputy Commissioner, Operations. George McClellan was brought from Alberta to become Deputy Commissioner, Administration.

My new duties placed me in administrative control of the two Directorates that I had commanded during my previous term in Ottawa – Operations and Criminal Investigations, and Security and Intelligence – the branches that direct all of the actual police work of the Force. My previous experience was of tremendous value in settling down to work at my new desk. George McClellan took over the supervision of the administrative Directorates and such branches of the Force as supply, personnel, training, Adjutant's Branch, finances, discipline, and the building program.

Our offices and those of the secretaries occupied a suite directly across the corridor from the Commissioner's office, an area of the building known to the staff as "the little Kremlin." There seemed to be a little wry retribution in the fact that McClellan and I, who on many occasions had plotted to outmanoeuvre Headquarters on matters that we thought were in the best interests of the Force, were now the "they" at headquarters and occupied the two desks against which most of our efforts had been directed. Now we were in the direct line of fire, and it remained to be seen whether we would do better or even as well as the previous incumbents.

Commissioner Rivett-Carnac was called on to make many inspection trips and to attend several conferences in England and the United States. As senior Deputy, it was my responsibility to act as Commissioner during his absence, and this gave me an opportunity to appreciate the variety and responsibilities of the work that Rivett-Carnac dealt with at "the top of the mountain." Since it is the Capital City and "the end of the line" for troubles and problems everywhere in the country, Ottawa is frequently in the throes of a crisis, particularly when the House is in session. We were not spared involvement in a few of these, but the officers had weathered many such storms and yet "another crisis" was taken pretty much in stride. As one old hand commented, "We don't really get bothered until they break three at a time."

The strains of office were telling on Rivett-Carnac's health. Doctors found that a heart condition, for which he had been hospitalized two years earlier, was becoming aggravated. He had served the Force for thirty-six years and had returned from retirement leave to meet the emergency caused by Nicholson's resignation. The emergency passed, and he decided to retire. On October 1, 1960, I was appointed Commissioner, the eleventh such appointment since the founding of the Force in 1873.

-》》-》》-》》-》》《-《-《-《-《-

Behind
the Commissioner's Desk

During my first few hours behind the Commissioner's desk, there were many welcome and pleasant interruptions. Officers and civilian friends dropped in or telephoned to offer their congratulations. Newsmen, photographers, and television crews came for interviews. The Orderly Sergeant brought a few urgent letters and these I signed, a little self-consciously, over the title "Commissioner." Eventually the hubbub died down and I had time to look around and appreciate what had happened to me. My recruit days were not so far back as to allow me to forget the awe with which I had held the Sergeant Major, an awe that I had never managed to fully overcome. In those days the Commissioner had seemed a mythical, far-off figure who wielded great power over my well-being from behind his desk. And here I was, sitting at that very desk! Somehow I had the feeling that I was an interloper.

The office was spacious, well-furnished, and comfortable. Looking up, I could see the buffalo head, the centrepiece of the crest of the Force, under which for many years a succession of Commissioners had carried out their work. On the walls were pictures that told of happenings in the history of the Force . . . March to the Mountain, 1874 . . . Graves of the Lost Patrol . . . Chief Crowfoot . . . Chief Sitting Bull . . . The *St. Roch* . . . Coronations . . . and a coloured reproduction of the Guidon listing the battle honours awarded the Force in every war since its inception. On the wall, to the left, were photographs of my ten predecessors. They looked directly at me, sternly and questioningly, as though asking, "What sort of a job will you do behind that desk?" It was a fair question. I wondered what the answer would be.

235

The bookcase contained a set of the Annual Reports of the Commissioners to Parliament. I could not resist the temptation to do a little reminiscing and started thumbing through the report for the year 1919. Memories of the awkward squad that had been relegated to the background and dubbed "prisoners" were stirred while reading Commissioner A. Bowen Perry's Report of the inspection by the Prince of Wales, in which the Prince said: "I know the men of the force of today are proving themselves worthy of those traditions and will ever uphold them." Commissioner Perry in his Report referred briefly to the recruiting campaign that had brought the strength of the Force from three hundred to fifteen hundred men and added a rather conservative comment on the problem that this had posed for him and his officers: 'It is no small task to absorb and train twelve hundred recruits and turn them into highly trained men of the Force, the members of which are called upon to act individually and at times collectively in the execution of their duties." The budget for that year was less than a million dollars. The work of the Force was carried out by ninety-six detachments, most of which were staffed by one man, and with the aid of three automobiles, 833 horses, ninety-three team dogs, and three boats. Radio, teletype, laboratories, airplanes, fingerprint bureaux, and other aids and refinements were still very much in the future.

Between 1919 and 1960, the budget of the Force had increased to seventy-five million dollars. Over eight thousand members staffed some seven hundred detachments. The fleet of three automobiles had grown to almost two thousand. Despite the introduction of mechanized transport, and planes in the north, opening the far reaches of Canada had brought the need for sled dogs up to 265. The last "mounted" detachment (Alexis Creek, British Columbia, with one saddle horse, one pack horse) had been supplied with a car a few years earlier when the roads in that area became passable. Horses now were used only for recruit training and "ceremonial" rides.

Crime-detection laboratories, an Air Division and Marine Division, an Identification and Fingerprint Branch, a Personnel Branch, Public-Relations Branch, and Radio and Telex communications networks had been added, and had advanced all operations to a state of smooth efficiency. Training had been broadened and intensified to meet the many new and complex demands made of the Force. The tiny Special Branch that had, despite lack of experience and training, produced important and valuable results, was now a well-staffed, efficient Security and Intelligence service which had earned and held a professional status equal to that of services in other countries. The challenge that had been tossed to the Force in the early twenties, "Develop to meet new demands and changing conditions – or go out of business," had been taken. The changes had not been accomplished without difficulty, nor as quickly or easily as might have been desired, but transition had kept pace with the development of the country and seemed likely to continue to do so.

Despite the many changes, it was still easy to see the influence that the old Force had exerted on the building of the modern organization. Loyalty, *esprit de corps*, great pride in the Force and its uniform, the role it had played and was playing in the history of Canada – all had survived, thanks to the strong traditions built in the early days. Recruits still exercised their undoubted right to grouse in the barrackrooms over the restrictions and discomforts of the tight discipline which had been inherited and perpetuated from the early days, but the grousing was a "within the family" matter which in no way affected anyone's pride in the fact that he belonged to a trained, tightly controlled corps.

While the Force had moved forward to meet new challenges, there were still areas in which it was called on to carry out the work of a frontier-police force. Exploration and development were opening up the northern regions, but there were hundreds of thousands of square miles that remainded almost untouched by the advance of civilization. Mounted Police posts served the people of those areas. The airplane had brought some relief from isolation, and some assistance in times of emergencies, but it could not replace the need for long, hard patrols that kept detachment men in touch with the widely scattered inhabitants. The Annual Report for 1959 showed that in the Yukon and Northwest Territories members had patrolled 53,443 miles by dog team, 27,850 on foot, and 74,179 by canoe and small boats. The Force was competent in its work of dealing with new and modern law-enforcement problems, but the policing of frontiers was still an important part of its functions.

When I had time to look into all branches of the organization, I realized that my predecessors had planned carefully and built well. My job within the Force was to keep the machine running smoothly and quietly with just a tightening here or alteration there to keep abreast of changing conditions. In this I had the willing advice, assistance, and support of excellent officers and NCO's, all of whom had come up through the ranks and were familiar with every part of the machine.

Outside the Force, my chief responsibilities were those of keeping the Minister and the Government fully informed of our work. It was my job also to get the funds, "the sinews" necessary to enable the work to be continued at a high level of efficiency. It was a relief to find that the Treasury people no longer started all discussions with a positive "no," thereby forcing an uphill fight. In line with their responsibilities to the taxpayers, they still insisted on examining every item in the estimate with minute care, but rather than the old "no," the attitude had changed to, "possibly – if you can prove the need." We had some fairly warm skirmishes but, on the whole, the results were satisfactory.

Committee meetings, conferences of police organizations, national and international, and visits to and by the heads of other police and intelligence organizations were time-consuming, but they served the useful and necessary function of keeping the Force in close touch with the policies of the Government and with international developments in the police and counter-intelligence fields. Divisional inspection trips brought close contact with the members who were carrying out the actual police work of the Force and had first-hand knowledge of conditions in the field. Discussions with the officers and personnel of the Divisions provided an opportunity to judge the quality of the administration efforts of Headquarters. Most officers and members were straight-forward and direct in their comments of the practicability and possibility of direction received from Ottawa, with sometimes a little more emphasis on those directives which, in their opinion, were "otherwise." Their frankness was helpful in bringing about any adjustments required.

Early in 1961, under the urging of Superintendent W. G. Fraser, Commanding G Division, who was justifiably proud of the work of his Division, which covered the Yukon and the Northwest Territories, I began to plan an inspection trip of that vast area. Arrangements were completed in March. When my plans were reported to the Minister, the Honourable E. Davey Fulton, he decided that he would come along in order to see and gather information about a part of Canada that was receiving a great deal of attention from the Government. His busy schedule could not be rearranged to give him enough time for the entire trip, but he managed to clear ten days, enough to allow him to visit fourteen settlements in the Eastern Arctic. Regretfully, he announced that he would have to return to Ottawa from Churchill, the half-way point, leaving us to carry on with the inspection of posts in the Western Arctic.

Many persons are eager to visit the north country, and this is particularly so of members of the diplomatic corps, from whom requests for an opportunity to "go down north" are frequently received. The most persistent of the diplomats was His Excellency A. H. J. "Tony" Lovink, Ambassador for the Netherlands, who for some years had been pressing my predecessors on this point. Lovink had developed a high regard for Canada and especially its hinterlands. As a member of the *Voyageurs*, he had made a number of difficult exploratory trips into the more accessible parts of the north country, but he was eager to get into the Arctic and see the people and the places about which he had read so much. Commissioner Nicholson had promised Tony first call in the event of a vacancy on a scheduled trip by a police plane into the north country, but he had not had an opportunity to fulfil his promise. Now with the Minister leaving the flight at Churchill, there would be available space throughout the inspection of posts in the Western Arctic. I invited His Excellency to join us at Churchill, an invitation that was quickly accepted.

In writing about the RCMP I have dealt almost entirely with changes and developments within that Force. In so doing, I might be giving the impression that the need for change was appreciated only by the RCMP – that other law-enforcement agencies in Canada were lagging behind. Certainly this has not been my intention, for the reverse is true. All major police organizations, and many of the smaller forces, had undergone tremendous changes in their efforts to keep abreast of new problems, and cope with increasingly difficult patterns of crime and shifting social conditions as they affected law enforcement.

Among experienced, top-flight police administrators and executives, it was appreciated that law enforcement could no longer be considered a purely local affair. A parochial outlook that held to the view, "I'll keep my area clean, you look after your own problems," might deal with home-grown, amateur talent, but the professional criminals were too mobile, and many of their activities were too complex and widespread to allow any one police force or any single community to rely solely on its own resources. This need for teamwork had been recognized and implemented. Centralized pools had been built up through the co-operation of all forces; information could be quickly exchanged on fingerprints, the *modus operandi* of individual criminals, their backgrounds, connections, cars and habits of professionals; their methods, fields of crime, and ramification of organized gangsters, and the movement of suspects. Through professional associations and the frequent exchange of views, the Forces were in close co-operation.

There were weak spots. Many of the smaller communities could not afford to set up adequate training facilities, and it was often the practice to hand a recruit a uniform, a revolver, and a pair of hand-cuffs, and expect him to be transformed, forthwith, into a capable policeman. And in some areas the proper maintenance of law and order was high in the expectations of councils and citizens but low on the list of priorities for expenditures. But this situation was changing. The federal and provincial Governments, through assistance in the highly important matter of training, and through policing contracts with municipalities, were helping to bring smaller forces to an acceptable standard of efficiency.

In the face of disturbing increases in crime, police forces had moved to close co-operation, nationally and internationally; long strides had been taken in improving administration, communication, scientific aids, and technical abilities. Crime-prevention programs had been developed. Aid had been sought and received from the universities, from scientists, from the medical profession and business organizations. The police had worked and were continuing to work closely with many groups and committees in studying various aspects of the crime situation and possible corrective measures. A great deal of effort had also been expended, with some limited success, toward improving relations between the police and the public.

It would be easy indeed to expand on the advances that had been made and to end this book with some indication of optimism and confidence that the police are now able to cope with the many problems of law enforcement, but to do this would be to strike a false note, to mislead, for there is very little real cause for confidence or optimism. Despite the strides that have been made, despite a great deal of work and study carried out by groups outside the actual field of law enforcement, and despite the dedicated efforts of thirty thousand policemen, crime in Canada continues to increase at a disturbing rate. Even more disturbing are clear indications that the increase in crime is accompanied by a falling off of respect for the authorities or regard for the law, the judicial system, the system of government and those who govern. If this seems a pessimistic way of putting it, we need only glance at the annual crime figures published by the Dominion Bureau of Statistics, or recall the space that has been taken up in the press and on radio and television with stories of brutal crimes, riots, unlawful assemblies, vandalism, and scandals. Surely there is little reason for those engaged in law-enforcement work, having brought their forces to a high degree of efficiency, to become complacent regarding the future.

During my term as Commissioner, I visited with police administrators in several European countries and at Interpol meetings and discussed mutual problems with them. Everywhere the story was the same. Crime was on the increase; the patterns of crime were becoming more involved and difficult; criminals were becoming better organized and, therefore, more powerful. And everywhere there was the accompanying phenomenon of a falling off of public support of the police and of authority in general.

Canada's geography dictates a cause for concern. The crime syndicates in the United States make up a sprawling empire which defies the efforts of the police, the revelations of innumerable committees and commissions and trials, and the mass of legislation that is intended to curb their activities and growth. Despite all the opposing forces, the syndicates have continued to expand. Many highly placed and expert authorities have publicly stated that the syndicates are more powerful, more sinister, and better protected now than they were in their heyday during the prohibition years.

These syndicates are not just haphazard groupings of hoodlums, murderers, and thugs intent on some immediate criminal activities. Hoodlums, thugs, and murderers, yes – but there is nothing haphazard or temporary about their organizations. The overlords are, for the most part, men who started out as hoodlums years ago and, by their ability to survive by picking the strongest – and, therefore, the winning side – and by their ruthlessness and dexterity in eliminating others have clawed their way to leadership and acquired vast fortunes.

Most of the overlords have criminal records earned during their early hoodlum days, but except for a few who have run afoul of contempt, income tax, or immigration laws, they have been free of prosecution for many years. They are protected and hidden by so many echelons of lower rank that they seem almost untouchable.

The syndicates operated by these overlords – according to evidence submitted to committees and commissions, and according to statements by government officials, prosecutors, and law-enforcement officials in the United States – are multi-million-dollar operations, tightly organized from the upper ranks right down to the lowliest hoodlum. Discipline and the rule of silence are strict and rigidly enforced. The leaders of these organizations wield a power greater in many ways than that of the heads of legitimate business enterprises. They have the assistance of bribed and corrupt officials; they have goon-squads on the payroll to enforce discipline within their own ranks and to put fear into the hearts of others; they have the power and ability to buy, ruin, or remove permanently many of those whose oppose them; they have ready access to highly priced legal help; and they have the strength of support from other syndicates.

Such gangs have learned much about organization during the prohibition years and since. Wars between syndicates fighting for new territories are no longer standard practice. The control of territories is apparently decided now at meetings of the overlords of crime. The leaders long since realized that open and widespread murder aroused public opinion. Extreme violence is used today only to eliminate competition from outside the syndicates; to discipline members of the syndicates who threaten the security of the organizations; to punish those who betray their colleagues or who disobey orders; to secure their ends where objectives cannot be achieved outside of the syndicates through bribery and corruption. Today bribery and corruption – not the tommygun – are the favourite weapons of the syndicates.

These things have been said many times by people engaged in the fight against the syndicates in the United States, but the point that impresses me – the point that I think we must keep in mind – is that these syndicates have flourished and grown in the face of all efforts to stop them, and only a long almost wide-open border separates them from Canada. Until a few years ago, we were very fortunate. It is true the syndicates have long been drawing large revenues from Canadian gambling organizations through the sale of such services as trackside information and lay-off arrangements or, as they are called, the bookies' bookmakers. A few years ago the Legs Diamond mob and later the Purple Gang provided Canadian criminal organizations with engineers and construction crews for the installation of the huge illicit stills. For some time after the Kefauver inquiry, several of the syndicates in the Eastern United

States moved their headquarters into Eastern Canada, and during that period it is said that it was impossible to place a bet east of Chicago that was not cleared through Canada, but this was a matter of convenience by which the American gangsters could evade American law-enforcement efforts. None of these operations brought the power of the syndicates into Canada for the purpose of taking over control of crime in Canada.

That picture has changed. The American syndicates have become increasingly interested in Canada and have moved to take over direct control of some existing criminal organizations. They are already active in the fields of gambling, narcotics trafficking, counterfeiting, stick and loan frauds, and in the protection racket. Beyond question, the syndicates working from headquarters in the United States will try to expand the already sizable beachheads that they have established in Canada, and it is equally certain that local mobsters will pattern their activities on the methods that have proven so successful across the border. Unless means are found to stop the growth of "mobs" – American or Canadian – we will, before many years, be faced with the problem of the multi- million dollar, powerful, seemingly indestructible syndicates of crime that thrive in the United States today.

There is nothing new or surprising in what I have said about the threat from organized crime, nor is there anything that has not been known and discussed by police officers for several years. I know something of the planning that has been done to meet the threat, and I have every confidence that the police forces of Canada will do their utmost to meet this particular problem, along with the general problem of reducing the crime rate. But the police cannot do the job alone. Unless legislators, the Bench, and the Bar – and most important of all, public opinion – take a stronger stand against the professional criminal than has been apparent in the past, the police will continue to fight a losing battle. A lifetime in the police business has instilled an understanding and sympathy for the beginner in crime, the people who make one or two slips before they get straightened out, but it has also taught me the utter fallacy and the dangers of extending sympathy to the professionals, of granting them the same protection and solicitude and safeguards that are rightly extended to first or second or even third offenders. The day may come when workers in the field of sociology will have eliminated conditions that throw up hoodlums, professional killers, and others who choose a life of crime, but that day has not yet arrived. In the meantime, we have the syndicates, the mobs, and the increasing power of organized crime. These are hard facts of today, and we must deal with them today, while continuing to hope that new theories and endeavours will eradicate the conditions that produced them. And it has been amply proven that professional crime will not be stopped by a soft approach.

Maximum service for senior officers in the Force is normally limited to thirty-five years, and I looked forward to April 22, 1963, the date on which I would achieve that service, with mixed feelings. On the one hand, there were many things that I had always wanted to do and several hobbies that I was anxious to pursue with more vigour than had been possible during my working years. On the other hand, retirement meant a sharp severing of direct and active connections with the Force and with friends with whom I had worked for many years. As the time for my retirement drew close, the Government paid me a tribute by asking me to remain at the Commissioner's desk. While I was pleased and flattered by the invitation to remain with the Force, I hesitated for a while before accepting. Promotion is fairly slow, and I was reluctant to hang onto office and slow the process further. I was not concerned for the work or future of the Force. Competent officers were available to move up, and the members, regular and civilian, were loyal and skilled in their work, and their morale was high. When the time came for me to drop out of the Force, it would be left in good, capable hands.

Toward the end of my service, friends and publishers suggested that – in view of my years with the Force, the many changes that I had witnessed taking place during those years, the fact that from time to time I had publicly expressed opinions regarding the increasing problems of law enforcement, and because I was the last serving member of the old Royal North West Mounted Police – I should attempt to write a book. The foregoing pages are the result. Since my retirement, however, the Munsinger, Spencer, Banks, and Rivard affairs have received a great deal of publicity, and as they were pending while I was still in office, and have given rise to a great deal of criticism of the Force, it seems fitting that I should write another chapter. Further, having been away from active interest and participation in the work of the Force, and in the police field generally for three years, I have been able to stand back and attempt an objective view of law enforcement and the difficulties that beset the police, and to try to find ways by which some of the present obstacles could be overcome or at least reduced. Retirement results in a lessening of personal involvement or direct concern with the problems and may enable a better perspective, but my views are still influenced by the work in which I was engaged for most of my life and are, therefore, still those of a policeman.

If this book attracts any attention, there will probably be a fair amount of disagreement and criticism regarding some of my suggestions, particularly from persons outside the law-enforcement field. They are not being advanced in the concluding chapter with confidence that there will be general acceptance, but rather in the hope that such controversy and criticism as they do arouse may lead to better opinions and better answers.

On October 31, 1963, I passed the reins to Commissioner George B. McClellan.

21

꿹꿹꿹꿹꿹

Let the Police Police

When I left the Force, there were thousands of investigations in various stages of development. All but four of these were brought to normal conclusions and caused little stir or concern except to the persons directly involved. But four cases – the Banks, Munsinger, Spencer, Rivard affairs – achieved international notoriety. The flood of criticism – a great deal of which was unfounded or, at best, the blowing up of a small grain of truth – rocked and, at times, threatened to upset the Government, which by its own actions on several occasions aggravated situations and brought on further accusations and criticisms. Clearly the Force could not escape involvement in the criticisms or avoid the role in which the police are so often cast – as "whipping boys." With the clear vision of hindsight and, at times, having recourse to the less-accurate practice of experienced guesswork, opposition parties thundered accusations of inept police methods and gestapo practice. Some of the details of these four cases were indeed important and interesting, but there is room for reasonable doubt that any one of them merited sensational and international coverage; most of which seems to have been brought on by political considerations rather than a concern with the facts at hand.

I am inclined to doubt that an involved investigation has ever been brought to a conclusion by such direct, efficient, and opportune procedures as to defy possible criticisms of any detail by persons making full use of the advantages of hindsight. Unfortunately, the police do not have a crystal ball that will place them in that advantageous position; nor do they have the power of the Royal Commissions to elicit information under oath; nor do they have weeks or months in which to arrive at a decision

244

as to the course of action. Looking back on the activities of the police in some of the four cases mentioned, it is possible to find points at which a different course might have produced quicker or more conclusive results, but the police were not engaged solely in examining the records of events that had already transpired – they were trying to anticipate action in which the initiative was in the hands of others. The success of their efforts depended on their ability to outguess – a task somewhat more difficult than second-guessing.

In the four cases, the Force came in for massive, severe, and sometimes harsh criticism because of its action or alleged action or lack of action in the conduct of the investigations. Now that the hubbub has died down and the unsavoury affairs are passing into history, I believe it important at least to attempt to set the records straight. This does not stem primarily from a desire to protect, justify or excuse the police, or to smooth feathers that may have been ruffled by unwarranted attacks. Policemen are not particularly thin-skinned. They know that the nature of their work makes them easy targets, and they should become accustomed if not entirely inured to criticism, fair and unfair. But widespread and unjustified criticism repeated over and over again, as it was in these cases, must bring about a reduction of public confidence in and support of the laws and law enforcement. For that reason, the charges of bungling inefficiency should be answered, if there are answers. Interesting information may be found by indulging in a little hindsight ourselves, now that the findings of Royal Commissions, and the evidence given before courts, have been published.

The Banks case provides a classic example of the manner in which a few ill-informed and ill-considered remarks during debates in the House of Commons may be repeated and embellished by the news media until they appear to establish a strong indictment against the police.

Harold Chamberlain Banks was a gross, tough, and unscrupulous labour organizer who came to Canada some years ago to take over leadership of the Seafarers International Union. There were heavy political overtones. It was alleged that the Government had brought him to Canada as an antidote to threats being posed to Canadian shipping by other unions. Be that as it may, he remained in Canada through several regimes. By 1962, following disruption of shipping on the Great Lakes, it became apparent that the antidote was worse than the original ailment. Mr. Justice F. G. Norris was appointed a Commissioner under the Industrial Relations and Disputes Act to investigate. In his Report, published in July 1963, Justice Norris recommended among other things that special counsel should be appointed to ascertain whether charges could be brought against Banks and others for having conspired to commit indictable offences, particularly in connection with the beating of Captain Francis Henry Walsh, the organizer of another union. This was alleged to have taken place in 1957. The Department of Justice requested that the Force carry out an investigation. Although six years had elapsed since the incident, the investigation succeeded in uncovering evidence that warranted the laying of charges against Banks and two of his cohorts.

Banks was convicted on May 5, 1964, and sentenced to five years' imprisonment. He immediately filed an appeal and, despite objections by Crown Council, was released on bail of twenty-five thousand dollars, not a large surety when the alternative of five years is considered. Then Banks fled the country. Banks' unsavoury reputation, the charges that this brutal man had been a tool of Government, the details of the merciless beating that had been administered to elderly Captain Walsh, and the fact that Banks had escaped just punishment – all these set the stage for a field-day for the Opposition parties. Charges and recriminations flew across the floor of the House and provided sensational and disturbing headlines, columns, and editorials. It was not to be expected that the police would be overlooked in the attempts to fix the responsibility in this miscarriage of justice.

The Force in particular and the police in general were charged with sins of omission and sins of commission: they had been careless and inept in allowing Banks to get across the border into the United States; there had been collusion in permitting his escape; they had made no real effort to pursue him in the United States. The efforts of the Force were made to look like those of Keystone Cops. This landslide of criticism almost buried two important and very relevant facts. First, but for the experienced and efficient work of the Force in unearthing facts concerning the beating six years earlier, Banks would not have been brought before the bar of justice. Second, having been released on bail – and it is worth repeating that this was done over the protest of Crown Counsel – Banks could have crossed the border with a brass band and dancing girls, and not a policeman in Canada could have laid a finger on him. Once in the United States, he could have continued to march at the head of a band, since he had absolutely nothing to fear from the Canadian authorities. The charge on which he had been convicted is not among those included in the Extradition Treaty with the United States.

On October 8, 1960, two Russian Intelligence "legals" – that is, spy masters working out of the Soviet Embassy in Ottawa, Lev Burdiukov and Rem Krassilnikov, slipped up in their usually cautious handling of "meets" with agents, and for a few minutes carried out their work in a very sloppy and most unprofessional manner. Unfortunately for them and their plans, they were being watched by members of the RCMP's Security and Intelligence Directorate who, taking advantage of the "break," were able to discover that the man with whom the Russians were holding a clandestine meeting was George Victor Spencer, a fifty-six-year-old postal clerk from Vancouver.

The Force already had some "traces" regarding Spencer. He had been a member of the Communist Party of Canada for some ten years, ending in 1946 when he was expelled, allegedly because of a tendency to argue with his confreres. This information was of interest in that it is a fairly routine precautionary measure in Communist circles to "expel" members from the "open" party when they are being considered for recruitment into the espionage apparatus. Whether the Spencer expulsion was genuine or trumped-up as a move to cover the connection of the Communist Party of Canada with the recruitment of agents, the reasons could not have been very serious since he was eventually brought into the espionage net – a move that would require the approval of the control centre in Moscow.

A second "trace" in the files of the counter-intelligence service showed that, in 1956, Spencer was seen talking to a Russian Intelligence Officer, Afanasiev, in Vancouver. That meeting may not have been very important or significant in that it took place openly, in the presence of several other persons, during welcoming ceremonies for a group of visiting Russians. After his meeting with the two Russian spy masters in Ottawa in October of 1960, Spencer was kept under observation by the Force. He returned to Ottawa on March 4 and again on August 5, 1961. On both these occasions, he met with the Russian, Burdiukov, and the surreptitious circumstances of their meetings followed the well-known pattern and made it clear that the arrangements had been carefully planned. Further, the Force was aware that Spencer had been busily engaged in gathering information which, while not of a classified nature, was material in which the Russians had often shown great interest.

At that point it was necessary to decide whether the matter was of sufficient importance to be allowed to go on or whether it should be brought to an end by an interview with Spencer and a request to the Government that the two Russians be declared *persona non grata*. With Assistant Commissioner W. Kelly and Deputy Commissioner McClellan, I discussed the matter at some length and agreed that the information being sought by the Russians indicated a possibility that they were planning to set up a new espionage net on the West Coast. It was decided that the matter should be allowed to develop until we had learned more regarding Soviet interests and objectives in British Columbia.

During 1961, 1962, and part of 1963, Spencer was quite active in supplying the Russians with the information requested by them. He made four more trips to Ottawa where he met secretly with espionage agents from the Soviet Embassy at times and places set by them through the exchange of seemingly innocent letters dealing with film showings. In view of Moscow's persistent denials of such involvement, it is interesting to note that Spencer's letters accepting the times and conditions of the meetings which were set by the spy masters were sent under assumed names and addressed to "The Film Editor, USSR Embassy, Ottawa," a rather careless but significant security arrangement.

The information gathered by Spencer fell into several categories. First, there were details that would have enabled the Russians to produce false "cover stories" or "legends," as they are called, through which Russian agents – as in the case of the spy in England, Lonsdale – could be supplied with documents and backgrounds that would be difficult to check and that would identify the bearer as a Canadian citizen. To this end, Spencer provided information secured from tombstones and archives about births and deaths and family backgrounds. From newspaper files and business records, he gathered details of old schools and residential areas that had been replaced by new building developments or industrial sites. His research included the records of bankruptcies and fires that might provide untraceable employment records for the "legends." The Russians also requested and received information regarding automobile and drivers' licences, local clothing and customs, procedures for crossing into the United States, and the forms required for emigrating to the United States. Spencer secured copies of these forms, along with maps of Southern British Columbia and tourist information regarding motels and points of interest.

The fact that the Soviets required this sort of information served to confirm our suspicions that they were planning to set up an "illegal" net in Southern British Columbia, and that their interest in farms close to the border and the desire for details regarding the formalities of border crossing indicated that they planned espionage on both sides of the border with headquarters located on one of the farms. "Legends" to be used by new agents and the training in local customs could have been drawn from the material provided by Spencer.

The Russians also assigned Spencer the task of supplying information regarding ethnic groups, a matter in which they often show considerable concern. This interest stems from standard tasks undertaken by Soviet agents: the recruitment of emigrés as spies through the use of such pressures as the threat of reprisals on relatives still in the home country; reporting on the attitude of ethnic groups towards the USSR; and where that attitude is hostile, to use disruptive tactics and character assassination in attempts to weaken the group. Among "targets" of a general nature, Spencer was given the task of providing photographs and details of the Trans-Mountain Pipeline which supplies the West Coast with oil and gasoline. The Russians were particularly anxious to get this information, and to oblige them Spencer devoted eight days of his vacation in 1961 to driving along the pipeline and taking photographs of it, including points where it crosses rivers, oil refineries, storage tanks, and pumping stations. He also was asked for and provided information regarding the security arrangements in force in the Vancouver Post Office and the water supply and distribution system for the city of Vancouver.

During his employment, Spencer was made acquainted with many of the methods of "trade-craft," or the tricks of espionage – the "live" and the "dead" letter box; "legal" and "illegal" agents, coded letters, means of evading surveillance and the use of cover-names, coded letters, and classified advertisements in order to avoid detection. The Russians received from him a great deal of information which, while not of a secret nature, would have been difficult for them to secure themselves. Their handling of Spencer did not always reflect credit on their training or ability as spy masters.

By the Spring of 1963, Spencer was becoming disillusioned with the Russians. During a visit to Ottawa, he committed the almost unforgivable sin – for an agent – of calling at the USSR embassy in an attempt to get clarification on several matters that were troubling him. They made it quite clear that he was unwelcome and had committed a blunder. From then on the relationship cooled off. Spencer made no more trips to Ottawa, and it became apparent to the counter-intelligence service that he was no longer actively engaged in gathering information. There remained the possibility that the Russians, alarmed by his indiscretion in visiting their Embassy, would leave him as a "sleeper" for some time and then re-activate the operation. The Force continued its observation on a reduced scale, since an investigation of this sort imposes a strain on available manpower and equipment. By the end of 1964, it was apparent that nothing would be gained by continuing the inquiry.

The first information to reach the public regarding the affair was contained in a brief announcement by the Government that two members of the staff of the Soviet Embassy had been engaged in espionage and had been asked to leave Canada. The announcement made very brief reference to the involvement of a civil servant in the espionage activities. Questions were asked in the House regarding the identity of the civil servant and the circumstances of the involvement. This, in time, lead to demands that the culprit be prosecuted. As public interest mounted, newsmen started an intensive search which ended when enterprising reporters in Vancouver located Spencer and secured from him an admission that he was the much-sought-after civil servant. They also learned that he had been dismissed from the postal service with loss of pension. However, in accordance with his rights under the statute, his contributions to the pension fund had been returned to him.

When the press located Spencer, he was a gravely sick man, having recently undergone major surgery for the removal of a cancerous lung. The Minister had been kept advised of Spencer's condition by the Force, and on May 11, 1965, he was given a copy of the following telex message:

> *Early today Spencer's prognosis obtained from Dr. Coy [Spencer's surgeon] after Coy had obtained Spencer's signature authorizing release of information to* RCMP. *Diagnosis is suspected malignancy in stump of removed lung and bronchial trunk leading to remaining one. Because of rapid growth of previous tumour, doctor's most pessimistic view is death within two to three months, when suspected malignancy could reach remaining lung. Most optimistic view, if cobalt therapy proves to be arresting, is one in ten chances of living up to five years. There is also the danger in lung cases that brain paralysis could occur at any time.*

Only callous inhumanity could have led to a decision to prosecute a man in such pitiful circumstances, even had the case against him been crystal clear, which it was not. Spencer had worked hard for the Russians and had supplied them with a great deal of information, but none of that material was of a secret or classified nature that would have brought his actions within the law relating to treason or offences under the Official Secrets Act. And in arriving at a decision against prosecution, the Government had yet another consideration. Spencer had served with distinction during the war and had been awarded the British Empire Medal.

When located by the press, Spencer had already given the RCMP a detailed statement of his work for the Russians. With the newsmen who originally located him, and later on television, he was quite frank in admitting his involvement in espionage and showed reluctance only when questioned regarding the amount of money he had received for his services.

In view of the facts of the matter – two Russian diplomats had been expelled for espionage; a civil servant who, by his own admission, had knowingly supplied them with a great deal of information and had been discharged from the civil service for misconduct – it might have been reasonable to expect that the affair would end rather quietly, probably with a condemnation of the Russians and a plea for some generosity toward a dying veteran who had erred but had paid a high penalty through the loss of his pension. Unfortunately the political stage was not set for a quiet ending. During the ensuing debates in the House, a barrage of criticism condemned everyone and everything connected with the affair – everyone, that is, except the instigators, the Russians. The Minister, the Government, the police, the civil service, Spencer – all came in as grist for the mill that was creating scandal where no scandal existed.

True, some compassionate members asked for a better deal for Spencer, but their pleas were almost buried by demands that he be prosecuted or given back his job.

Amazingly, since the facts were so clear and readily obtainable, it was held that the Government and police had fabricated the story of Spencer's critical physical condition in order to avoid prosecution because knowledge in his possession would cause "heads to roll." Conversely, there were insinuations that Spencer had done no wrong, but that the police had engaged in a silly witch-hunt after an innocent postal clerk who had merely sent postcards to the Russian Embassy. According to some versions, the police were "hounding" an innocent man and had used pressures to secure a confession. Others clamoured for prosecution.

At the height of the clamour, Spencer, probably encouraged or confused by his sudden notoriety, publicly complained about his dismissal and loss of pension. The complaints were not very clear or forceful, but they did provide more grist for the mill. Critics in and out of Parliament, still unmindful of the facts that had been supplied in the House, now centred their attention on demands for a Commission of Inquiry. Justice Minister Cardin, possibly mindful of the cost to the taxpayers, resisted the demands for several days but was eventually overruled. On March 7, 1966, Mr. Justice Dalton Courtwright Wells of the Supreme Court of Ontario was by Order-in-Council appointed a Commissioner, "to inquire into and report upon the complaints made by George Victor Spencer and related matters."

The inquiry had just got under way when, on April 9, Spencer was found dead in the kitchen of his house in Vancouver. From all appearances, death had occurred about forty-eight hours before the finding of the body. Despite the public knowledge that the unfortunate man had been suffering the final stages of cancer, the circumstances of his death brought another spate of rumour and sensational insinuation. Had there been foul play? Had he been silenced because of his knowledge of Soviet espionage methods? And, conveniently forgetting that there had been no charges against the man, and that any invasion of his privacy would have justified stories that the police had been "hounding" him, the police were accused of having failed to provide adequate protection. These utterly ridiculous rumours were ended with the publication of the findings of the coroner's jury which established that there had been no foul play. Nor could any amount of protection have saved the poor man. He had come to death, "as a result of pulmonary thrombosis secondary to resection of the left lung." His death was certified as "natural."

Justice Well's report was submitted on July 18, 1966. His Lordship's findings go into every aspect of the case with such thoroughness as to rout the critics and satisfy the public that justice was done. So clearly are the facts drawn out in the report that one is forced to wonder, politics aside, how they could have led to the setting up of a Commission.

If there was witch-hunting in the Spencer affair, it was carried out by the debates in the House and the resultant publicity not by the police. The far-ranging debates forced the setting up of the Commission of Inquiry, and the report of Mr. Justice Wells provided conclusive answers to the many questions and suspicions that had been raised. The Report contained few facts that were not known or readily obtainable to Members of Parliament at the time of the debates. A little more trust and confidence, and a shade less interest in getting into the limelight, would have avoided sensationalism. One might paraphrase the old wartime question by asking, "Was this inquiry really necessary?"

The Rivard affair was actually two interlocking, vastly involved, and serious inquiries. The first concerned the arrest, escape, and rearrest of Rivard; and the second, which arose during the Rivard case, hinged on allegations of attempted bribery and corruption in high places.

The Rivard case would have been sensational without the injection of allegations of bribery. Lucien Rivard was a leader among the criminals of Montreal. A list of his associates would read like a *Who's Who* of the underworld not only in Montreal but on the international crime scene as well. For some years it had been suspected that, apart from other criminal activities, he was a member of an international organization engaged in smuggling narcotic drugs from Europe into Mexico, and from there into the United States and Canada.

On October 10, 1963, one Joseph M. Caron was arrested in Laredo, Texas, when found in possession of a very large amount of heroin. Investigations by the RCMP and the United States Federal Bureau of Narcotics established proof that Caron was one of Lucien Rivard's couriers. A charge was laid against Rivard in Laredo, Texas, and the Force was requested to apprehend him. He was taken into custody by the RCMP on a provisional warrant, pending the outcome of extradition proceedings. Having discharged its duty by apprehending Rivard, the Force had no further direct interest or responsibility in the matter. The federal Government does not become involved in extradition cases at the judicial level. All judicial processes, including custody of the person under detention, are carried out in provincial courts and institutions, the provincial courts being designated Extradition Courts for the purposes of the Extradition Act. Counsel to represent the interests of the foreign state desiring custody of the detainee is appointed by that state. The federal Government only acts in the area of the required diplomatic representations, and the Minister of Justice signs the final surrender warrant if that has been the decision of the provincial – more properly, the Extradition – Court.

The proceedings regarding Rivard's surrender to the United States followed the usual lengthy and protracted course before the courts, but toward the end of July a new element was added which brought the Force back into the picture. Pierre Lamontagne, the lawyer representing the United States in the Rivard action, and who had appeared as Counsel for the RCMP in a number of narcotics cases, claimed that about three and a half weeks earlier he had been offered a bribe of twenty-thousand dollars if he would withdraw his objection to bail for Rivard. The offer was said to the have been made by Raymond Denis, a lawyer who was Executive Assistant to the Minister of Citizenship and Immigration. This was reported to the Minister of Justice who instructed that an investigation of Lamontagne's charges be started forthwith. On November 23, 1964, the allegations regarding attempts at bribery were brought up in the House of Commons.

The Rivard case had been receiving a considerable amount of attention from the press. Now it leapt into headlines and became, as indeed it was, a major and sensational scandal. After further debates in the House and demands for a public inquiry, the Honourable Frederic Dorion, Chief Justice of the Superior Court for the Province of Quebec, was appointed Commissioner, in conformity with the Inquiries Act, to inquire into the alleged bribe and the behaviour of both the Minister of Justice and the RCMP.

In the meantime, the attempts at bribery having failed, Lucien Rivard was still in Bordeaux jail in Montreal awaiting the outcome of the extradition proceedings. While the two matters – the allegations of attempted bribery and the extradition of Rivard interlock – it may be clearer to dispose of Rivard before returning to the Special Public Inquiry, particularly in that the affair was to become more involved and sensational.

On September 25, 1964, Rivard was finally committed for extradition. Through his lawyers, he had fought every step of the way, and he continued his efforts to avoid facing a court in the United States. An appeal was entered against the commital order, and it was not until March 8, 1965, that the appeal was dismissed and the order committing him for extradition was upheld. However, Rivard was not available for deportation. At approximately 7:00 p.m., March 2, accompanied by another criminal, André Durocher, he escaped from Bordeaux Jail.

The method of escape, it was said, had been amazingly easy. Rivard, a notorious criminal, whose name had become almost a household word because of the bribery scandal, with his companion Durocher, quite notorious in his own right (there were some seventeen charges outstanding against him), had simply borrowed a hose from a guard and climbed over the high prison wall. The hose had been lent to them to flood the skating rink, although the temperature at the time was well above freezing.

For some weeks, Rivard replaced world news in Canadian headlines, and certainly the series of scandals that had followed his arrest was newsworthy. From time to time, the news media carried stories that Rivard had been seen in Mexico, in Spain, in Switzerland, and at various other points around the world. Some of these stories were started by Rivard's wife who showed newsmen letters that she claimed to have received from her husband. The letters were carried in the press and gave a fillip to the news stories. They also provided an excellent and ingenious method whereby Mrs. Rivard could get messages to her husband who was, in fact, hiding out in Canada. In trying to fix responsibility for the escape, questions were asked in the House and in the press regarding the police. Why had they not provided special guards to keep Rivard in jail? These questions added a little colour to the affair, but the answers were too obvious for them to be taken very seriously. The RCMP have nothing to do with the administration or operation of prisons. They have their own staffs, and the police may move in to assist them only on the request of the prison authorities. The police at all levels, federal, provincial, and municipal, worked in close co-operation in the search for Rivard. When he was recaptured on July 16, 1965, in a summer cottage near Montreal, with him were two other known criminals, against whom there were outstanding warrants.

Rivard was escorted to the border and handed over to the United States authorities six days later. He was subsequently convicted in Texas on November 12, 1965, and sentenced to imprisonment for twenty years and a fine of twenty thousand dollars. Three other Canadian criminals, Joseph Raymond Jones, Charles Emile Groleau, and Julien Gagnon were extradited to Laredo, Texas, on charges arising from the seizure of heroin. All were found guilty. Gagnon and Jones were sentenced to fifteen years, and Groleau to twelve years imprisonment.

André Durocher, who escaped with Rivard, was recaptured on May 11, 1966. On May 18, he was sentenced to one year on charges of possession of firearms and explosives. Subsequently, witnesses before a coroner's jury gave evidence that Durocher had been responsible for the deaths of two girls, Alice Rious and Audre Payuette. Before any further action could be taken in that regard, Durocher, against whom there were seventeen charges, including robbery while armed and theft, committed suicide in Bordeaux jail.

Rivard's escape, the series of revelations regarding his criminal activities and those of his associates, stories of large sums of money put up by the underworld to assist him in his efforts to evade justice, and the allegations that the underworld had been able to reach into high echelons of Government had alarmed the public and brought greater pressures to bear on the Commission of Inquiry. The Commissioner, the Honourable Frederic Dorion, submitted his report in June of 1965, a massive record of thirty-six volumes and more than seven thousand pages of evidence, comment, and opinion. The nub of the report was the first question raised in the terms of reference of the Commission: "The truth of certain allegations concerning the offer of a bribe to a lawyer whom the American Government had retained to take action before the Courts for the extradition of a certain Lucien Rivard." The questions raised by the terms of reference regarding the behaviour of the Royal Canadian Mounted Police and the Minister of Justice, while of great importance, were ancillary to that central question.

When questioned before the Inquiry, RCMP Commissioner McClellan said that he was inclined to believe the greater part of Lamontange's statement that he had been offered a bribe and that he had been subjected to threats by Rivard's cohorts. But McClellan's opinion would not provide evidence before the Criminal Courts, and he had grave doubts about Lamontagne's evidence standing up under cross-examination.

The Inquiry Commissioner was quite critical of the investigation carried out by the RCMP and the fact that on the instructions of the Minister, it had not been pursued beyond the point when it was decided that Lamontagne's statement would not stand up in court. However, any shortcomings in the police investigation were, surely, corrected by the Inquiry during which it is reasonable to assume that the Honourable Justice Dorion, exercising powers and authority far greater than those enjoyed by the police, went into every available scrap of evidence. Having ended his investigation, the Inquiry Commissioner concluded that McClellan had been wrong in advising the Minister that there was not sufficient proof on which to prosecute, and that the Minister had erred in his decision that the available evidence was not strong enough to lead to a conviction. The Inquiry Commissioner was strong and decided in his views that evidence necessary to corroborate the Lamontagne statement was available.

I would not have the temerity to question the opinions of the Honourable Frederic Dorion. However, as a result of the Report of the Inquiry, Lawyer Raymond Denis, the former Executive Assistant to the Minister of Citizenship and Immigration, was charged with having offered a bribe and conspiracy. The trial was the longest in the history of Ottawa. After thirty-one days of hearings, it ended in a mistrial.

Blackmail has always been a weapon of Communist espionage. In recent years it has become one of their chief methods of forcing information out of reluctant sources. Most counter-intelligence services, including the Royal Canadian Mounted Police, can produce hard proof of this from cases within their experience.

Before coming to Canada Gerda Munsinger, a convicted thief and prostitute, was employed by an Iron-Curtain espionage net. If her trip to Canada was an extension of her work for the Communists in Germany, or if she had been re-recruited in Canada, her job would not have been the actual gathering of information. Prominent persons involved in the notorious Munsinger Affair attempted to ridicule the espionage theory on the grounds that she had never attempted to pry secrets from them. This is patent nonsense.

It seems obvious that a highly skilled and secretive group of spies would not endanger their organization by bringing into their inner circles a woman of her background and character. One of the first and best observed rules of espionage is that knowledge of the group's activities will be distributed only on a strict, "need-to-know" basis. Her masters would indicate the persons they were interested in. Her job would have been the setting up of the "pigeons for plucking." The actual "plucking" would have been attended to by persons trained in and with a thorough knowledge of the interests and requirements of their country. Gerda Munsinger had had no such training.

During debate of the affair in the House of Commons, and later during the Spence Inquiry, there was great play on the words "breach" and "risk." At various times, attempts were made to imply that in the context of security these two words were synonymous. Since it could not be established that there had been a breach of security, it followed that there was no risk. These fallacious arguments did not receive full acceptance, but they did cloud and confuse the issues.

There is no proof — or even clear indication – that Munsinger's effort led to a "breach" of security. There is ample proof that there was a "risk". Records show that some men have had the courage to resist threats of exposure, but this has not always been the case. It would have been a very simple matter for the espionage agency to secure photographs of Gerda's visitors, and there were many. Some were in a position to supply important information. Others might have been forced into aiding the spies in other directions. And it is known that espionage agents visited another apartment in the same building.

There was risk from another unsavoury group. Gerda Munsinger is known to have had highly placed contacts in the Montreal underworld. Criminals usually blackmail for cash, but the highly organized underworld of today can and does use threats and pressures for larger profits than might be secured from immediate payment. If in the process they should come into possession of state secrets, does anyone doubt that they would sell these to the highest bidder?

Beyond question, the Munsinger Affair was a potential threat to security. Fortunately, as far as is known, it was stopped before the risk led to the handing over of secrets. Gerda Munsinger appeared to have possessed considerable ability in her ancient profession. Had she been allowed to continue in the exercise of that ability, it is altogether possible that she would have used her charms on persons through whom her espionage masters could have breached the security of the state.

While the Munsinger affair was receiving wide publicity, many stories were circulated about compromising photographs taken in Gerda's bedroom. These stories may have stemmed from rumours that were current in Montreal's underworld for several months. I do not know if such photographs exist, but I am certain that if they do they were not taken by the Royal Canadian Mounted Police. The Force is concerned with security – not pornography or blackmail.

From time to time critics attempt to make much of the existence of secret police files. In this regard the Munsinger case established two points. First, the Force does and must keep secret dossiers; second, in some cases the country is better served if the files remain secret.

During a life spent in police work, there were many times when I felt that the scales of justice were weighted heavily, too heavily, against the police. On many occasions when criminals were set free, not for want of proof but because of ritualistic adherence to jurisprudence drawn from a different era, I was almost ready to agree with the old adage about the law being an "ass."

But a practising policeman may be too close to the scene to arrive at sound, objective opinions regarding the overall effectiveness and fairness of the law. He may have mastered the sometimes difficult task of being completely impartial in the carrying out of his duties, but only a superman could remain free of prejudice against crime and violence when day in and day out he is witnessing their effects and talking to their innocent victims. The fact that learned judges, lawyers, legislators, sociologists, and a host of others, including a large section of the news media, championed the existing methods of administering justice raised the possibility that I was not seeing the entire picture.

I have been in retirement for more than three years. My interest in law enforcement is now that of a citizen and taxpayer. It is altogther possible that some of the old prejudices against crime and violence remain, but I am free of any personal involvement or direct interest other than the desire shared by most other Canadians to see reversed the trend toward increasing crime in Canada.

My wider point of view has served only to strengthen my opinion that the criminal – the hardened, professional, career criminal; not the beginner – gets too many breaks and too much help. I am still unwilling to accept that "the law is an ass." However, when it tends to handcuff the police instead of the criminal, when at times it shows maudlin sympathy for the hoodlum and scant regard for his victims, it comes perilously close to qualifying for that description.

In this fast-moving atomic age, when in other fields every institution and practice is being questioned and changed to meet present conditions, in law enforcement there is a determined clinging to methods that were designed to meet the problems of the horse-and-buggy days; a dependence on rulings and judgments of generations or even centuries ago under circumstances and conditions that have no semblance to our times. The scales of justice have become so enmeshed in cobwebs of the past as to prevent them balancing freely for the protection of honest citizens and law-abiding, peaceful communities.

Cobwebs of the past? Certainly our courts must draw on sound, basic principles established through the years, but this inbred habit of looking backward seems to have cluttered our legal processes with a mass of material which no longer has practical or reasonable application and serves only to provide counsel with arguments with which to confuse and confound the issue. One quick example comes to mind.

Some years ago I was involved in an investigation and prosecution that developed into one of the longest preliminary hearings in Canadian history. A number of well-known citizens were charged with having conspired to defraud the Government of six million dollars. The evidence dealt with the ownership of vessels active in the Atlantic coast "Rum-Row" of prohibition days; with rum-laden schooners plying an illegal traffic between the West Indies and Canada; with secret codes and clandestine radio stations; with stocks of liquor worth many millions of dollars stored on offshore islands; and with all the systems and devices of a huge, modern smuggling organization.

The Crown employed two lawyers; the Defence sixteen. Among the latter were specialists in every branch of law that might be touched on during the hearings. Legal argument took up more time than the presentation of evidence.

At one stage of the proceedings, the Defence in arguing a rather remote point of law referred to a case that had occured in England almost a century earlier as a result of an unfortunate man getting his thumb caught in the door of a railway carriage. For two entire days the time of the Court was taken up while this poor wight – sore thumb, bandages, pain, and all – was verbally paraded up and down the courtroom. I am sure that if he could have been there in the flesh, he would have been as perplexed as I was as to how his trifling and rather silly accident in the nineteenth century could have landed him in "Rum-Row," or how his aching thumb could have any interest to a court studying an alleged conspiracy of major proportions.

There is a bit of humour in that story, but there in nothing funny in the fact that the enervating ritualism of the courts opens many loopholes for those criminals who can afford to hire counsel experienced in seeking out escape routes. Anyone familiar with the courts can relate many instances in which, because of a seemingly ridiculous ruling based on antiquated jurisprudence, guilty men have walked from the court-room free to ply their trades in crime again. I recall an instance in which thirteen dealers in illegal narcotic drugs were turned loose because the formal charges against them, while detailing the appropriate offence under the Opium and Narcotic Drug Act, did not contain the words, "without lawful authority," words that had not been held as essential in previous prosecutions.

A policeman encounters difficulty with antiquated and often contradictory rulings long before he is able to bring an accused person to court and, indeed, he is frequently defeated in his efforts to bring about that desirable end by the very laws and ruling which, in theory, are supposed to have been designed in the cause of justice and law and order. At almost every step of an investigation, a policeman is faced by legal rulings practices, and procedures which stifle the gathering of evidence and often prevent its presentation before the courts.

It has been held by some critics that the problems of the police stem from lack of training; that with adequate training an investigator could pick his way quickly and firmly through the morass of laws and court rulings. Such critics over simplify the situation. Judges are learned in the law and have spent many years in its practice and yet are in frequent disagreement. Lawyers are trained and skilled in their work, and one of the most noticeable effects of their skill and training is that it enables defence and prosecution counsel to advance opposite and contradictory views on any point of fact or law brought before the Courts. Today's policemen are better trained, better equipped, and have a wider appreciation of the limits placed on the powers of a peace officer and of the rights of a citizen in the enjoyment of his liberties than at any time in the past. But it is asking a great deal – even to the point of flattery – to suggest that a policeman, during an investigation or fracas, should on the spur of the moment arrive at firm positive decisions which have been beyond the reach and ability of the Bench and Bar.

Apart from outmoded laws and legal procedures, there are many other factors that raise problems for the police and that have a direct bearing on increasing criminality – and growing opposition to law enforcement. Within individual forces, through police organizations and in collaboration with other professions, law-enforcement agencies have tried to pinpoint these factors. Other groups and committees from the Bench, the Bar, sociologists, criminologists, psychologists, social workers, have tried to come up with some reasons for the phenomenon of increasing crime and the accompanying public opposition to law enforcement; and, more important, all these groups have attempted to find answers.

Blame has been placed on a feeling of insecurity in an unsettled world: a breakdown in home life; a weakening of religious influence; poverty; a too affluent society; Communist propaganda; growing protest and resentment of authority; that the police are enforcing an increasing number of restrictive rather than criminal laws; soft treatment of criminals by the courts; and a host of other reasons.

Despite all this study and effort, solutions have not been found; rather the reverse. There is a continuing and growing attitude that if we avoid looking directly at the problem it will go away – and that, in any event, law enforcement concerns only the police and the criminals, and that in such a contest it is desirable that the odds should be weighted heavily in favour of the criminals.

More and more the police seem to be regarded as a body somehow separate from the public, bent on imposing disciplines and restrictions of their own making. Somewhere along the line it seems to have been forgotten that policemen are simply citizens who have been put into uniform to enforce laws passed by legislators elected by the people and; that, far from being a law unto themselves, they are the most closely controlled and restricted of all public servants responsible to their immediate superiors, to Crown Counsel to the Courts, to the Governments at all levels, and ultimately to Parliament itself. These very simple facts are to an increasing extent being overlooked.

It is often charged that the police have been over-zealous or – that favourite charge of defence counsel – that they have used "Gestapo" tactics – simply because they enforced some unpopular law or tried to maintain order in the face of a rioting mob. Sometimes enthusiastic critics follow up such charges by expressing fears of a "police state."

It should be obvious that the time to start worrying about a "police state" is when the police stop enforcing the laws enacted by the elected representatives of the people. Police states start when the police are given or take unto themselves the authority to enforce only laws of their own choosing or making. Law-enforcement authorities may express their views to their governments, but so long as a law remains on the books it is the duty of the police to enforce it.

Other attitudes have developed to hinder the police. The use – or overuse – by the news media and sometimes in the Courts of such words as "stoolpigeon," "informer," "police agent," has built up in the minds of many people the feeling that in some way they are breaking the rules of some game if they assist the police in their efforts to make our communities safe. It is a dangerous and costly attitude, but it is fairly widespread.

Then there is the quick and ready assumption on the part of large sections of the public that every charge levelled against the police is based on fact. Certainly the police make mistakes; of course there have been crooked policemen. Police men are known to have used undue pressures. They are no better – and certainly no worse – than the members of any other group or profession, and they are under stricter control and subject to more rapid and severe punishment than most others, and their work makes them ready targets for false accusations while, for the most part, it denies them an opportunity to refute the charges.

Every cub reporter knows that a favourite gambit of defence counsel, when he faces strong police evidence against his client, is to raise the much used cries of "police brutality," "third-degree methods," or "police harassment" in an attempt to destroy or weaken the case against his client. Evidence to support the defence claims is rarely forthcoming, but the accusations themselves make sensational reading and quite often are made the subject of news reports and broadcasts.

In a very important case some years ago, I was the subject of such charges when the defence counsel attempted to prevent the presentation of evidence in documents found in a safety deposit box. The evidence contained in the documents was damning against his client, and in his efforts to earn his fee, counsel felt called on to accuse me of great wrongdoing and brutality. The case had attracted a great deal of public interest, and the defence counsel's accusations were sensational and outrageous. The press made the most of the opportunity. News stories were headlined across the country, and these lead to editorials condemning the police. One of these, carried in a leading Canadian magazine, expressed deep regret that the police of Canada had "stooped to the use of American methods of brutality and third degree." Eventually the Court interrupted the trial in order to give the defence an opportunity to substantiate the charges that had been made. Having listened to all the defence had to say, the Judge concluded that "not one tittle" of evidence had been produced to indicate that the police had not conducted their inquiry in a perfectly proper and legal manner. As far as I am aware, the only attention given by the press to that part of the story was a one-paragraph article on a back page of one of the local papers.

A great deal has been said and written about the "police image" in recent years. Concern has been expressed because that image has been tarnished. The image *has* been tarnished, and there is cause for concern – not because of any tender feeling of the police or because their morale may be directly effected, but because the changed image and the continuing carping criticism, usually unfounded, has caused a falling off in the co-operation and support of the public. The police may train their members, increase their staffs, improve their equipment, and be completely competent in the mechanics of their work, but they will continue to lose the battle against crime unless they enjoy the confidence and support of the public and through the public, the deserved support of legislators and courts.

Criminals will not disappear of their own accord. The disturbing increase in crime will not be reversed until drastic steps have been taken, and it seems that such steps will be taken only when an aroused public – sick and tired of robbery, murder, cheating, and gangsterism – and sick and tired of paying the heavy costs – demand such action. The hard and obvious fact is that, despite efforts to remove the causes of crime and despite efforts to reduce crime through the rehabilitation of prisoners, the criminal population is growing, crime is becoming better organized, the American syndicates of crime are increasing their activities and influence in Canada.

Our answers to these problems are weak and inadequate. The police are often hamstrung in their investigations by laws that do not contemplate or recognize the machinations of organized and syndicated crime, or the vast changes in the patterns of crime that have been brought about my modern methods of speedy transportation and communication, or the aid and comfort given professional criminals by many of their rulings. Provided with so many breaks and loopholes by the law, the possibility is great that the criminal will escape detection and arrest. If the police succeed in finding their way through the maze of restrictive laws and bring the criminal before the Courts, chances are that he will win an acquittal not for want of evidence but because some ancient ruling has not been brought into line with existing conditions. The administration of justice has become to a large extent a sort of game presided over by referees who are much more intent in seeing that all concerned – and particularly the police – abide by the rules of his complicated and outmoded rule book than in bringing the book up to date.

Opinions such as these are frequently dismissed out of hand on the grounds that they are the result of "police thinking" or "the police mind," as though that were argument enough. Lest my views be so lightly dismissed, I will bolster them with a few excerpts from an address given by Lord Shawcross to the Chicago Crime Commission in 1965. Lord Shawcross is one of Britain's most distinguished lawyers. His career embraces business, university, and Government service. He was Attorney-General in the Labour Government from 1945 to 1951. During his address "The Criminal is Living in a Golden Age," he said:

> Nor is the problem only one of detection. Once a criminal is apprehended he still has to be tried. If he pleads not guilty, the chances are over fifty per cent in his favour of being acquitted. Newspapers usually herald the result by saying that "Mr. so and so has been cleared." It is not that at all. There is not the least doubt that the great majority of those acquitted by juries were in fact guilty of the crimes with which they were charged. What has happened is that somewhere, at some stage in the game, the prosecution has lost a point or two under the rules. . . . What some of us in England are beginning to ask ourselves is whether the criminal law is not too heavily

weighted in favour of the criminal. . . . The barriers protect-
ing suspected and accused persons are being steadily rein-
forced. I believe our law has become hopelessly unrealistic in
its attitude towards the prevention and detection of crime. We
put illusory fears about the impairment of liberty before the
promotion of justice. Indeed, our whole idea of justice is,
when you come to think of it, a bit odd.

It would be interesting to have the views of Lord Shawcross on the now famous decision of the Supreme Court of the United States in the matter of "Miranda versus Arizona" which dealt with the matter of self-incrimination. An immediate result of that sweeping judgment was the release in Miami of seven men charged with rape: in Los Angeles, a confessed murderer went free: in Cincinnati, a robbery suspect was let go, until he promptly committed another crime. The long range effect – and since rulings of courts in the United States are quoted and have a bearing in Canadian Courts, law enforcement here will feel the effects – will be far more serious.

This matter of self-incrimination of statements and confessions has long been the subject of much controversy before the courts and one of the most troublesome problems facing the police. Courts at all levels have disagreed as to the conditions under which a statement or confession might be legally taken by the police. There have been many and widely varied rulings as to what constituted "undue pressure." Often the rulings that undue pressure had been used by the police were utterly ridiculous to a point that bordered on the assinine.

I recall a case in Montreal in which a man was arrested on a very serious charge and brought to our office. Without pressure or promise of any sort, and having been properly warned that he need not say anything, but that anything he did say might be used in evidence, he spent more than two hours writing a confession in longhand. By the time he had finished, it was too late to give him lunch in the police dining room, and the policemen knew that it would be too late for him to get a meal in the courthouse cells. On the way to the courthouse, they stopped at a small restaurant and bought him a meal. It was a hot August day and he asked that he be allowed to have a glass of beer with his meal. The policemen bought him a beer. At the trial, his lawyer argued that the police had used undue pressure to secure the confession by promising his client a meal and a glass of beer. Was it ridiculous to hold that a man would confess to a serious crime in return for a lunch and a drink? The Judge did not think so. He threw out the confession – and the case.

On this point of confessions, the famous English jurist, Lord Devlin, had this to say; "But I think there has been too much tenderness towards prisoners in this matter. I confess that I cannot look at the decisions without some shame when I consider what objections have prevailed to prevent the reception of confessions in evidence."

Much of the confusion that has surrounded the matter of statements and confessions was removed by the decision of the United States Supreme Court in the Miranda case. When, in handing down his judgment, Chief Justice Warren said that a suspect in "police custody, surrounded by antagonistic forces, and subjected to the techniques of persuasion cannot be otherwise than under compulsion," and went on to hold that the very atmosphere of a police station carries its own "badge of intimidation," he effectively protected suspects from any questioning by police in the United States – and in Canada to the extent to which the judgment of his Court may be followed in this country. It is interesting to ponder the fact that four of the nine Justices who made up the Supreme Court were in complete disagreement with the decision.

One of the first questions that should come under close examination when eventually we are compelled to amend our laws to meet the problems of today is this matter of privilege against self-incrimination. It has been truly said that the privilege has ancient and honourable origins, but so has the desire of citizens for safe, peaceful communities. The administration of justice should be aimed at providing such communities – not on embalming justice. But so firmly is this concept against self-incrimination embedded in our laws and procedures that it seems almost an act of sacrilege to raise the slightest question regarding its applications under today's conditions.

I believe that the administration of justice and law enforcement would benefit greatly if we recalled that the privilege against self incrimination arose in mediaeval times when illiterate prisoners were often subjected to torture in order to extract confessions, and when trials and "Star Chambers" sat in secret session to receive the confessions, and when news of brutal practices being carried out in the name of justice could be spread only by word of mouth at the risk of the teller, and when downtrodden people had no recourse to real justice. Are these the conditions today? Is this "ancient and honourable tradition" a valid reason for extending the privilege against self-incrimination to the protection of professional criminals of the twentieth century who are tried in open court, who can depend on the power of the press to widely publicize any indication of injustice, and who have skilled counsel to advise them before and during trial – and, indeed, sometimes before the commission of the offence.

I believe that the rule against self-incrimination should go and that by substituting laws closer to the requirements of the modern world we would take a long step forward in the interests of true justice. Justice is offended if an innocent man is convicted, but the rule against self-incrimination no longer protects innocent persons. And justice is also offended when a guilty man escapes – and this happens every day. Of course, it is better that ten guilty men go free than that one innocent man be found guilty, but the rule against self-incrimination has no bearing on that truism. An innocent person is helped and not jeopardized by telling the truth.

I should point out that the suggestion that the rule against self-incrimination should go is not new, nor is it limited to police thinking. Several jurists, among them Lord Shawcross, have expressed the opinion that the rule is badly outdated. Over a hundred years ago Jeremy Bentham, the great philosopher, lawyer, and liberal law reformer, called the rule, "One of the most pernicious and irrational rules that has ever found its way into the human mind. . . . If all criminals of every class had assembled and framed a system after their own wishes, is not this the first rule they would have established for their security? Innocence never claims advantage of it: Innocence claims the right of speaking, as guilt invokes the privilege of silence." The rule is still on law books, and each year crime increases and criminals go free while we pay deeper obeisance to an ancient, hampering shibboleth.

Is it an invasion of individual freedom to allow the police, without promise, threat, or pressure, to ask an individual who on reasonable grounds is suspected of having committed an offence to account for his actions? Would it be an horrendous abrogation of the rights of an accused if the Courts were empowered at some stage of the hearings to invite the accused to tell the truth. The Judge may not do this at the present time, nor may he, or Counsel, comment if the accused does not take advantage of the ever-present opportunity to take the witness stand on his own behalf. It is difficult to imagine how an innocent man could incriminate himself, but it is obvious that a guilty man would have good reason to fear the witness box.

There are a number of other rulings and laws that hinder the police and in the face of increasing crime give aid and comfort to the criminals. Suggestions that some police forces resort to illegal methods such as wiretapping, interference with the mails, and the use of microphones have brought about loud cries of protest and disturbed many people. Certainly such methods are illegal and any policeman using them is breaking the law – but should this be so? Should there be an absolute prohibition of the use of any or all of these methods at any time under any circumstances.

Could anyone who has not been entirely carried away by fear of a wholesale invasion of privacy contend that the Queen's Mail, or the telephone, or a locked room should provide sanctuary for the planning of crime and treason? Can it be sensibly argued that criminals and spies should be able to get together and conspire, safe in the knowledge that the police are forbidden to listen in on their plotting? I would be opposed to the removal of all restrictions. However, a strong case can be made for the use of these methods under carefully controlled conditions. There would be no real threat to privacy – except the privacy of criminals – if judges, having assured themselves that the police have reasonable grounds for requesting such action, were empowered to issue orders or warrants authorizing the police to proceed.

Some years ago, Parliament passed the Habitual Criminals Act under which an individual, after having been convicted of four indictable offences, may be charged and sentenced as an habitual criminal. The law has not been widely used, nor has it proven very effective when attempts were made to use it. But that law made a distinction between the professional criminal and the beginner. If the thinking back of that act was sound and just, why not apply the same reasoning in other ways? Why not take the gangster, the professional who has chosen a life of crime, the hoodlum, who carries a gun during the commission of his crimes, or the syndicate man out from under the umbrella of protection that has been raised to protect the innocent or to give beginners a chance at rehabilitation. Should we extend the same sympathy and help to the top brass of crime as we do to beginners?

I said earlier that a few policemen have been guilty of misbehaviour. But do a few isolated cases justify laws and regulation that hamper and hamstring the thirty thousand dedicated policemen who are doing their utmost to uphold the laws of the land. Surely it would be more realistic and reasonable to pass stricter laws for the disciplining of those few men who misuse their authority.

One more suggestion. It would be very helpful to the police and, therefore, to the public if critics, whether they be judges, lawyers, legislators, newsmen, or private citizens, would make sure of their facts before indulging in the easy – and publicity-gathering – practice of condemning the police. If the police have been guilty of wrong-doing, they should be exposed. But first give them at least the same break as we insist on giving criminals by making sure that the judgment is based on fact and not on rumours that spring from self-interest of some individual or group. The police cannot do even a fair job without the support and confidence of the public. Statements that deprive them of that should in the interests of the public be well considered and based on fact – not sensationalism.

Someday we will be forced to drastically overhaul our system of administering justice. Some day the public will be compelled by deteriorating conditions to look directly at the problem, rather than looking away in the hope that it will disappear. And some day the law-makers and the judges will be forced by public opinion to look ahead rather than backwards in the formulating of our rules and laws.

That day has not arrived. Across the border we can see the results of delayed decisions in the sprawling empires of the crime syndicates which seem untouchable. We are more fortunate. We may still have time to head off those end-results. It will not be done by wishful thinking.